Words of Praise for *The*

"Bold, earnest and heartfelt…"

— Roshan R. Billimoria, Former ⸻ ⸻cutive Committee of Non-Government⸻ ⸻s

ဪၥဪၥဪၥ

"Leaders need an integrity check-up and Dr. David Gruder is just the man to do it. Too many well-meaning leaders haven't made the connection between their personal and relationship development and their effectiveness in the collective arena. Dr. Gruder's simple yet powerful integrity model provides a much-needed shot in the arm."

— Ken Blanchard, Co-author of *The One Minute Manager*

ဪၥဪၥဪၥ

"Any human resources executive in the role of being the organization's moral compass or 'canary in the coal mine' should make this a must read, among the more standard business literature."

— Victoria Berger-Gross, Senior Vice President, Tiffany & Co.

ဪၥဪၥဪၥ

"The New IQ brings clarity to the complexities of personal development that is not available from any other source. Dr. Gruder's disciplined, transparent organization of factors that both expand and impinge upon a personally satisfying and productive life, combined with his wide ranging international personal and professional experience, has created an excellent step-by-step guide for finding one's own formula for a complete, confident and productive life. Because so many of today's global leaders are creating devastating results due to their lack of synergy and collaboration skills, I particularly appreciate and applaud how Dr. Gruder applies those qualities and skills to international politics. The New IQ is a most excellent and important read, both for today's leaders and the leaders of tomorrow."

— Mort Mondale, National Educational Association, Professional Development Specialist Emeritus

ဪၥဪၥဪၥ

"Timely and provocative, touching on the underpinnings of a world in change: both our inner worlds and our outer worlds, and teaching us how to become sustainable human beings while at the same time sustaining our planet!"

—Jeanne House, President, SOL Communication

∞☙∞☙∞☙

"The New IQ organizes the many steps in personal, relationship and leadership development into a unified whole, explaining how they fit into a grand developmental scheme. David's insights may result in him one day being regarded as 'The Sigmund Freud of the twenty-first century.'"

—Dawson Church, Ph.D., Author of *The Genie in Your Genes*

∞☙∞☙∞☙

"The book of the decade! This long-overdue system for dealing with all of today's hugely damaging social and political issues through upgrading our understanding of integrity offers the gold it would otherwise take ten other books to reveal."

—C. Norman Shealy, MD, Ph.D., Founding President, American Holistic Medical Association

∞☙∞☙∞☙

"The instruction manual for life that we all wish came with."

—Dana Ansell, Director of Honesty, A Way of Life

∞☙∞☙∞☙

"A vital contribution as our culture tries to find its way back to a sustainable course."

—David Feinstein, Ph.D. and Donna Eden, Co-authors, *Energy Medicine* and *The Promise of Energy Psychology*

∞☙∞☙∞☙

"The New IQ *may well set the standard for a huge transformation in our beleaguered world.*"

—Sharon Cass Toole, Ph.D., CEO, Meridian Seminars

∞☙∞☙∞☙

"A most valuable book for our time, giving us insightful ways to reconsider our values, see how they have been out of balance, and what we can do about it."

—Henry Grayson, Ph.D., Founder and Chairman, National Institute for the Psychotherapies

ಬಂದಬಂದಬಂದ

"What a remarkable book for each and every one of us! A dynamic blueprint for change written with ease and simplicity. Turns a very complex subject into a dynamic hands-on learning experience. It is hard to put this book down – you just want to keep on reading!"

—Bala Jaison, Ph.D., Author of *Integrating Experiential and Brief Therapy*

ಬಂದಬಂದಬಂದ

"Exceptional and very timely…a profound education in being an authentic human."

—William Tiller, Ph.D., Professor Emeritus, Stanford University

ಬಂದಬಂದಬಂದ

"A landmark contribution…"

—Margaret Moore, Founder & CEO, Wellcoaches Corporation

ಬಂದಬಂದಬಂದ

"The 21st Century's first sensible, down-to-earth and comprehensive guide for integrity-based adult development during perilous times, The New IQ *needs to become a key book for all patients in any kind of mind-body treatment program."*

—Jude Gladstone Cade, Ph.D., Director, Sanoviv Medical Institute

ಬಂದಬಂದಬಂದ

"If you are a physician or other helping professional, place The New IQ *at the top of your recommendations list for both patients and colleagues."*

—Bruno Cortis, M.D., Author of *Heart & Soul*

ಬಂದಬಂದಬಂದ

"David walks the talk and is 'the change he wishes to see in the world.' Integrity shines through every written word. If you too want to learn how to be 'the change you wish to see in the world,' this book is for you. It will also become a must have in every coach's toolbox."

—Sarah Bird, C.EHP, Certified Conflict Resolution Coach

ஐ௸ஐ௸ஐ௸

"A powerful guide for restoring and upgrading integrity, this timely book deserves to have a deep positive impact on our collective lives."

—Rusty Wells, Professional Coach

ஐ௸ஐ௸ஐ௸

"Profound, well written, and easy to follow, this cornerstone for the advancement of society, regardless of racial, social political or religious identity propels us toward a more responsible, caring and higher consciousness society. A must-read book for all."

—Maria Becker, M.D., Author of *Awareness, Acceptance and Transformation*

ஐ௸ஐ௸ஐ௸

"A profound roadmap for healing the blocks to living a life of joy and integrity."

—Margaret Paul, Ph.D., Author of *Do I Have To Give Up Me To Be Loved By You*

ஐ௸ஐ௸ஐ௸

"Thoughtful and provocative, this book proposes wise and insightful ways to understand our personal, relational and societal problems and innovative ways we can address them as individuals and as a global community."

—Daniel J. Benor, M.D., Author of *Personal Spirituality*

ஐ௸ஐ௸ஐ௸

"This seminal, practical work leads us beyond understanding ourselves and our personal relationships to grasping the vital role we have in leading with integrity to create an upshift in our collective consciousness. The depth and originality of the Seven WisePassions Dr. Gruder describes, how they build upon each other, and the wisdom of linking integrity to these key life skills, is a great gift to all of us. The New IQ is required reading for all who care about human life, even survival, in this 21st century."

—Dorothea Hover-Kramer, Ed.D., Author of five books on energy healing

৪৩৪৩৪৩৪৩

"Take this exceptional, heart-warming, engaging and practical guide home and start reading it! You'll be so grateful you did!"

— Wendy Anne McCarty, Ph.D., Core Faculty, Santa Barbara
  Graduate Institute

৪৩৪৩৪৩৪৩

"If you only read one book this year about your own development as a truly three-dimensional human being, this is the one!"

— George J. Pratt, Ph.D., Chairman, Psychology, Scripps
  Memorial Hospital

৪৩৪৩৪৩৪৩

"A smart, thoughtful, well-written resource for developing and sustaining integrity, with practical applications and clear direction for the reader...a sorely needed book in these morally and ethically ambiguous times."

— Belleruth Naparstek, Author of *Invisible Heroes*

৪৩৪৩৪৩৪৩

"You can read 10 self-help books or you can read The New IQ, *which is much more than a self-help book. This compassionate guidebook is full of practical wisdom for becoming complete human beings."*

— Larry Stoler, Ph.D., President, Association for
  Comprehensive Energy Psychology

৪৩৪৩৪৩৪৩

"A very deep and broad book, The New IQ *is for people from all walks of life. It illuminates the human condition with unusual clarity and offers a wonderfully accessible and easily applied road map for living. Provides an excellent template for therapists and their clients to use. This book receives my highest recommendation."*

— Nicolee Jikyo McMahon, Head Teacher at the
  Three Treasures Zen Community and Marriage and
  Family Therapist

৪৩৪৩৪৩৪৩

"This important book needs to be on everyone's bookshelf!"

— Peggy McColl, Author of *Your Destiny Switch*

৪৩৪৩৪৩৪৩

ജ ⚇ ജ ⚇ ജ ⚇

"The New IQ *is right on target! If policy makers and leaders from both the developed and developing world took Gruder's words of wisdom to heart, we would see less political game playing and rhetoric on the international stage and a real movement towards fulfilling the human rights and dignity of vulnerable populations in our world.*"

—Aileen Kwa, Co-author of *Behind the Scenes at the WTO*

ജ ⚇ ജ ⚇ ജ ⚇

"*Principle centered and value driven,* The New IQ *is an effective guide for living an aware, authentic, and accountable life and a great contribution to co-creating a better world for individuals, groups, companies and nations.*"

—Eric Allenbaugh, Ph.D., Author of *Deliberate Success*

ജ ⚇ ജ ⚇ ജ ⚇

"*This is truly a ground-breaking work to be savored by everyone! Dr. David Gruder offers an enlightening aerial view for charting an exact course to integrity, authenticity, and fulfillment. This map and these tools will help to positively transform your life, your relationships, your organizations, and the world.*"

—Fred P. Gallo, Ph.D., Author of *Energy Psychology*

ജ ⚇ ജ ⚇ ജ ⚇

THE
NEW IQ

by David Gruder, Ph.D.

www.TheNewIQ.com

Elite Books

Santa Rosa, CA 95403

www.EliteBooksOnline.com

Library of Congress Cataloging-in-Publication Data

Gruder, David.

The new IQ / by David Gruder.— 1st ed.
   p. cm.

ISBN: 978-1-60415-013-1
1. Integrity. 2. Conduct of life. I. Title.
BJ1533.158G78 2008
170'.44—dc22

2007048636

Cover design by Victoria Valentine

Typesetting by Karin Kinsey

Copyedited by Jane Engel

Typeset in Cochin

Printed in USA

First Edition

10 9 8 7 6 5 4 3 2 1

Printed on recycled paper.

An Important Note

The case histories and other examples in this book are derived from actual interviews and research. Most are single individuals. Some are composites of more than one person to preserve anonymity. The relevant facts are real, but except when explicit permission was provided or the example is a matter of public record, all of the names and other identifying details have been changed to protect the privacy of the individuals.

All content in this book is purely informational and educational. You alone are responsible for how you understand and utilize this material, and for the results you do or don't obtain through utilizing it.

The publisher and author are not responsible for any goods and/or services referred to in this book and expressly disclaim all liability in connection with the fulfillment of orders for any such goods and/or services and for any damage, loss, or expense to person or property arising out of or relating to them.

Reading this book does not create a client-therapist relationship of any kind between the reader and David Gruder, Ph.D. This book is in no way intended as a substitute for seeking appropriate professional assistance for physical, psychological, spiritual, relationship, career, leadership or other challenges.

Should you be utilizing helping professionals of any kind, you are strongly encouraged to use this book's content to collaborate more effectively with them. (Helping professionals include, but are not limited to, mainstream and alternative mental health and physical health care providers, certified wellness, life, executive, career and sports coaches, recovery programs, and religious/spiritual advisors.)

This New IQ is Dedicated to...

1. All the *natural developers* who taught me what to teach deliberate developers.

2. All the *deliberate developers* who taught me how to help them succeed in the ways natural developers intuitively do to become their true selves, create the connection with others they most yearn for, have a powerfully positive impact in the world, step into more enlightened leadership, and live a life of true integrity.

3. All of my too-many-to-name *trailblazers* and *teachers* on whose shoulders I stand in bringing forth the road map this book provides. (You will find them in the Best Resources section of my website, www.TheNewIQ.com.)

ACKNOWLEDGMENTS

Expressing my gratitude to all those who have directly or indirectly influenced this book would fill a book all on its own. Here are but a few of those wonderful people I want to honor:

- Wayne Germain for being relentless in pushing me to write this book.

- All of my many clients and workshop attendees over the decades for teaching me what works.

- Dr. Rebecca Grace and Lerissa Patrick for co-creating with me some of the important antecedents to this book in the book *Sensible Self-Help: The First Road Map for the Healing Journey*.

- Christine Benton who proposed "self-improvers, connectors and do-gooders" as the names of the three main groups that development-oriented people split into after the 1960s.

- Dawson Church, publisher of Elite Books and its imprint, Energy Psychology Press, for believing in the importance of this book, and his entire staff for being such wonderful people to collaborate with through the birthing and release process, including but not limited to Courtney Arnold and Jeanne House.

- Midpoint Trade Books for all they do to make sure that this book reaches booksellers.

- Jane Engel and Lerissa Patrick for their expertise in helping me slim down to an agreeable length what began as a much-too-long manuscript, and for their talent at doing this in ways that strengthened the potency of the messages.

- Nagila Manfrim-Hajjar for her outstanding and rapid final proofreading.

- Karin Kinsey for her typesetting finesse and also for her extraordinarily patient collaboration in inserting all the last-minute tweaks that needed to be made.

- My book publicists, S. A. "Sam" Jernigan and Jeanne House for going "above and beyond" in helping this book become visible amidst a seemingly endless sea of titles.

- My assistant, Tracey Lott, co-owner of Str8eye Personal Concierges, for her passion, optimism and tireless efforts on behalf of this book.

- All those who provided extremely valuable input as my manuscript evolved (you know who you are!), and especially Constance Wells, Josh Beckman, and Roshan Billimoria for their excellent in-depth input, as well as the focus group who provided me with inspiration and support early in this project.

- My wife Laurie who inspires me to remain love-based and life-balanced. I love you dearly.

- The members of my ManKind Project iGroup, who consistently inspire me to be a better man on behalf of both men and women.

- My mother, Gloria "Steffi" Gruder, not only for bringing me into this world and for her steadfast love, but for her remarkable personal support throughout this project. My late father, Alex Gruder, for gifting me with far more than he ever realized during his life. My brother Ben, whose courage in the face of ongoing adversity inspires me. My aunts, Ruth Portnoy and Sylvia Leskowitz, for their unwavering love during both my joyous and difficult life chapters.

CONTENTS

SECTION THREE
DEMYSTIFYING THE RHYTHM OF ADULT LIFE

SECTION FOUR
THE SEVEN KEY LIFE SKILLS NATURAL DEVELOPERS
DEVELOP...AND HOW YOU CAN DEVELOP THEM TOO

SECTION FIVE
THE GRAND UPSHIFT IN HUMANITY
AND YOUR ROLE IN HELPING IT EMERGE

Appendices

INTRODUCTION

Even though this is the introduction, it is that part of a book that authors tend to write last. I am no exception. The day I began writing this introduction I watched a man pull into a handicapped spot, hang a handicap placard on his rearview mirror, get out of his car, and walk swiftly and sure-footedly down the block like a non-handicapped person. I watched in amazement as he entered the pizza place I had just left. I was reasonably confident he had not gone there to pick up a handicapped person because there was an empty loading zone right beside the pizza place whereas the handicapped spot was much further away. This particularly caught my attention because I had just days before read an article in the newspaper about handicap placard fraud.

I see this as but one small manifestation of a problem of pandemic proportions. Lack of integrity occurs in everyday ways in all walks of life around this planet of ours. Lack of integrity is not limited to certain leaders. It is an equal opportunity opportunist, damaging all cultures, religions, political orientations, socioeconomic status and careers. Integrity is about every one of us.

The age of rampant lack of integrity we currently live in is not a sustainable path. We can no longer afford to overlook our pervasive integrity issues. To succeed, our understanding of integrity must be transformed from a narrow philosophical concept to a complete set of very specific actions that we take on behalf of ourselves, those with whom we are in relationship and the larger collective of which we are a part.

I wrote *The New IQ* to illuminate precisely how lack of integrity develops and to propose a comprehensive road map that everyone from everyday people to world leaders can use to upgrade their personal, relationship, collective and leadership integrity. The title is both a play on words and a social statement. It is now well-known that there are many forms of intelligence that go beyond what the original IQ, or Intelligence Quotient, measures. One of the more well-known of these is Emotional Intelligence, also known as EQ.

We live in times when another form of intelligence has become more important than ever: Integrity Intelligence. I believe this form of intelligence is so vital to our collective future that I have come to call it "the new IQ." In this case, "IQ" stands for Integrity Quotient. *The New IQ* is about upgrading your Integrity Quotient in ways that make life far more fulfilling: for your own life and for the lives of us all.

I wrote *The New IQ* to provide you with practical ways to upgrade your integrity for your own sake, for the sake of those you care about and work with, and for the sake of the collectives of which we all are a part. Please join me in ushering in a new and much-needed age of integrity.

Looking forward to sharing the journey with you,

David Gruder

November, 2007

How to Use This Book

The New IQ is designed to be a reference guide to help you remain on track with all aspects of your development for the rest of your life. Each time you revisit this book, expect new insights to emerge and different sections to speak to your current needs.

Even though *The New IQ* is written in a step-by-step way, feel free to skip around, especially if you are not a step-by-step kind of person. I wrote the Table of Contents in a way that I hope helps make this easier to do.

The New IQ is one-third of an interconnected trilogy of resources, although this book also stands on its own by providing you with a comprehensive road map to guide your integrated personal, relationship, leadership and integrity development.

The New IQ Integrity Makeover Workbook (referred to in *The New IQ* as "the Workbook") offers extensive in-depth self-assessments and exercises for each section in *The New IQ*. These are designed to assist you in bringing what you learn in *The New IQ* into your life in a deeply personal way.

TheNewIQ.com website provides you with extensive specialized resources for delving more deeply into each of the topics covered in *The New IQ*. Consult the *Best Resources* section of www.TheNewIQ. com for my most up-to-date list of the finest resources I have found on that topic. Because I am constantly updating my resources list, a website is far better adapted to doing this than a book.

Dividing this material into this trilogy of resources became necessary because there was simply too much information to include in a single book.

For more information about additional resources connected with this book, please consult the *Going Further* section of the Appendix.

SECTION ONE

LIFE IN AN AGE OF LACK OF INTEGRITY

CHAPTER 1

YOU ARE A
THREE-DIMENSIONAL SELF

*What does it take to feel truly authentic, lovable
and to make a difference?*

*I was only trying to live in accord with
the promptings that came from my deepest self.
Why was that so very difficult?*

I was seventeen when I first read that line in the novel *Demian* by the brilliant existential novelist Hermann Hesse. It struck a chord deep within me. What I did not know at that time was how this sentence would also almost single-handedly set the direction my career would take. Not until twenty years after I completed my Ph.D. had I learned enough from my clients and my own life to respond to Hesse's question in ways that have proved useful to many others — and hopefully will to you as well.

I have noticed three "promptings from our deepest self" that we carry throughout our lives:

1. "How much am I living in accord with my deepest, truest self?"

2. "How much connection do I co-create with other people?"

3. "How much positive impact do I have in my world?"

Answer the following three questions honestly. Take your time and make sure your responses are true.

- *Are you deeply satisfied with and fulfilled by your self-expression, your self-care and your ability to manifest your intentions?*

- *Are your relationships with others as deep, durable and embodied with joyfulness and creativity as you would like?*

27

- *Do you feel aligned with, and able to act upon, your inner (or divine) life purpose?*

- *If you answered yes to ALL three questions, pass this book on to a friend and continue living fully.*

- *If you answered no to ANY of these questions, or weren't absolutely sure about your answer, you are about to discover what I hope will be an eye-opening picture of why this may be so. You are also about to discover some practical strategies for getting to "yes" with your answers. Buckle your seatbelt, though, because we are going to cover a lot of territory.*

- *But, first close your eyes for a few moments and imagine how your life would be if you COULD answer yes to all three of the proposed questions...*

We want the freedom to be authentic, to be able to express who we really are. We want to experience nourishment and co-creation through respectful and collaborative connection with others. We want to feel like we are doing our part to help the world become a better place.

These wants reflect our Three Core Drives: 1) Authenticity; 2) Connection; and 3) Impact. They guide our personal, relationship, leadership and integrity development.

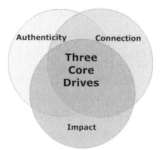

Collectively, these three drives form the three-dimensional self that we are: one part personal authenticity, one part relatedness with others (through mastering the art of co-creation or "synergy"), and one part service to the larger collectives of which we all are a part ("stewardship").

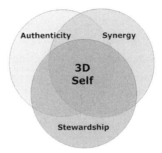

Our three core drives are deeply interconnected. Yet, because it can seem as though they are distinctly different from one another, they often feel in conflict within many of us. *Can we be our truest, most authentic self, enjoy deeply nourishing and rewarding connection with others, and make a positive difference in the world, all at the same time?*

My decades as a psychologist working with individuals, couples, businesses and leaders has taught me that all of us *need* to: 1) feel personal well-being; 2) enjoy connection with others; and 3) make a positive difference in the world. Yet, few of us *are* in integrity with all three of these core drives.

Imagine how personally fulfilled you would feel if you lived in integrity with all three of your core drives. Imagine what our world would be like if more of us lived in integrity with all three of them. The more we are in integrity with all three, the higher our "New IQ" (Integrity Quotient) becomes.

How do we fall out of integrity with our three core drives? More importantly, how do we come back into alignment with them? The secret to accomplishing this is developing 3D Integrity: aligning all three of your core drives so they work with each other rather than compete against each other.

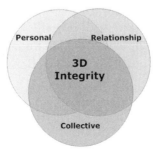

In a way, this competition among our three core drives is rather odd. It is odd because the same basic ingredients are needed for personal authenticity, relationship synergy and serving highest good. You will discover in this book what these ingredients are and how developing them is your key to harnessing the vast power of what could aptly be called "The Integrity Effect."

3D Integrity is not only the key to personal fulfillment. It is, I believe, what personal, relationship and leadership development is meant to be all about; indeed what it *needs* to be about, for the sake of humanity and the planet as much as for the sake of your own personal fulfillment and relationship success.

Are you ready to move into full expression and alignment among all three of your Core Drives? Are you ready to raise your "New IQ?"

The Self-Improver, the Connector and the Do-Gooder

Carl, a millionaire business executive, came to me in profound pain because his wife and children left him. He understood the business world inside out and had achieved success beyond many people's wildest dreams. He was also valued and respected in the community as a philanthropist and a caring person who truly wanted to make a positive difference in the world. But he couldn't figure out how to love his wife and children in ways that felt like love to them.

How could he be so beloved by so many and yet so baffled by his own family?

This was Carl's integrity crisis. The core drive that was Carl's primary focus was his drive to have an impact in the world. His way of living revolved around being a Do-Gooder. He and his family suffered because Carl was not sufficiently attending to the connection dimension of his 3D Self: he did not know that the "connection" aspect of his integrity intelligence was suffering.

Once Carl laid the inner groundwork necessary for successfully co-creating and synergizing with others, he began to experience relationship success for the first time in his life. His integrity quotient leaped higher. He and his children are now closer than they have ever been. Even though Carl's changes came too late to save his marriage, he developed a lovely post-marriage friendship with his ex-wife.

Melissa wanted my psychospiritual support in recovering from cancer. She was certain she had developed it as the direct result of having spent far too many years being there for others. Her husband and her children and her church community all adored her. She felt as though the severity with which she neglected her own self-care and personal needs had finally caught up with her in the form of cancer. She did not know that the "authenticity" aspect of her integrity intelligence was suffering. This was Melissa's integrity crisis.

Melissa struck me as someone whose way of being in the world was primarily as a Connector. Her health suffered greatly because she was not attending sufficiently to the authenticity dimension of her 3D Self. Her self-neglect showed that she did not like herself nearly as much as those who adored her.

Once Melissa freed herself from the old programming that had required her to be so self-neglectful she started to overcome her cancer. As Melissa tapped into her own forms of creative self-expression and authenticity, she began feeling more whole and complete in ways she had never experienced while she relied solely on connection with others to feel lovable and valid. Her integrity quotient rose significantly.

Sam was a brilliant artist and musician whose level of creative self-expression was as remarkable as his devotion to his own self-development. I remember feeling nearly overwhelmed as I listened to him recount the dozens of self-help books he had read, all the workshops he had attended and all the spiritual development practices he used. Despite all this, he sought my assistance for two reasons. First, he did not feel he was making any kind of meaningful difference in the world; and second, his romantic partners always left him after a relatively short period of time, accusing him of being self-absorbed and self-centered. This was Sam's integrity crisis.

Sam's main life focus seemed to be that of a Self-Improver. He was suffering because he was not sufficiently honoring the connection or service dimensions of his 3D Self. These aspects of his integrity intelligence were suffering. Once he digested and harvested the untapped gifts embedded within his adverse childhood experiences, the long-standing wall he had erected between himself and the world began to dissolve. His integrity quotient skyrocketed.

The Price I Paid for Being
Out of Integrity with my Three Core Drives

Collectively, the self-improvers, connectors and do-gooders I have worked with taught me that focusing on any one of our three core drives at the expense of the other two is a prescription for suffering and lack of fulfillment as an adult. I did not fully appreciate the importance of what folks like Carl, Melissa and Sam were teaching me until after my own first marriage ended.

My primary role in contributing to its demise stemmed from severely neglecting my self-care in favor of focusing on being of service in the world. I had figured that since I was pretty healthy I wasn't being dangerously self-neglectful. Boy, was I wrong. I became so depleted inwardly that my wife was able to connect with my heart less and less of the time. Eventually, she transferred her heart elsewhere. Until my marriage ended I never appreciated how grave the *non*-physical consequences of self-neglect could be.

This was also a huge lesson in integrity. Following in my parents' footsteps, I have always been an honest and ethical man in the usual meanings of those terms. Only through digesting the loss of my marriage and my life as I had known it for more than fifteen years did I come to appreciate the subtleties of integrity. I hadn't had an affair; I had remained devoted to my wife; and did all I could to handle our life logistics that she could not handle due to the life-threatening illness from which she was focused on healing.

Not only had I become more and more emotionally unavailable to the person I had loved the most; I also became increasingly irritable and critical as a consequence of my internal depletion. Those qualities are no fun to be around. I was in an integrity crisis of major proportion.

Even though my leadership integrity stayed reasonably sound (despite falling out of integrity with myself), my relationship integrity went down the tubes.

Only after it was too late for my first marriage did I begin to appreciate that personal wellbeing is the integrity foundation upon which everything else depends. A few years later some cancer cells were found in my prostate. It had turned out that my stamina had not been as strong as I had imagined.

The Price of Being a Self-Improver, a Connector or a Do-Gooder

Carl, Melissa, Sam and I all excelled in our own ways. Yet all of us also suffered and were unfulfilled. Our integrity intelligence was impaired in ways we had never imagined because we each almost exclusively focused on one of our three core drives while being out of integrity with the other two.

It turns out that self-improvers, connectors and do-gooders all have only a slice of a larger picture.

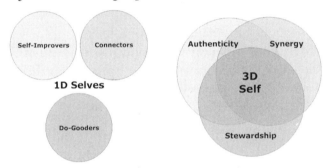

Self-Improvers live for the sake of personal growth, freedom and creative expression. While they may be in integrity with themselves, they tend toward being out of integrity with others and the collective.

Connectors live for the sake of love and close relationships. While they may be in integrity with others, they tend to be out of integrity with themselves and the collective.

Do-Gooders live for the sake of serving others and making the world a better place for all. While they may be in integrity with portions of the collective, they tend to be out of integrity with themselves and those they most love.

Self-improvers, connectors and do-gooders tend to have a certain disdain for one another.

Self-Improvers tend to believe that larger collectives can only change as a result of individual consciousness changing first. They are often skeptical about how much positive impact activists and leaders can have, especially those who themselves are wounded people who refuse to do their own inner work. Besides, those who focus on self-development and personal freedom don't want "Big Brother" telling them what to do.

Connectors tend to believe that change can only happen two by two — or at most in small groups such as families. They distrust do-gooders because they see how badly most of them neglect their relationships; and they view self-improvers as too self-centered to be capable of having good relationships.

Do-Gooders tend to believe that only when larger collectives improve can the individuals within them live better lives. They tend to view love and close relationships as a luxury that they cannot afford. They view self-improvers as indulging the kind of self-centered entitlement that they are fighting against; and they tend to view the personal development and self-esteem movements as having harmed society rather than helped it.

Which are you primarily?

❏ *A Self-Improver*

❏ *A Connector*

❏ *A Do-Gooder*

❏ *I am trying to be all three but do not know how to do this without feeling stretched too thin...*

A note about labels: Naming an elusive phenomenon makes it easier to spot and do something about it. I offer labels such as self-improver, connector and do-gooder throughout this book so you can learn more about yourself and spot danger signs in your relationships with others. I do not offer labels to be used to judge, shame, manipulate or control others. Please do not use the knowledge you gain from this book as a weapon against other people.

Rather, I implore you to use this material to develop a more compassionate attitude toward yourself and others and to expand your own effectiveness and integrity.

CHAPTER 2

WHAT HAPPENS WHEN YOU ARE LESS THAN YOUR THREE-DIMENSIONAL SELF

*"Is integrity merely a vague philosophical concept that
no one can actually define?"*

The Relentless Media Barrage

We live in times of international cultural and economic turmoil. Self-Improvers, Connectors and Do-Gooders are at odds with one another about what to do about this and what to focus on first. Many do-gooders, especially social activists, despair at institutional and governmental lack of integrity. Personal fulfillment continues to seem elusive to many self-improvers, despite all their attempts to unify mind, body and spirit, and connectors lament the high divorce rate and the deterioration of the family.

Not a day goes by without yet another news story appearing about how we're going to hell in a handbasket. It's corporate greed or government corruption today. It's global warming and Internet scams tomorrow. It's fanaticism and terrorism the next day. It's health crises and the high divorce rate the day after. And it's over-consumption, poverty and other economic crises following that. Then the stories recycle all over again with new variations.

The daily media barrage of "the problems and the pundits" has blurred into a broken record. The same song is sung day after day, albeit with an unending parade of different specifics.

Do-Gooders advocate that each of these seemingly separate issues urgently needs to be addressed. Many cannot see these issues as symptoms of a larger problem; and most do not see what that larger problem is. Instead, the number of issues seemingly needing to be handled separately overwhelms the average leader. The number of do-gooders who have sacrificed their ethics and principles in order to continue to have impact in the world is staggering.

Connectors advocate that love conquers all. But the do-gooders counter that loving one another doesn't magically translate into action steps that create social change.

Self-Improvers advocate that change can only occur one person at a time. But the connectors and do-gooders claim that this is precisely the kind of self-centeredness that has created our collective problems in the first place.

Too many of us feel so overwhelmed by the daily media barrage of the problems and the pundits that we throw up our hands in disgust and defeat. Too many of us deteriorate into *Self-Preservers* and abandon all three of our core drives. Self-preservers feel reduced to looking out for themselves as best they can. Many self-preservers wish there were something more they could do, but this wish retreats further and further under ground, being replaced by toxic self-centeredness. This only makes our individual, relationship and collective problems worse.

The Secret Source of Personal, Relationship and Societal Suffering

What if all of the separate problems in the world are actually variations on a theme? What if the root cause of lack of personal fulfillment, relationship distress and social problems is all the same? And if there is a single cause, is there something practical that everyday people can do about it?

We have seen that when we focus on any one aspect of our 3D Self at the expense of either or both of the other aspects, our sense of personal fulfillment suffers, our relationships suffer and we become selfish in the world. Most important of all, our integrity suffers. Indeed, conflicts among our three core drives are responsible for many of the personal, relationship and leadership problems we are individually and collectively struggling with today.

Framed this way, does it not seem a matter of common sense that we would be wise to develop our three core drives in a coordinated, integrated way? Does it not seem clear that one of the root causes of all of our seemingly separate problems is that too many people are out of integrity with one or more of their three core drives?

In 1969, I ended up at the infamous Woodstock music festival at 15 years old because it was a special trip provided by the summer camp for the performing arts I attended. Experiencing a half a million people attend to one another and to collective highest good impacted me quite deeply.

For me, and many I knew, Woodstock began to rekindle the fires of social responsibility that had been doused the previous year by the assassinations of two leading voices for social responsibility during that era: Martin Luther King in April of 1968 and Bobby Kennedy just two months later. Then the Kent State massacre occurred less than a year after Woodstock.

Timothy Leary's injunction to "Turn on, tune in and drop out" — rather than Woodstock's lessons about social responsibility — finally won out in many circles over wiser voices. Too few of us knew it yet, but this refocusing toward inner exploration at the expense of social responsibility would mark the beginning of the rampant self-centeredness we collectively suffer from today. In hindsight, I believe that this series of events had a huge influence on me, feeding a fascination with personal development during the years that followed, despite my more natural interest in collective highest good.

During the second half of the 20th century, the self-improvement movement inadvertently drifted off course. Our culture came to a fork in the road around the time of Woodstock. Many, perhaps most, took the personal fork and largely set aside the social responsibility path. We came to focus primarily on the first of our three core drives, and self-esteem, self-expression, personal development and lifestyle creation became the primary focus of many people's lives.

This self-improvement focus created huge problems. By single-mindedly pursuing personal expression, authenticity and self-esteem, self-improvers tended to neglect their needs for mutually respectful collaboration with others and serving collective highest good. What happens when we only define our sense of self in this one-dimensional way? The result is narcissism, greed, a sense of entitlement and lack of integrity. These in turn contribute significantly to our culture's current list of problems.

Also during the second half of the 20th century, many leaders were overpowered by the self-centered orientations of their own companies or constituents. This happened in large part because they rejected the idea that their own abilities as leaders had anything to do with the un-dealt-with inner issues they carried. Do-gooders thereby ended up being far greedier and embodying far less integrity than was good for the collective or for everyday individuals.

In short, *when we define ourselves, or our integrity, primarily through any one of the three dimensions of our 3D Self, we ourselves suffer, those around us suffer, and the world suffers.* When we focus on developing only one or two dimensions of our 3D Self, we end up feeling unfulfilled no matter how hard we try, no matter how successful we are, and no matter how much self-improvement we do, and we will remain confused about why we are not getting the results we're after.

What is Integrity?

Many people I know, from everyday people to influential leaders, believe the word "integrity" is a vague and abstract philosophical concept rather than a practical and action-oriented way of life.

Integrity is a kind of intelligence that most of us do not grasp until it is pointed out to us. In hindsight, though, integrity turns out to be one of the most important forms of intelligence there is.

The word "integrity" originates from the word "integration." Dictionaries define integrity as "steadfast adherence to an ethical code," "a state of being unimpaired and sound," and "a condition of being whole and complete."

Yet, as important as being ethical is, integrity is much more than that; it is more than only treating others as we would like to be treated. Integrity is also about saying what you mean and doing what you say; yet it is also much more than "only" aligning our intentions, words and actions. All of these aspects are most definitely part of what integrity is; however, they are not all of what it is.

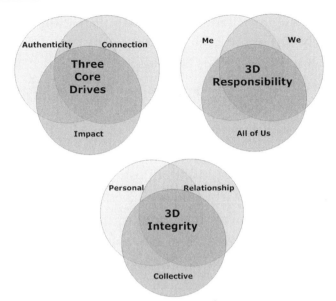

Integrity builds upon our three core drives.

When looked at through the perspective of our three core drives, a remarkable clarity about integrity emerges. *Integrity is the wholeness that comes when we are fully authentic as an individual, compassionate and effective co-creators with others, and servants of collective highest good. The essence of integrity is this three-dimensional alignment.*

Integrity Intelligence is our ability to align our personal authenticity, our ability to co-create mutually satisfying and effective relationships, and our attentiveness to making the world a better place. 3D Integrity means being aligned among all three of these integrity dimensions in the decisions we make and the actions we take. 3D Integrity is authenticity, love, leadership and spirituality made practical. This is why integrity and fulfillment are the same thing. They are inseparable. Understanding this is part of Integrity Intelligence.

The Full-Spectrum Opposite of Integrity

Consider the following symptoms that most of us either personally struggle with or read about on a daily basis:

- Not eating enough food that gives you what your body needs — or overeating
- Not getting enough sleep to function well

- Not exercising enough to maintain your strength and stamina

- Not doing what you tell someone you will do

- Ignoring your own personal boundaries and becoming resentful and depleted as a result

- The high divorce rate

- Over-consuming on the one hand and poverty on the other hand

- Internet spam and scams

- Global warming and littering

- The AIDS epidemic and other health crises

- Chronic over-spending and debt by individuals, couples, businesses and governments

- Corporate greed and government corruption

- Fanaticism and terrorism

Even though these may seem like separate issues, each of them is a form of lack of integrity.

Lack of integrity is, of course, nothing new. It has existed throughout history, cultures and religions. What is new is the potential impact of this lack. We have gathered so much power from science, technology, and global interconnection that we now have the capacity to damage or destroy humanity — and indeed our planet itself…all because of our lack of integrity.

What exactly does it mean to have a lack of integrity? No single word in the English language captures all of what being out of integrity includes. Instead, we have many different words for various aspects of being out of integrity, such as, corruption, dishonesty, manipulation, lying, and so on. These words do not describe other important aspects and flavors of lack of integrity described in this book, such as lack of self-care.

Linguists call this an "empty category": something occurs, and there is no word to describe it. Imagine being brought to the 21st century from the 1700s and seeing someone talking on a cell phone; the phenomenon would be right there before your very eyes, yet you would have absolutely no way to name it. You would be unable to have an intelligent useful conversation about what you were seeing. Empty categories make it nearly impossible to talk about something. And if you can't talk about it, you can't do anything about it.

And so it is with our empty category — the full-spectrum opposite of integrity. Think about the implications of this. The pandemic of lack of integrity, because we don't have a word for it, is nearly impossible to recognize, talk about or do anything about. The terms for the opposite of integrity I use in this book are lack of integrity and "out of integrity" (in contrast to being "in integrity").

Our Three Core Drives and the Era of Lack of Integrity

Think about what happens to cultures when lots of everyday people, and lots of those who are highly influential, are out of integrity. You do not have to imagine too hard; look around you in your personal life and in the news. What is happening immediately becomes painfully clear.

Some time ago, I was hired to provide training in negotiation skills to a group of ambassadors and other delegates to the World Trade Organization from developing countries. I was chosen because, as an outsider, I was considered to be untainted by WTO politics and because my orientation is psychologically based and collaboration-oriented.

I was warmly welcomed in individual meetings with the ambassadors beforehand, even though some of them expressed a bit of concern that I would be doing psychotherapy with them. Their faces showed great relief when I assured them that they were going to be attending a training experience and not group psychotherapy. I was told that the director of a major WTO advisory organization had said that personal development is, and I quote, "bullshit" and that it has no relevance for change agents (activists) or for the international community. I was definitely an alien outsider.

During my interviews, each ambassador told me that the "negotiation" style they saw being used most prevalently in the WTO was coercion, and they reported that compromise seemed to be the backup plan if coercion didn't work. The negotiation style that was least used was collaboration.

They shared with me their perceptions about the power politics they believed were the standard operating procedure in the WTO. They spoke of the pressure they felt from their home governments to take certain positions on behalf of their countries that might help a modest number of people in the short run but would be harmful to their countries in the long run. Many felt that if they spoke up authentically regarding the broader wisdom about international trade that they were gathering through their position in the WTO, they would be fired.

Once I noticed these trends in the feedback I was receiving, I began to ask more directly in my remaining pre-workshop interviews how the question of collective highest good was being addressed in the WTO. Every ambassador responded the same way: a blank look, followed by a thoughtful admission that it wasn't being addressed at all.

I well understood that the day-to-day business of the WTO was to hammer out difficult and complex trade agreements among the world community. I knew that politicians and business leaders tend to approach negotiations with the intention of getting as much as possible for the people and organizations that most influence them. I nonetheless found it appalling that an international organization responsible for guiding the delicate process of trade globalization might not be in an ongoing explicit dialogue to co-discover what might serve collective highest good.

As I completed constructing the workshop around what the ambassadors had shared, a wave of sad clarity washed over me; every ambassador I had interviewed struck me as a person of good will and good intention who wanted to do the right thing, and each seemed to be valiantly struggling to do that within the constraints they felt their role placed upon them.

They had quickly taught me three things:

1. They could not afford to be authentic in how they carried out their role.

2. They were not trained in the art of co-creation and synergy with others because this is not how negotiations are done in the WTO.

3. They did not see the WTO as being actively involved in discovering how to truly be a steward of collective highest good.

The picture of the WTO the ambassadors had collectively created for me was that it is a dog-eat-dog environment. The prime directive was therefore to get as many short-term benefits as they could regardless of the probable long-term costs to their own countries or other countries.

Though they did not recognize it, these ambassadors were teaching me that *an international organization responsible for wielding a huge amount of planetary power was doing so from a survival orientation frighteningly similar to what children do to survive difficult experiences.* As these ambassadors described it, the WTO's operating style was contrary to everything that my successful psychotherapy and leadership mentoring clients have taught me about successful adult development. Yet, the prevailing vision in the world community appeared to be that world leaders were above the need for adult development. Organizations like the WTO could do its job perfectly well without adult development nonsense, thank you very much.

Thankfully, this was not the attitude most of those who attended the workshop had by the end. The workshop turned out to be quite an eye-opener for the attendees, who were uniformly grateful for what they had learned.

The experience affirmed for me how vitally important it is to help people in positions of influence and leadership understand the profound extent to which their own level of adult development controls their ability to fulfill their roles.

You Can Help End Our Current Era of Global Lack-of-Integrity

Integrity has not been a particularly sexy topic even though lack of integrity has reached pandemic proportions globally. In fact, my publisher told me that it would be difficult to sell a large number of books on the topic of integrity.

Why? Because everyday versions of lack of integrity go largely unnoticed. Because most people don't recognize the connection between a lack of integrity, a lack of personal and relationship fulfillment, and a chronic absence of solutions to our most pressing global problems. And also because most of us have been used to being out of integrity with ourselves, others and the collective since we were children.

Our current attitudes about integrity, and mechanisms for dealing with it, are actually spawning even more lack of integrity.

Virtually all of us know we have big problems today: individually, in relationships and collectively. We focus on coping with them and surviving despite them. We use aspirin to cover up our headaches. Media sound bites oversimplify stories because they believe we do not want to understand issues deeply enough to develop educated perspectives about what real solutions might entail. We look for quick surface "fixes" and when we don't find them we blame others for the problems rather than joining together to co-create solutions that resolve and transform the issues at a root cause level. This "quick fix" attitude pervades every realm of adult development: personal, relationship and leadership.

Lack of integrity is not merely a government issue, a business issue, or a relationship issue; it is an extremely personal issue. Lack of integrity damages our inner capacity for fulfillment in significant ways that most people have never considered.

Integrity is not just another entry on a laundry list of traits people ought to have. Rather, integrity is the glue that binds together the various facets of a person's character.

- *In what ways do you tend to be out of integrity with yourself?*
- *In what ways do you tend to be out of integrity with your relationships? Which ones?*
- *In what ways do you tend to be out of integrity with your responsibilities to the collectives of which you are a part — from your own communities to humanity as a whole?*

Low integrity intelligence is devastating: to all of us, to our relationships, our families, our communities, our nation, the international community and to our very planet itself and in all conceivable ways. Don't know what I mean? Review the checklist from a few pages back.

The "Integrity Effect" is equally powerful. *The Integrity Effect is the profound surge in personal authenticity, relationship effectiveness and ability to serve collective highest good that comes from full expression and alignment among all three of your core drives.* This is what you are about to learn how to create.

Imagine the impact even one person has when s/he moves into 3D Integrity:

- Think about the personal fulfillment you feel in moments when you are truly embodying your own authentic self-expression and personal power.

- Think about how enjoyable being in relationship is when you and another person are co-creating closeness and generating collaborative, mutually honorable solutions to the challenges you face together. Think about how enjoyable a person you are, or would be to be with, when you are able to co-create this kind of synergy.

- Imagine being motivated to make a difference in the world because you have a deep inner knowing that self-interest is only true self-interest when it is also compatible with collective highest good.

- Imagine a world populated by both leaders and citizens who live in 3D Integrity: people like Oprah Winfrey, Billy Graham, Sidney Poitier, Queen Noor of Jordan, Jimmy Carter, Dennis Prager, Barack Obama, Diane Sawyer, Jon Bon Jovi, LaDanian Tomlinson and Stephen Covey. What would that world be like?

CHAPTER 3

WHAT NATURAL DEVELOPERS DO
THAT THE REST OF US WOULD
BENEFIT FROM DOING ALSO

*"Can I really learn to do intentionally what
natural developers do intuitively?"*

Integrated Personal,
Relationship and Leadership Development

Personal, relationship and collective well-being all depend on the way we express, balance and coordinate among our Three Core Drives: 1) Authentic self-expression; 2) Connection with others; and 3) Making a positive difference in the world.

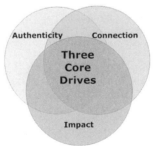

The fields of personal, relationship and leadership development evolved by leaps and bounds during the second half of the 20th century. As a result, we now have an unprecedented opportunity to integrate all three of these aspects of human development for the first time in history. Aligning our three core drives makes it clear how integrity and fulfillment to go hand in hand. Through this integrated approach to developing ourselves, we can make great strides toward eliminating the lack of integrity that has been damaging all aspects of life while simultaneously developing a more solid sense of inner fulfillment.

There is also a practical reason for 3D development: efficiency. It is no secret that all of us have only so much time, energy and money to devote to our development. The number of personal, relationship and leadership development resources that have become available during the past couple of decades is staggering. This blessing presents a significant challenge: how to select the most useful resources for you at each point in your development.

The more resources that are available, the more sophisticated consumers need to become in their ability to select among them. The less someone knows how to do this, the more "Resource Overwhelm" they are likely to feel.

Think about how much time, energy, money and needless frustration you would save if you knew the secret to avoiding resource overwhelm. Think about what it would be like to feel more confident in your ability to select the most helpful development resources for yourself at each point in your development. A valuable starting place for eliminating resource overwhelm is to learn the keys to pursuing your personal, relationship and leadership development in an integrated way.

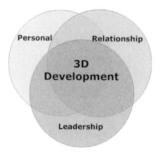

Natural Developers and Deliberate Developers

Since the late 1970s, I have been intrigued with the question of why some people are able to transform into extraordinary adults while others remain stuck no matter what they try.

This led to my doctoral dissertation: a research study designed to identify the qualities that clients, rather than therapists, brought into psychotherapy that correlated with positive outcome. I continued to be fascinated with this question long after completing my dissertation. In the twenty-five years since, one of the key lessons my psychotherapy and leadership coaching clients taught me is that there are Natural Developers and Deliberate Developers.

Natural developers seem to know intuitively how to free themselves from their baggage and mature into effective, empowered, authentic, creative, loving, service-oriented, integrity-oriented adults who are particularly good at manifesting their intentions. The strategies they instinctively use allow them to develop more effectively and efficiently than the rest of us.

Deliberate developers are the majority of us (including me) who need to learn the art of integrated adult development. When we do *on purpose* what natural developers do *intuitively*, we get similar results and become what I call Successful Deliberate Developers.

An Amazing Example of an Everyday Natural Developer

Here is a particularly moving example of a natural developer, pulled straight from the news:

Arwen, a twenty-four-year-old woman, was riding in her boyfriend's car when a five-pound piece of concrete smashed through the windshield, crushing every bone in her face and destroying one of her eyes. As Asher, her uninjured boyfriend, helped guide the car to the shoulder, another car rear-ended them, and their car rolled down an embankment, further compounding Arwen's injuries.

In the hospital, a very complex series of reconstructive surgeries began. The plastic and reconstructive surgeon said her injuries were among the worst facial fractures he had ever treated. "I used enough plates and screws to set off security devices in department stores," he said.

Titanium and grafts from Arwen's hip replaced the crushed bones. Her nose was rebuilt. Her jaw was wired shut. A glass eye was inserted into the rebuilt eye socket. A periodontist performed gum surgery. An orthodontist performed a root canal and a dentist bonded her teeth. A chiropractor started working to repair Arwen's back and neck.

For days after the initial surgeries, Arwen was almost unrecognizable. For almost three weeks she couldn't breathe on her own. She could not walk, talk or even open her mouth. She was in extreme physical pain. And she had no medical insurance.

Despite all that, Arwen somehow maintained such a winning attitude that her team of doctors decided she should not have to pay anything for their services. They told her that whatever costs were not covered by a stopgap insurance program and other county medical benefits were going to be gratis, including all follow-up visits. Arwen's plastic and reconstructive surgeon observed, "She had the best attitude I have ever seen" for someone who had a life-altering accident, adding that he was "amazed by her spirit."

Arwen's attitude was so infectious that friends, family and complete strangers alike rallied around her. They surrounded her with hundreds of floral arrangements and they produced several fundraisers that raised tens of thousands of dollars for her.

Why did the entire medical staff adopt Arwen in this way? Why did so many strangers reach out to her? Because she had intuitively mastered the art of digesting life experiences in such a way that she transformed not only herself through this unexpected and life-changing event, but what she modeled also deeply impacted and inspired those around her.

Arwen's attitude was, "How you react to the hand you are dealt is what makes or breaks you." She saw herself as a positive, self-aware person who could see the bigger picture. She focused on accepting the experience and transforming as a result of it: "The sooner you accept reality, the quicker you can grow from it," she added.

Arwen focused on her blessings: "I survived. I'm not paralyzed and I have no brain damage."

Dance had been her life since she was eight and she was also a model. Despite all that, she allowed this experience to upgrade her sense of identity and purpose, rather than destroy it. Arwen chose to focus less on what she looked like and more on her deep belief that she had been spared for a reason. As she put it, "It's not just about being a dancer, but affecting other people."

Arwen had been expected to remain in the hospital for up to three months. Her capacity to rapidly and deeply digest this life experience helped make it possible for her to leave in just seventeen days. As she so accurately put it, "I think you make a decision and your body follows."

Arwen did more than accept an experience; she turned it into a gift for herself and for those around her as well.

She found a way to transcend a human tendency to identify herself through her now-damaged physical attributes and then to use her experience to inspire others.

In a split second, this woman's life changed completely and dramatically. At just twenty-four, Arwen's days of dancing professionally were over forever, because the loss of her eye affected her depth perception and balance. Her modeling career was also over because of the damage to her face. So, what did she do? She started teaching dance at an elementary school (authentic self-expression), while touching the lives of those she meets (service), and continuing to be in a mutually nourishing relationship with her boyfriend (connection).

Arwen is a natural developer. She provides us with an exquisite example of what being in integrity with all three of our core drives looks like, even in the face of a particularly dramatic life upheaval.

Natural developers like Arwen are my heroes; they are our role models for how adult development is designed to occur.

What Natural Developers Taught Me and Can Teach You

My experience has taught me that the reason so many people feel deeply unfulfilled today, no matter how hard they try, is because they focus on only one or two of their three core drives.

It saddens my heart when I notice so many people have given up on trying to flourish with even one of their three core drives, and live primarily in survival mode.

Like a psychotherapeutic Robin Hood, I have learned from natural developers what works and I have brought these strategies to deliberate developers, including myself. The strategies work equally well for self-improvers, connectors and do-gooders, turning them into Successful Deliberate Developers. Of the many eye-opening lessons my clients and workshop attendees have taught me, three stand out as the most stunning of all:

1. **Fulfillment Has Three Ingredients:** The more a person's three core drives (authenticity, connection and impact) work together, the more whole, happy and fulfilled the person feels.

2. **Integrity Matters:** Everyone suffers when someone is out of integrity with him/herself. That person suffers. Those with whom that person is in direct (and sometimes indirect) relationship suffer. The larger systems of which that person is a part suffer.

3. **One Set of Life Skills Does It All:** Natural developers have taught me that the same skills are needed for personal, relationship and leadership integrity and success. One of the big keys to eliminating resource overwhelm is learning these skills and how to develop them more efficiently.

Becoming a 3D Self is what I believe all well-meaning people most want in their heart of hearts. The challenge shared by virtually all of those whom I have served is how to align their personal, relationship and leadership integrity in order to create true life balance; and for the longest time, I shared their confusion.

My Dream

Early in the 1980s, I had a dream.

I come out the end of a long, dark and difficult tunnel and find myself high on a mountaintop, with a panoramic view of what in the dream is called "the end," and "the path" to get there.

With great elation and relief I eagerly set out on the path, down the mountain into the valley below. I arrive in the valley and I come upon a girl dancing with utter joy and total abandon. I am told by a spiritual presence traveling beside me that the girl is "dancing the Dance of Life."

As I stand transfixed and in awe, I notice that this girl has no face. My guide suggests that I look again. I do, and realize that I had been lying to myself about her having no face: the truth, which feels too terrifying for me to acknowledge, is that she actually has no head at all. At the top of her neck, where her head ought to be attached, is a smooth flap of skin. My awe shifts to frozen terror. My mind begins to race: How can someone without a head even be alive, let alone exude total joy in dancing the Dance of Life with utter abandon?

The spiritual presence suggests that, in light of my reaction, it would be wise for me to stay with her awhile and let her be my teacher.

I refuse, arrogantly stating that I have already seen "the end" and "the path" and that I am unwilling to allow anything to stop me from getting there as quickly as possible.

In my dream, I was so focused on wanting to get to my destination that I did not recognize the only way for me to truly get there: allowing myself to be transformed by my life experiences and developing the skills that would be gifted to me by doing this. Not surprisingly, this was a perfect reflection of the way I was living my life at that time — almost totally with my head, and not enough with my heart and gut. The time had come for me to expand beyond being such a serious, results-driven, intellectually-based man. The time had come for me to learn how to also walk through life in more playful and lighthearted ways. Such is the brilliance of dreams.

Your Dream

Whoever you are — a social activist, a leader, a helping professional, a parent, someone new to personal healing and development, or a self-improvement veteran striving for high level well-being — I invite you to use my dream as a jumping-off point to your own dream.

Imagine slipping out of yourself, wherever you currently are on your life's journey. Allow yourself to imagine coming with me to a nearby mountaintop high enough for you to have a panoramic view of your entire life path. Imagine this mountaintop as a beautifully breathtaking place from which you can safely see where you came from, where you are now, where you are currently heading, and where your deepest heart of hearts means for you to go.

Imagine it is a beautiful clear day and that you have a forever view. What do you notice? Are you able to see how your past experiences brought you to where you are today? Now, from here on this high mountaintop, are you able to see where you are currently heading? Are you able to see where your deepest heart of hearts means for you to go? With your own personal development? With your relationship abilities? With making a difference in the world?

Any one of four things might have happened for you in this very brief exercise. 1) You might have had difficulty allowing an image to form; 2) It might have been difficult for you to "see" some of the elements in this image; 3) You may not have liked parts of what you saw; or 4) You may have been delighted with all aspects of what this image revealed.

No matter which of these was true for you, I invite you to ask yourself these six questions, based on your experience with this imagery:

1. To what extent do I have difficulty seeing the big picture of my life, or what life is for?

2. To what extent am I clear about both where I am currently heading and where my heart most means for me to go: personally, in my relationships and in my desire to make a positive difference in the world?

3. To what extent can I accurately pinpoint where I currently am, relative to the bigger picture of where my heart most means for me to go?

4. To what extent am I aligned in where I am heading and where my heart most means for me to go?

5. To what extent do I have heart-felt appreciation for all that has occurred in my life before now (the good, the bad and the ugly), and am I grateful for how these experiences

(especially the "bad" and "ugly" ones) have propelled me toward where my heart most means for me to go?

6. Out of the vast overwhelming sea of personal, relationship and leadership development resources available today, to what extent do I feel confident in my ability to select the ones best suited to moving me forward from where I currently am?

What Brought You to Where You Are Today?

What brought you to where you are today is most likely a combination of:

- Universal human drives such as your three core drives

- Your individual temperament (your basic psychological and biological wiring)

- Your ability to digest your life experiences (that is, to turn the unexpected, unasked-for and unacceptable into profound blessings)

- What you believe about what life experience is for

You may be so locked into your worldview (your paradigm) that you have lost sight of where you truly, in your deepest heart of hearts, mean to be heading. Or, you may be locked into inefficient or self-defeating strategies for getting there. You may have your own version of the theme in my dream in which there is a disconnection between where I was heading and how I was trying to get there. Or, you may have decided that what your soul most deeply wants isn't possible in "real life." You may have watered down the yearnings that come from your deepest heart of hearts, causing you to settle for pursuing something less than your deepest yearnings.

Like Sam in Chapter 1, you may have been so focused on your inner development or personal or career success, that the parts of you that thirst for deeper connection with others or making a positive difference in the world have been ignored. You may have been like Melissa: so focused on your relationships (finding a partner, raising children, etc.) that your inner life, career or financial success, or desire to be of service in the world, has suffered. Or like Carl, you may have been so focused on having a positive impact in the world that you have been self-neglectful, or those you love have been starved for your heart or your time.

To whatever extent any of these are true, you are out of integrity with yourself; and if you are, rest assured, you have a planet full of company. The good news is that you, and all of us, can do something about this — something really powerful about this — beginning today.

You can learn how to do on purpose what natural developers intuitively do and successful deliberate developers have learned to do to emulate them. You will begin to do precisely this starting in the next chapter.

CHAPTER 4

REVERSE ENGINEERING THE
SECRETS OF NATURAL DEVELOPERS

*"What is revealed by looking at development
with a rearview mirror?"*

So far, you've discovered how all of us have three core drives around which our lives apparently are meant to revolve:

1. To experience personal well-being and authenticity.

2. To enjoy connection with others.

3. To make a positive difference in the world and serve highest collective good.

You have also viewed a small sampling of the personal, relationship and societal symptoms that inevitably erupt when we are individually and collectively out of integrity with one or more of our three core drives. The impact is far-reaching and pervasive, touching every aspect of life.

It follows, then, that for the sake of individuals, relationships and the collective, *the most central purpose of adult development is to move into increasing integrity with all three of your core drives, aligning them so they complement rather than compete against each another.*

This not only makes common sense; it also reflects what I have seen natural developers do.

Defining Development Based on End Results

Most conventional Developmental Psychology models begin in childhood and move forward from there. Many seem to assume that our development ends in late adolescence; others do their best to include the entire lifespan.

Most models of adult development describe the *themes* we deal with in each stage of adult life rather than *how* we develop as adults. *No Developmental Psychology theory that I know of approaches the development process as a reverse engineering challenge.* Nor do any of them seem to focus in an equal and integrated way on personal, relationship and leadership development.

My most successful clients taught me that frequently the best way to understand development is to look from the end backward rather than the beginning forward. The advantage in looking at the development process in reverse is that it allows you to discover the real meaning of childhood experiences and the best steps to become the adult you want to be. The meaning of prior life events is quite different when looked at from the end backward.

The Wisdom of 20/20 Hindsight

Let me offer you a personal example. I grew up feeling as though I had been born into the wrong family. By all accounts from others I was, by temperament, a naturally happy and contented little boy. I smiled when someone came into the room; I didn't get upset when they left the room; I played happily on my own; I played happily with other young children; and I played and interacted happily with adults.

Until I was around the age of three, I lived largely in a world of imagination, parts of which I still remember quite well. My inner world was far more vivid, engaging and three-dimensional than my outer word.

That turns out to have been a good thing. My parents were miserable; they each were dealing with — or spending a lot of energy avoiding — their own inner demons. As a couple, their marriage was all but dead emotionally. Between their cultural background, the standards of the time and their own conformist natures, divorce was not an option.

Growing up in my parents' house was not a happy experience for me. The exception was how alive my mother seemed to be when she and I were alone together. This alone time with my mother was a relief from the more pervasive pain permeating our little apartment, but it also carried a hefty price tag: I felt responsible for saving my mom from the pain she was obviously in.

My brother came along when I was three. His temperament was in some ways the opposite of mine. He wanted nothing to do with the outer world. He retreated into an inner world in such a profound way that, despite having more IQ points than me, it was not until he was four that he finally started to develop language. The big hope I had when my brother was born was that he would be a companion of light in a dark family. I had no way of knowing that he would end up needing me to save him, too. My hopes for the kind of brother I wanted were soon dashed.

By the age of four or so, I began living my days in deep inner pain. I did my best not to show it. I hated school. Connecting with other kids my age became increasingly difficult for me as well. By the time I was ten, I had defined my role with my peers as an outcast who was regularly taunted and beaten up. I refused to fight back. I judged fighting to be barbaric. I wore "martyr" on my sleeve and "taunt me" on my forehead. I judged myself to be stupid and increasingly had the grades to prove it. I would not begin my gradual process of outgrowing this script until my senior year of high school.

For years, the story I told myself about my childhood, was that it was miserable because I was sentenced to coming to this planet. It was my punishment for something horrible I must have done.

My perspective did not shift until I found ways to harvest the profound gifts concealed within both my painful and joyous childhood experiences.

Not until I could see my childhood experiences in the larger context of my life purpose and what adult development is about did I find enduring gratitude for all of the unacceptable things that occurred during my childhood. I saw how without these experiences my ability to empathize with others would not have developed as deeply as it did. I saw how important it was to view life experiences from a higher perspective. I saw more clearly what my life mission was.

Had I not harvested these and other gifts from my "adverse childhood experiences," (a term that comes from a landmark psychological study you will read about at the beginning of Section Four), the quality of my life would have been diminished.

How this New Understanding
of Adult Development Was Birthed

For more than twenty years my natural developer clients were teaching me how to do this bit by bit. I learned the following from them:

- ❑ A *mind-set* to adopt toward my life that allows this transformation to occur.

- ❑ A set of *life skills* that this transformation process seems to require.

- ❑ The most efficient *sequence* for developing or upgrading these skills.

- ❑ The specific kinds of *meaning* that need to be found in prior life experiences in order to be successful in the developmental journey toward 3D Living.

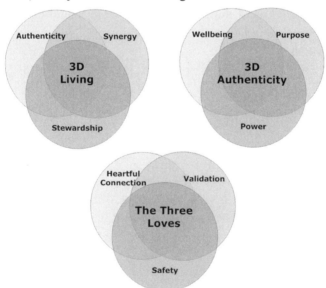

My successful deliberate developer clients taught me they could learn to do on purpose and with similar results what my natural developers did by instinct. They taught me how the rest of us could most efficiently develop these skills.

By 1996, I had already written about much of what I had learned from these clients in *Sensible Self-Help*, but I did not yet fully comprehend what my clients had taught me. That appreciation did not occur until after 2002, with the single most humiliating experience of my adult life — the end of my marriage. Only after I rose from the ashes of that disaster did I begin to fully appreciate the huge price of not attending to one of more of our core drives.

I subsequently read *Good to Great* by Jim Collins. It reveals what businesses that sustain their leaps into greatness do and what businesses that don't sustain those leaps should do. Collins reverse engineered the steps companies took that had enabled them to leap from good to great companies…or not. That got me thinking about what developmental psychology might look like if it was reverse engineered.

Around the same time, I heard a story about a successful, respected CEO who was asked after he retired how he turned his company into the huge success that it became. He replied that he began by asking himself the question, "What do I want this company to look like when it's 'done'?" When he had a clear and detailed vision of that end result, he then imagined having already arrived there. From that vantage point in the future, he imagined looking backward at the steps he had taken to get there. He then noticed the order in which he had taken those steps.

How Adult Development Occurs
From a Reverse Engineering Perspective

When I heard this story, a light bulb went off. I began reflecting on all of my natural developers and successful deliberate developers from this perspective. As I did this, the following question emerged: "What have my most successful clients consistently shown me adult development is for?"

The purpose of integrated adult development is to expand the extent to which we experience deep inner fulfillment, love and wisdom. The way to accomplish this is by moving into integrity with our three core drives. This is the secret to living in ever-increasing alignment with our most heartfelt values, vision and sense of purpose.

63

Based on this goal, a fascinating picture began to emerge about how integrated adult development occurs. That picture contained three main elements:

1. The *path* successful personal, relationship and leadership developers take that gets them to this outcome.

2. The *skills* these developers most rely on to get them there.

3. The *resources and techniques* that were consistently best at helping them develop each of those skills.

Here is the growth path most natural developers seem to take:

- As virtually all of us do, natural developers cultivate a Survival Plan and a Redemption Plan. Our survival plan enables us to cope as children with unresolved life experiences that all of us have growing up. Our redemption plan refers not to anything religious but rather to a strategy for proving as adults that we are worthy of experiencing fulfillment and love. Life issues all of us with Wakeup Calls, which are invitations to outgrow our survival and redemption plans as adults.

- Natural developers respond to their first powerful wakeup call in a specific way that is different from most of the rest of us. They move into their first adulthood Transformation Chapter. This is an intensive inner growth spurt during which they begin the process of outgrowing their survival and redemption plans. To succeed they intuitively develop a very specific set of skills in a very specific sequence. Upon completing this Transformation Chapter, they go through a Consolidation Period during which they integrate their gains into the fabric of all three of their core drives.

- After their first sojourn through the cycle of adult development, natural developers tend to repeat this cycle throughout the rest of their lives with increasing effectiveness and speed.

Wakeup Call → *Transformation Chapter* →
Consolidation Period → *Next Wakeup Call*

Natural developers become increasingly graceful with this rhythm each time they cycle through it. This is partly due to experience and partly due to the fact that the skills they develop keep getting stronger and stronger. This makes adult development increasingly efficient and effective with each cycle that natural developers go through for the rest of their lives.

The Seven Essential Life Skills Natural Developers Use to Succeed

One of the most eye-opening revelations I had in studying natural developers is that there appear to be seven key life skills they intuitively develop to move into integrity with their three core drives. They are the basic ingredients that build wisdom and compassion, the vehicles through which it becomes possible to passionately live a life of personal, relationship and leadership integrity.

I wanted to give a name to this set of key life skills that readily conveys how they combine wisdom, compassion and passion. As a result, I now call these common sense skill sets *The Seven WisePassions*. They appear to form the bedrock of personal, relationship and leadership development. They seem to be the master switches for 3D Integrity and fulfillment. This makes them the key building blocks that enable us to express and coordinate all of our three core drives.

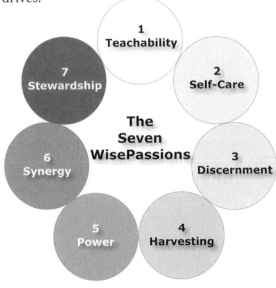

Here is the essence of the Seven WisePassions:

1. *Teachability* is where integrity and true adult development begins.

2. Personal, relationship, collective and leadership integrity all require that you honor your *Self-Care* needs impeccably.

3. Learn *Discernment* because this brings you into right relationship with the inner and outer input you will need in order to grow into full integrity.

4. *Harvesting* precious gifts from all your life experiences is the key to upgrading your integrity and more fully living your life purpose.

5. Embracing your full *Power* and light makes personal, relationship and leadership success and integrity possible.

6. The key to fulfilling, productive, integrity-based relationships of all kinds is *Synergy* rather than coercion, capitulation or compromise.

7. *Stewardship* of collective highest good is a crucial component of personal fulfillment.

Secret Wisdom of Successful Developers

Those who succeed with their personal, relationship and leadership development, whether intuitively or deliberately, have a different perspective about this process than my other clients. Successful developers understand that:

Adult Development Requires Inner Courage: Face that which you least want to face within you because that is where the greatest gold is.

Meaning and Gratitude are Inseparable: You cannot know what a life experience was truly for as long as you view it as having been a horrible thing to have happened to you. Get to a point with each life experience where you feel deeply grateful for it — not merely in your head but in the cells of your being. There is no such thing as a life experience too awful to be capable of ultimately transforming into a blessing.

The Habits That Build Fulfillment and Integrity are the Same: Develop habits that enable you to face what you don't want to face, and convert these undesired experiences into blessings that enable you to live in increasing integrity with all three of your core drives. Do this as efficiently as possible so your life can *focus on thriving rather than on surviving* and so your life can focus on living rather than healing. Learning to be practical about how you conduct your development process is far more important than reading high-minded philosophies about how life should be.

Life is Not a Burden, But a Blessing: There is nothing more important than the combination of an inner sense of well-being and lightheartedness, deeply loving others, developing higher wisdom about how to view life, serving highest good, and embodying integrity in all that you do, especially when others aren't looking.

The clients of mine who approached their life and their development with these attitudes made the most progress in the shortest time and were the happiest with the results they got from the therapy and coaching I did with them. These are the attitudes that helped me heal from my divorce.

Integrated Adult Development in a Nutshell

My curiosity about reverse engineering the adult development process led me to the following discoveries:

- *Most people are, to varying degrees, out of integrity* with their three core drives (individual well-being and authenticity, connection with others and positive impact in the world through serving collective highest good).

- *Sacrificing aspects of our integrity begins in childhood for the sake of survival.* The survival patterns we develop in childhood become unconscious and automatic, as is the inherent nature of all habits. Our survival plan in childhood develops into our redemption plan in adulthood. Adult development is about replacing these strategies with personal authenticity and well-being, co-creative synergy with others, and service to the collective.

- *Integrated Adult Development (personal, relationship and leadership) requires a significantly different set of skills than those that comprise our Survival and Redemption Plans.* Integrated Adult Development comprises a lifelong series of cycles to restore our integrity with our three core drives (authenticity, connection and impact). Successful cycles require a different set of skills from the ones our survival and redemptions plans use. Developing and upgrading these skills is the mechanism by which our souls and our authenticity grow, our love expands, our capacity to be of service expands, and our feelings of fulfillment deepen.

We will next look at how you fell out of integrity with your three core drives to begin with.

SECTION TWO

HOW LACK OF INTEGRITY BECAME SO COMMONPLACE

CHAPTER 5

WHY WE FALL
OUT OF INTEGRITY

*"What causes us to sacrifice our authenticity
and our sense of right and wrong?"*

There is a perfectly understandable reason why so few of us live in integrity with all of our Three Core Drives (authenticity, connection and impact). This reason goes back further than you might imagine.

We compromise our integrity for the sake of childhood survival. Coping with having sacrificed our integrity requires a specific set of skills. These childhood survival patterns become automatic, unconscious habits that we unintentionally carry into our adult lives where they begin to sabotage rather than serve us. Adult fulfillment largely depends on outgrowing our childhood Survival Plan and upgrading the life skills, the Seven WisePassions, that enable us to live in full integrity with all three of our core drives.

The more you understand your own version of the childhood survival patterns you brought with you into adulthood, the more focused and effective you will be with your adult development. My experience with natural developers has revealed that the more you can frame your childhood experiences and choices from the reverse engineering perspective I described in the last chapter, the easier it will be for you to outgrow your Survival Plan and upgrade your WisePassions.

Read the questions below and notice your reactions:

1. What would it mean if your parents were *supposed* to be imperfect in how they raised you?

2. What would it mean if falling out of integrity to one extent or another was actually an important part of your development journey, rather than something that interfered with it?

3. What would it mean if your life was supposed to include some amount of trauma and upheaval beginning in childhood?

4. What would it mean if some of your childhood experiences were supposed to remain undigested until you became an adult?

Do you bristle at any of these questions? How would your perspective about your life, especially about your most difficult experiences, be different if you embraced all of these perspectives? Write your answers in this book or on a piece of paper. Bear the questions in mind as you read this chapter and beyond. When you complete *The New IQ*, return to these questions to see how your answers have evolved. Check if you have found a way to embrace these seeming paradoxes.

What is Worse Than Loss of Innocence?

A popularly accepted notion about childhood is that we come into life innocent and pure, and as our childhood unfolds, we gradually lose more and more of our innocence. Many people lament this and nostalgically long for a return of innocence. Fewer of us dwell on the consequences this loss of innocence might have on how we live our lives as adults. Most of us believe the loss of innocence is simply part of what happens as we mature.

All of my clients taught me that something far more powerful than innocence diminishes beginning in childhood. It is far less glamorous than the loss of innocence. Yet it far more directly influences the difficulties we have as adults. That "something" is integrity. We don't merely begin to lose our innocence as children. We begin to lose our integrity.

Isabel's Childhood Survival Plan

Isabel's mom was a ballerina. Her dad was a successful and wealthy businessman. She grew up in a financially privileged family, wanting for nothing on the material level. Yet, in looking back, she discovered she had lived her childhood, and most of her adulthood as well, in a state of profound emotional and spiritual poverty.

Isabel's parents did not get along very well. Her mother was extremely self-centered and prone to bouts of depression. She was gone for months at a time each year. When she was home, the thing she most needed from Isabel was for Isabel not to need anything from her. Her father looked to Isabel for two seemingly contradictory things. One was for Isabel to be his substitute wife, by being his companion and date (though fortunately not through meeting his sexual needs). The other was for Isabel to be the son he never had.

Isabel felt extremely alone. There were many times when she was left alone for hours on end in her large family home, frequently at night. The seconds, minutes and hours crawled by, as they do for lonely, bored children. In the dark, time seemed to go by even more slowly. Her only company was the terror that her parents would never return — a terror that grew stronger with each tick of the clock. Being repeatedly left alone in these ways traumatized Isabel. Not being able to get her parents to truly feel what she was going through traumatized her even further. She felt disconnected and alone. By age seven, Isabel's anxiety attacks became so severe that even at that tender age she asked her parents to take her to see a therapist.

Isabel was growing up without enough of the kinds of connection and validation she most needed from each of her parents. She did what any self-respecting child does under such circumstances. She decided there had to be more love available from her parents than she was receiving. She tried to figure out the rules she needed to follow in order to get more connection and validation from each of them.

Those rules included becoming a tomboy for her dad by day. They included being an escort for him at night when mom was working, away or too depressed to function. Isabel became a "good girl" for her mom as well. The rule with her mom was to try her best to need nothing from her. Following these rules did provide Isabel with some semblance of greater *connection, validation and/or safety.* However, by following them, Isabel became a little adult at an age when she was supposed to be in the midst of her childhood. As part of this she learned to hide her heart.

Isabel sacrificed significant amounts of the authenticity aspect of her integrity in order to follow the rules she believed had the best chance of earning her the *connection, validation and/or safety* she most deeply needed from each of her parents. She gave up herself to be loved by them through "serving" them, which meant performing for them rather than being fully authentic. She did this by becoming who she believed they needed her to be at an age when what she most needed was to be served *by* them.

What We Most Need as Children

Any one of us who has spent a reasonable amount of time around young children will have noticed how their young lives revolve around four things (other than food and sleep):

1. **Normal children want to cuddle.** They instinctively understand that to develop properly they need nurturance. Human beings, and in fact all primates, quite literally cannot survive without physical affection. Even rats do better when they are held 15 minutes a day as babies for the first few weeks of life. Later in life they manage stress more efficiently, have better health and live longer than rats that were not held. (*Why Zebras Don't Get Ulcers*, Robert M. Sapolsky, page 388.) Connection, in all its forms, is a large part of how children learn they are lovable. There is obviously much more to connection than only cuddling but our basic wiring makes cuddling a great starting place. (One exception to this may be children who tend toward autism and therefore find cuddling too intense to manage.)

2. **Normal children seek validation.** They go through a phase when their battle cry is, "Look at me." This reflects their need to register deep in their bones that their authentic joy is welcome. They need to know that their own version of discovery and success will earn them validation rather than rejection. They need to experience that they can

indeed have a positive impact on the world around them. As you can see, our three core drives are already driving us in childhood.

3. **Normal children have painful experiences.** "Ouch" is an unavoidable part of growing up. The only children who are significantly shielded from pain, difficult experiences and traumas are those who are overprotected. This becomes a problem in and of itself because it teaches these children to believe they are too fragile to cope with how the world is. Children having "ouch" experiences need two things in order for these experiences to become gifts. First, they need to be kept company so they learn how to naturally cycle through difficult inner feelings. They need to learn they can handle the entire range of their feelings without becoming overwhelmed by them or repressing and denying them. Second, they need help in learning how to turn painful experiences into teachable moments. Through these forms of connection and validation, children learn the vital life lesson of how to turn lemons into lemonade, lead into gold. Their adventures with "ouch" also teach them another crucial life lesson: how to better balance their desire for discovery with their need for safety.

4. **Normal children learn the word "no."** Through *hearing* this word, children learn about other people's limits and boundaries. Through *using* this word, they learn how to teach others about their own limits and boundaries. Developing a friendly and inquisitive relationship with the word "no" is one of the ways children learn about their own authenticity, about how to honor other people's needs, about how to remain safe, and about the impact we all have on one another.

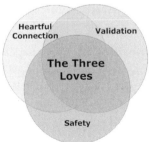

There are many forms of love that children need, such as food, clothing, shelter, health care, and the like. But, *there are only three forms of love that children actually experience as love: 1) Connection; 2) Validation; and 3) Safety.* These are the three loves of childhood.

When children experience sufficient amounts of the three forms of love, they can thrive quite well with even a minimum of food, clothing and shelter. Sidney Poitier shares a deeply moving and elegant portrait about this important truth in his extraordinary autobiography, *The Measure of a Man*. He does a magnificent job of connecting childhood experiences with adulthood integrity. He also beautifully describes some particularly poignant life experiences in which his desire for discovery collided with his need for safety. I hope you make a point of reading his book. Better yet, consider listening to him read it in the audiobook version — listening to Poitier's story in his own wonderful voice is a true treat!

Connection and Disconnection Experiences

Imagine yourself as a small child. You come upon what to you is a huge dog; a collie. Imagine this is the first time in your life you have ever met a dog "up close and personal." The dog comes running toward you, barking, with its tail wagging.

Your heart is suddenly pounding. You look to the big person with you, a man you know well who cares about your safety. He is smiling at you as he encourages the dog to come closer. As the dog comes to within a couple of feet of you, the big person notices your apprehension. He crouches down, gently holding your hand. With his other hand he keeps the dog far enough away so it can't touch you. He provides the time and safety you need to begin discovering for yourself that hanging out with a dog can be a pretty fun experience.

Not long afterward, you ask your parents if you can have a collie of your very own.

This is an example of a digested life experience. In this example, your reaction was compassionately noticed by someone who kept you safe. He also kept you company and helped you discover something precious about love and life from your experience. You would have learned about more than just dogs from this experience. You would have taken one step closer to learning how to keep company with your own feelings on your own. You would have learned it could be a good thing to remain open to learning during future difficult situations, as long as you could keep yourself relatively safe.

Now, imagine this same situation unfolding in a different way. In this example, as the collie comes toward you, there is no big person there. This animal is huge, making a loud noise and galloping at you. You are afraid it will knock you down or eat you or who knows what. Your heart starts racing and your adrenaline starts pumping. You scream and cry as you run away in terror. As soon thereafter as you can, you tell an adult what happened to you. You relive your terror as you describe what happened. You start crying all over again. You can't help it. You're only a child.

The adult tells you to stop being a sissy and says, "I'll give you something to cry about," and then spanks you for having been scared. This is violation.

Or he walks away shaking his head in disgust. He leaves you all alone with feelings you don't know how to manage; he leaves you alone to glean whatever learning you can. This is abandonment, which is also how Isabel felt as a child, terrified to be left home alone at night. What her Mom most needed from her was to not have any needs — also a form of abandonment.

Or he tells you what a nasty, bad dog that was, that what it did to you was a horrible thing, and that you were just an innocent victim. This is indulgence.

Or he becomes emotionally overwrought, recalling the time he had been viciously bitten by a German shepherd as a boy. You begin to try to comfort and soothe him rather than cycling through your own feelings and discovering the gifts hidden within your difficult life experience. This is stealing the attention, as when Isabel's father needed her to be his substitute wife rather than the little girl that she was.

These are examples of the four main varieties of disconnection that result in an undigested life experience: **Violation, Abandonment, Indulgence**, and **Stealing the Attention**.

The Four Forms of Disconnection

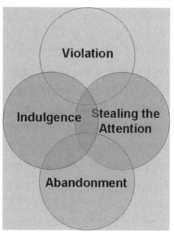

Life experiences do not create scars. Disconnection does. Life experiences do not create lasting trauma. Disconnection does because it results in an undigested life experience. Undigested life experiences are the traumas that keep on re-traumatizing.

Chronic disconnection, no matter what forms it takes, prevents children from developing the Seven WisePassions they need to develop for adult success and fulfillment. Children who re-experience chronic disconnection from others have difficulty being teachable because they never discover how to learn properly from their life experiences. They don't know how to care for themselves adequately because they are too busy learning how to protect themselves from life experiences they don't know how to digest. They have a diminished capacity for discernment because they never learn right relationship with their own sensations, emotions and interpretations. They never learn how to harvest true gifts from life experiences because they never learn the art of life experience digestion. They either become afraid of their power or they develop an indulgent relationship with their personal power. They have difficulty synergizing with others because they didn't experience sufficient connection as children to learn how to do this. And they do not know how to recognize collective highest good because it's all they can do to simply survive.

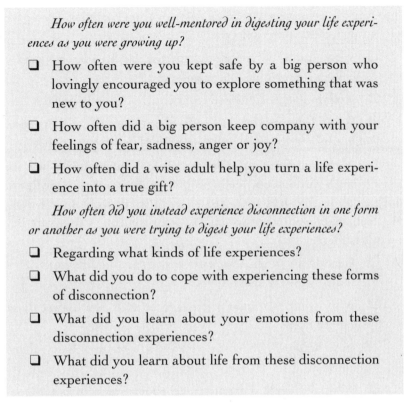

How often were you well-mentored in digesting your life experiences as you were growing up?

❑ How often were you kept safe by a big person who lovingly encouraged you to explore something that was new to you?

❑ How often did a big person keep company with your feelings of fear, sadness, anger or joy?

❑ How often did a wise adult help you turn a life experience into a true gift?

How often did you instead experience disconnection in one form or another as you were trying to digest your life experiences?

❑ Regarding what kinds of life experiences?

❑ What did you do to cope with experiencing these forms of disconnection?

❑ What did you learn about your emotions from these disconnection experiences?

❑ What did you learn about life from these disconnection experiences?

A Closer Look at the Four Forms of Disconnection

In addition to company keeping, the most basic of all connection responses, there are four disconnection responses we all experience as children. Each is a variety of disconnection response. These responses come in the four descriptions you have already read about: violation, abandonment, indulgence and stealing the attention. They are widely available in all areas of our life: relatives, friends, school, church, etc.

Review the disconnection experiences you had as a child as you read the descriptions of the following Four Forms of Disconnection.

1. **Violation:** As children, we feel intruded upon or violated when someone older than us makes us wrong or punishes us for having an emotional reaction to a life experience. We feel intruded upon or violated when someone older than us decides for us what we should learn from a life experience, rather than helping us

discover our own sacred learning. We are also violated when we are physically, emotionally, spiritually or sexually abused.

- ❏ What kinds of violation experiences did you have as a child? With whom? At what ages?
- ❏ How humiliated did you feel because of being violated?
- ❏ What decisions did you make about yourself, other people, life and/or God as a result of each violation experience?

2. Abandonment: As children, we feel abandoned when we have to work through our feelings about a life experience, or figure out the life lessons it is supposed to teach us, entirely on our own. We feel abandoned when we deeply want someone's company but no one is there.

- ❏ What kinds of abandonment experiences did you have as a child? At what ages?
- ❏ Who would you have wanted to be with you during these experiences?
- ❏ How "unworthwhile" did you feel as a result of being abandoned?
- ❏ What decisions did you make about yourself, other people, life and/or God as a result of each abandonment experience?

3. Indulgence: We were indulged as children whenever someone blamed another person, or other external circumstances, for how we felt, how we reacted, or what we learned from a life experience.

- ❏ What kinds of indulgent experiences did you have as a child?
- ❏ Regarding what events did you receive the direct or indirect message that you were an innocent victim of circumstance or of another person's actions, when you actually had even a small role in what occurred?
- ❏ Who indulged you in these ways? At what ages?
- ❏ What did you learn about entitlement as a result of being indulged?

What decisions did you make about yourself, other people, life and/or God as a result of the experiences in which you were indulged?

4. **Stealing the Attention:** Someone stole the attention from us as children when they became emotionally overwhelmed by our reactions, resulting in our setting aside our own reactions to care for them, even though we were the one with the life experience to digest. For instance, you might have been approached by a stranger who scared you and even though you got away, you were still shaking and upset when you told your mother about what happened. If your mother had burst into tears or became furious about this stranger while you were still in the middle of your own reactions, this would be an example of stealing the attention.

- ❑ Who reacted to your own difficulties by stealing the attention?
- ❑ Regarding what experiences? At what ages?
- ❑ What decisions did you make about yourself, other people, life and/or God as a result of your "stealing the attention" experiences?

The Lessons of Disconnection

If you had any of these kinds of disconnection experiences frequently enough as a child, you likely did not learn how to properly digest your life experiences. If disconnection experiences occurred during your most difficult childhood life experiences, they turned into traumas. You are likely to be impaired by them as an adult unless you made a point of properly digesting them.

Here are three of the most common and significant lessons we learn from our disconnection experiences:

1. Aspects of our authentic self are too much for others to handle.

2. We must therefore disconnect from or hide certain feelings or aspects of ourselves.

3. If we figure out how to disconnect from those feelings or aspects, people will finally love us: they will connect more with us, validate us more, and keep us safe more often.

You will find more exercises related to this in *The New IQ Integrity Makeover Workbook*.

More About Digested and Undigested Life Experiences

There are two types of life experiences: those we successfully digest and those we do not.

Digestion means harvesting from a life experience hidden gifts that truly make the experience worthwhile, even if it was horrible or unacceptable at the time. This is how we stop being harmed by life experience. Emotional indigestion means anything short of this.

It is never too late to finish digesting a life experience. In fact, the capacity to properly digest life experiences is one of the cornerstones of integrated adult development.

Life experience digestion occurs via connection; life experience indigestion occurs via disconnection.

Connection is the catalyst necessary for digesting Life Experiences. This is as true for adults as it is for children. It is true whether someone else offers it to us, we experience it from spiritual sources (God, angels, etc.), or we learn how to offer it to ourselves. Connection is the experience of being joined with another person, with ourselves and with our spiritual resources, all also known as bonding. Connection is the heart of parenting; disconnection impairs a child's capacity to develop all seven WisePassions that you will learn about later in this book.

(The term "spiritual resources" is used throughout this book as a sort of shorthand to refer to the many spiritual frames of reference people use. Feel free to mentally substitute whatever term works for you. For example, Higher Power, Greater Power, God, Goddess, Spirit, Natural Law, Higher Self, True Self, the Tao, Krishna, Guide, Mother Nature, Gaia, Holy Spirit, the Cosmic Christ, Jesus, the Buddha, the Cosmos, personal Truth, the Force, etc.)

More About Connection

The more frequently and effectively we are offered connection as children, the more we become able to offer connection to ourselves as adults. The more connection we experience as children, the more likely we will be as adults to seek people to be close to who also know how to do this for themselves and for others. The more connection we experience as children, the better we will be at synergizing with others as adults instead of coercing or giving in. (Again, synergizing is co-creating agreements with others and finding solutions that are mutually beneficial.)

Connection is not simply love. Many loving parents were not sufficiently trained by their parents, teachers, clergy or peers, in the art of emotional connection or company keeping. If most had this skill, far fewer couples would remain together miserably, or divorce. If most had this skill, there would not be nearly as much conflict or war on our planet as there is.

An adequate supply of Connection is crucial to proper development. Connection is like money in the bank. When a parent has built up his/her connection bank account with a child and the parent then does not keep company with the child during a particular life experience, the child will ordinarily be fine anyway. S/he might accumulate an undigested life experience, but it will be much easier to digest that experience later.

Effective and consistent Connection, both when a child is in joy and when s/he is expressing his/her gifts, reinforces the gold in him/her. It reinforces that it is okay for the child to feel happy. This in turn develops adults who feel free to be authentic and who welcome their happiness.

Effective and consistent Connection during difficult life experiences teaches us as children to be unafraid of life experiences or of our interior reactions to them. It teaches us how to keep ourselves company during such experiences so we can properly digest them (harvest their gifts). It teaches us to remain in full embrace of our deepest heart, our true temperament and our personal truths, even during difficult life experiences.

Keeping Company

The most basic connection response is "Keeping Company:" the art of being a tenderhearted witness who listens attentively and compassionately to your own or someone else's feelings without saying how to feel or what to do. Keeping company with someone means being fully heart-present to them in ways that encourage them to explore, resolve and learn from their inner reactions. (Eugene Gendlin, the originator of an extremely important discernment development tool called Focusing, coined the term "keeping company.")

There are two broad categories of life experiences during which it is important to keep company with a child:

1. *When s/he is in joy or expressing his/her gifts.* Company-keeping under these circumstances validates the child's inner "gold." It teaches him/her that it is safe to show the full measure of his/her light. It teaches the child that it is OK to enjoy feeling happiness and joy.

2. *When s/he is going through, or trying to make sense out of, a difficult Life Experience.* Company-keeping under these circumstances validates the child's lovability and okay-ness. It teaches him/her that even when s/he has dark and difficult feelings, they can be worked through. It teaches the child that good things can come from struggling with inner parts and reactions that might not seem socially acceptable.

We need lots of company-keeping as children while we explore our emotions, boundaries, wants, reactions and various aspects of ourselves. We need company-keeping as children in order to discover our talents, gifts and personal power. Company-keeping is what teaches us to trust our ability to deal with challenging life experiences. It is what teaches us to feel safe with the emotions we feel in response to those experiences. Because of all this, company-keeping teaches children a priceless skill that will come in handy for the rest of their lives.

In order to grow up being able to digest our Life Experiences properly, adults must show us as children how to:

1. Keep company with and safely release our entire range of feelings and reactions. This teaches us not to be afraid of our insides. It teaches us how to learn from our insides.

2. Turn the life experience into a gift that expands our capacity for authentic self-expression, connectedness with others and having a positive impact in our world because we had that experience.

The more we learn as children how to digest our life experiences, the more capable we are at doing this for ourselves as adults. The more we can do this for ourselves as adults, the more we can assist others in digesting their life experiences. The less we were kept company as children, the more damage we inadvertently do to others and ourselves as adults...until we learn differently as part of our adult development.

The more frequently and effectively we experience Connection as children the more capable we become as adults to:

1. Listen to and honor our own inner experiences and wisdom; this makes us unafraid to face any inner feelings, thoughts, reactions or wants we might have.

2. Choose people to be close with who know also how to do this for themselves and others. We can also choose to remain more distant from those who do not know how to do this for themselves, unless we are in a helping role with them.

3. Digest our life experiences in ways that enhance our authenticity, our capacity to lovingly connect and collaborate with others, and our ability to serve the collective highest good.

You might recall that in the last chapter I mentioned that this capacity was something that natural developers instinctively knew how to do with relatively little help from me. Harvesting gifts from our life experiences through properly digesting them enables all of us to embrace our deepest heart, our true temperament and our personal truths. In this sense, it is the key to authenticity.

Undigested life experiences disrupt our energy field, our psyche and our body. They disrupt our authenticity, our capacity for connection with others and the ways we go about trying to be of service in the world.

What happens if a child has an undigested life experience that is particularly extreme? A big emotional scar, that's what. A

THE NEW IQ

consistent stream of undigested life experiences produces an even bigger emotional scar, except now it is more difficult to trace back because the scar is not linked to a single dramatic life experience.

Life is structured so that disconnection is inevitable during at least some life experiences. This is no one's fault. It often occurs despite the best of intentions. Because disconnection is inevitable, so are undigested life experiences.

As children, we need a mechanism to cope with Disconnection and Undigested Life Experiences. As adults, a significant portion of our development involves outgrowing this mechanism and digesting our backlog of undigested life experiences so we can at last harvest the gifts they have been waiting to give us. The mechanism is a Survival Plan.

To Recap...

❑   Life experience digestion occurs via connection.

❑   Life experience indigestion occurs via disconnection.

❑   Life is structured so that disconnection is inevitable during at least some life experiences.

❑   This is no one's fault and it often occurs despite the best of intentions.

❑   Because disconnection is inevitable, so are undigested life experiences.

Because undigested life experiences occur, a survival plan becomes necessary.

CHAPTER 6

HOW YOU WERE A
CHILDHOOD GENIUS

*"What are the five universal survival strategies that
we come to think of as 'who I am?'"*

Introducing Your Survival Plan:
A Temporary But Sacred Childhood Coping Strategy

A brilliant childhood mechanism enables us to search for ways
to get more connection, validation and safety. It also allows us to
cope with our growing backlog of undigested life experiences. This
amazing mechanism is called a Survival Plan. We do not create it as
children through foresight; rather, our innate inner wisdom invents
it to save our lives as children.

To varying extents, depending on our individual circumstances
as children, our survival plan:

❑ Enables us to place aspects of ourselves in *hiding*.

❑ Replaces our authenticity and integrity with *coping* mechanisms that allow us to live with an accumulating backlog of
undigested life experiences.

❑ Provides us with *substitutes* for the Connection we lack.

The Five Elements of a Survival Plan

A survival plan includes five sets of skills:

1. The ability to manufacture hope through a **Happy Ending
    Fantasy.** This is a core childhood lifesaving belief that life
    will get better if I can only figure out what to do differently
    in order to get more *connection, acceptance and/or safety.*

2. The **Rules** I believe I need to follow in order to do that "something different" that will make my happy ending fantasy come true.

3. A **Pandora's box,** into which I hide:

   a. Gifts and talents of mine that I believe are too much for others.

   b. Aspects of myself that I have judged awful or unacceptable.

   c. My growing backlog of undigested life experiences.

      (The term "Pandora's box" comes from Greco-Roman mythology. A classic version of the Pandora's box myth holds that this box contains things you believe are harmful, and it also contains hope.)

4. A **Mask** that gets you to see me as the person I think you need me to be, or that I wish I was. The purpose of this inner "press agent" is to make sure you don't see what I have hidden in my Pandora's box.

5. **Anesthesias** that numb the pain I feel because:

   a. No amount of trying to figure out and follow the rules ever makes my happy ending fantasy come true.

   b. I have given up portions of my authenticity, integrity, and sometimes even spiritual connection, in order to survive the effects of disconnection and undigested life experiences.

Developing a Survival Plan is part of the architecture of life. When viewed from the reverse engineering development perspective, a survival plan must serve a sacred purpose or it would not be developed by virtually all of us.

What is that purpose? *The purpose of a Survival Plan is to buy us time to become capable of truly digesting our life experiences, and of moving into full integrity with all three of our Core Drives.* Our survival plan is not built to last forever; planned obsolescence is built into its architecture. It is only designed to serve us until we become adults. We are meant to outgrow our survival plan once we become adults. We are not meant to strengthen it further, as so many of us end up doing.

The Elements of the Survival Plan

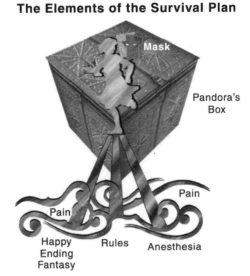

Everyone Develops a Survival Plan

Each one of us, *no matter how wonderful a home we came from*, carries within us a growing backlog of undigested life experiences. This comes from all parts of our lives as children: home, friends, school, extracurricular activities, and experiences we have alone, even in our places of worship. How pervasive our survival plan becomes depends on how extensively we feel the need to stifle or distort one or more of our three core drives to effectively cope with not experiencing as much *connection, validation and/or safety* as we need.

Survival Trumps Integrity

As children, we develop the capacity to connect with our spiritual resources and ourselves only to the extent that others connect with us. We digest our life experiences only as well as adults around us know how to help us do that. We remain authentic only to the extent that the most important adults in our life encourage this.

In other words, our spiritual, psychological and physical lives are on the line during our early development. While the amount that each child does this varies, all of us to one extent or another need to find ways to survive:

💣 Childhood disconnection experiences.

💣 A growing backlog of undigested life experiences.

💣 Becoming less-than authentic.

Survival needs to be a higher priority during childhood than living in integrity. We sacrifice our integrity as children, to whatever extent we need to, in order to survive. And it works...for a while....

This principle of development is vitally important to understand. Only to the extent that you have unmasked and freed yourself from the spell of your survival plan can you become capable of living in 3D Integrity. Only to the extent that you have unmasked and freed yourself from the spell of your survival plan can you fully digest your life experiences. Only to the extent that you have replaced your survival plan (and your subsequent redemption plan) with the Seven WisePassions of 3D Living (first mentioned in Chapter Four) can your adult development unfold as efficiently as possible.

You will find an exercise to help you reveal to yourself some of the ways you sacrificed your integrity as a child for the sake of survival in the companion book: *The New IQ Integrity Makeover Workbook* (which will be described in detail in the "Going Further" Appendix and meanwhile will be referred to as the *Workbook*).

Our Genius as Children

It should now be clear that all of us experience a blend of connection and disconnection experiences as children, of validation and invalidation experiences, and of safe and unsafe experiences. What varies from child to child is how much we have of each. What varies is the extent to which we are successfully assisted as children in turning undesired experiences into teachable lead-into-gold moments.

Each moment of our life, from the moment we are born to the moment we die, is a teachable moment. The only question in each moment is, "What will we learn?" Teachability is the first of the Seven WisePassions of 3D Living.

What do we do with the disconnection, invalidation and lack of safety experiences we have as children? What do we do with all the life experiences we were unable to successfully transform into teachable lead-into-gold moments? *The answer is both simple and obvious. We learn how to survive despite, rather than because of, these life experiences.* We learn to survive despite these experiences remaining incompletely or improperly digested within us.

Surviving *despite* our experiences is not thriving. Flourishing *because* of our experiences is thriving.

Our capacity for survival, for adaptation, is hard-wired into all but the most physiologically damaged children. It is part of our genius as children. *The purpose of childhood survival and adaptation in response to disconnection, invalidation and lack of safety experiences is to buy us time until we grow old enough to become capable of digesting these experiences in more useful ways than we could do as children.*

We gain a huge life gift by learning how to keep such experiences locked inside our inner Pandora's box until we grow older. We learn that we can trust our ability to endure the exigencies of life. In other words, *having to find a way to survive despite carrying Undigested Life Experiences teaches us the gift of resilience.*

Without the gift of difficult and even undigested life experiences, we do not develop a capacity to navigate whatever deeply painful experiences will naturally and inevitably be woven into our adulthood tapestry of experiences. Without this gift, we do not develop the capacity to keep moving toward achieving our most precious goals and dreams as adults, despite the hardships that are frequently built into the journey.

Yet, as precious as the gift of becoming an excellent survivor is, our survival plan comes with a price tag. Fortunately, that price can be eliminated once we become adults. Recognizing the price you have been paying in adulthood, while still living in childhood survival mode, is your admission ticket into true adulthood.

This is why we are looking at the anatomy of childhood survival before turning our attention more directly to integrated adult development a few chapters from now. Understanding the anatomy of childhood survival reveals important secrets about why we have the integrity problems we have. This clarity will contribute immeasurably to your understanding of why integrated adult development involves what it involves, as you will soon see.

The picture you will develop about yourself in the next couple of chapters will illuminate what you need to outgrow in order to become who you truly are. The Seven WisePassions of 3D Living will be your key to accomplishing that.

CHAPTER 7

THE SURVIVAL PLAN IN ACTION: THREE PORTRAITS

*"How can I acquire some clues about
my own hidden survival plan?"*

Remember Isabel? Her story illustrated some common ways people move away from their integrity beginning in childhood. It also provides a powerful portrait of a childhood survival plan.

Isabel's happy ending fantasy revolved around connection and validation from her dad and safety with her mom. She believed her father could connect with her and validate her more fully than he was doing. She believed she would feel safer with her mother if she stopped abandoning her through her long periods of time away from the family.

The rules Isabel believed would help get her more connection and validation with her father were to become a tomboy by day and his escort by night. The rule she believed would help her get more safety with her mother was to have no needs.

Isabel's parents' expectations that she behave like an adult while she was still a child pushed underground a wide range of aspects of her authenticity. To follow the rules she created to make her happy ending fantasy come true, Isabel had to place many aspects of herself into her Pandora's box. These included:

💣 Her femininity: Isabel's father wanted her to be the son he never had, and her femininity threatened her mother's fragile sense of worth. Her best solution was to hide her femininity by wearing a tomboy mask.

- ✹ Her emotional needs: her father needed her to be an adult and her mother needed Isabel not to need anything from her.

- ✹ Her intuition: her parents were threatened by her intuitive gifts.

- ✹ Her spiritual connection: neither of her parents were religiously or spiritually focused so this aspect of was her not welcome.

The mask Isabel developed was that of a good "adultified" tomboy who didn't really need anything from anyone. Her mask helped her appear to others as though she did not need connection when in reality she was connection-starved. It helped her hide the "unacceptable" parts of her so she could follow the rules she hoped would make her happy ending fantasy come true.

As a child, it was impossible for Isabel to maintain her mask all the time. Periodically, her profound emotional pain erupted into incapacitating anxiety attacks. She desperately needed company-keeping and to be loved just as she was, things her parents did not provide. Isabel needed to develop anesthesias to cope with this pain. One of Isabel's strengths was that she was an unusually intuitive child. She discovered that animals, especially horses, loved her in the ways she so desperately needed from both her parents. This made animals her perfect first anesthesia and she spent more and more time with her animals and less and less time with people.

Isabel's regular panic episodes made her too afraid of the world to take important risks. However, as a young adult she found the love of her life and to be with this man, she needed to break free of her survival plan's shackles to become who she really was. Instead, her rules overpowered her intuition that this man was the one for her. Isabel lived with deep regret throughout most of her adulthood because she had been unable to find the inner strength to break her rules and follow her inner guidance.

Isabel's tragic lost love was followed by two failed marriages and a failed relationship. Despite having become a talented and well-regarded psychotherapist, her practice was so small it barely supported her. Her pain was at last deep enough that she came to me to begin freeing herself from the bondage of her childhood survival plan. She was in her sixties.

Isabel began to replace her childhood survival plan and adulthood redemption plan with the Seven WisePassions of 3D Living. The more she did this, the more her career finally began flourishing and her love life finally began nourishing her. Isabel wants readers of this book not to wait as long as she did to do this transformation work. She also wants those who do wait until later in life to know that it's never too late for it to be more than worthwhile.

A Story about Being Unable to Invent a Happy Ending Fantasy

As a young child, my mother had already become certain that her parents had virtually no interest in who she really was. When she was in her eighties, I asked her to tell me about this. She gave me permission to share what she had never before confessed to anyone.

About her parents, Mom said, "They didn't know me. They wanted me to be what they wanted me to be, so that is how I acted. I was a good girl and gave them the agreeable self they wanted, except for my periodic episodes of stubbornness."

In these few words, Mom told me volumes about her rules and mask. From everything I could piece together, it looked to me like Mom was right; I never saw indications that her parents had any interest in who she was except insofar as she could be who they needed her to be.

Mom told me that she felt safe enough with her parents, so she did not need to invent hope that there was more safety than there really was. But she grew up without virtually any true connection or validation.

When I asked her how she developed false hope to help survive as a child she burst into tears, telling me she had never been able to do that. "As a child I never thought things would be better. I had no hope," she said. Without false hope, Mom never developed a happy ending fantasy. I wondered how she had survived without one.

From the time she was a young girl until she was around sixteen or seventeen, Mom believed she could not be fully authentic with anyone. She never even tried to have impact on anyone; she tried to be as invisible as possible. She didn't try to build deep emotional connection with anyone. Mom was filling out her portrait of the rules she followed.

Mom told me that even though she knew she was being who her parents needed her to be, she never knew which aspects of her own authenticity she was covering up. Instead, she said she spent her childhood feeling internally dark, impervious, and numb. This woman in her eighties again reiterated that she had never confessed to anyone anything about her Pandora's box. She seemed relieved that someone was finally hearing the true version of her story.

I asked Mom what anesthesias she had used as a little girl to numb her pain about all this. She said that even though it didn't feel exactly comfortable to her, she felt strangely soothed by a sense of physical paralysis she experienced most nights as she slipped into sleep. She also told me that the other Anesthesia she discovered as a child was fondling herself. She said she received a deep sense of comfort from this when she was quite young. (Fortunately, it seems that she discovered this on her own rather than through having been fondled by someone else.)

Mom revealed that she never felt she had found herself; she never developed the hope that her life could ever be any different from how it was for her as a child. She didn't develop a happy ending fantasy that connection or validation was possible for her to get. Still, her need to remain safe with her parents caused her to develop rules, a Pandora's box, a mask and anesthesia.

As an adult, Mom never found another adult with whom she could get some of her connection and validation needs met. The man she married was a great provider. My father provided her with safety as long as she didn't demand much else from him. Safety was all she got.

I asked her why she had not married a man who could connect with and validate her. Mom replied that this would have been too disloyal to her parents for her to bear. Mom also never developed spiritual resources that might have given her at least some sense of being loved for who she is. Instead, this essentially spiritual person viewed herself as an atheist. She truly was alone her entire life except for the light her two boys brought to her.

What saddened me the most was that Mom never developed hope that her life would be better someday. She instead adopted the script of the living dead: "Buck up. This is just how life is." She had no happy ending fantasy to transfer to goals, dreams or other people. When she reached the age when others were converting their childhood happy ending fantasy into an adulthood redemption plan, she was resigned to a lifetime of emptiness.

Mom never found herself; she never reached her potential, and she never felt like she made a difference in the world except through her two sons. Despite a couple of stints in therapy and attending a number of personal development workshops beginning in her fifties, Mom never found a way to harvest gifts from her rather gigantic backlog of undigested life experiences. She therefore remained extremely limited in her authenticity, her capacity to connect with others and her ability to make a positive difference in the world. She never experienced 3D Living.

Thankfully, after my dad died when Mom was in her sixties, she finally found a man who loved her just as she was. Now, in her final years, she has found a way to make peace with her life and her choices. This did not make up for a lifetime of not finding a way to (as Hesse put it) "live in accord with the promptings that came from my deepest self." But at least she found some measure of inner peace.

Mom wanted me to tell her story in this book. She hoped it would help you more fully appreciate the importance of discovering the anatomy of your childhood survival plan so you can see what you need to outgrow as an adult. She believed that, had she undertaken the process of integrated adult development described in this book, her life would have been markedly happier and more fulfilling. Although still very much alive as of my writing this book, at eighty-two Mom viewed sharing her secret story with you as one of her final acts of service in wanting to help make the world a better place.

Dean's Survival Plan

Dean was another story entirely. His father, who was apparently anything but a kind man, may have done him a favor by leaving when Dean was fairly young. His parents' divorce left Dean's mom relatively destitute, and extremely angry that a man was not around to take care of her. She turned to Dean to fill that void. But, because she also carried a lot of hatred and fear toward men, she turned toward him with a mixture of neediness, anger and fear.

Dean, on the other hand, was rightly leery of her desires to draw him closer. He saw much more hope in developing a happy ending fantasy with his grandfather than with his mother. As Dean busied himself figuring out the rules for creating as much *connection, validation and/or safety* as he could with his grandfather, Dean's mother became increasingly angry and vindictive toward Dean for abandoning her.

The situation with Dean's mother became quite extreme. Dean had to devote a huge amount of his attention to figuring out and enacting the rules for containing his mother. Hoping it would take some pressure off her, Dean took a job to pay his own way beginning as a young teenager. He hoped his independence would keep him relatively safe for however long he would continue to live under her roof. Like Isabel, Dean wore a mask of being more mature than could ever be true for his young age.

Holding down a half-time job as a young teen while going to school took a lot of Dean's energy. He was regularly humiliated by peers and found himself at a disadvantage academically as well.

Despite his best efforts, Dean's mother proved uncontainable. She made Dean her scapegoat for her profound hatred of men. For his part, Dean contributed to the mix the rage building up inside him about having to stuff his authenticity into his Pandora's box. They eventually landed in court. Part of what helped save Dean was his gifts as a problem solver and inventor. His science experiments eventually became his primary childhood anesthesia. By the end of high school, he was winning national science awards, although his overall academic development, as well as his people skills, remained stunted. As a result, he was unable to succeed in college and dropped out.

A powerful and wealthy man took Dean under his wing. Dean was deeply grateful to this man, with whom he bonded more deeply than with either of his parents. Making money became his second anesthesia. Ultimately that man turned on Dean just as his mother had and abandoned Dean just as his father had.

As a result of all these experiences, by the time he was a young man, Dean had become locked into viewing himself as an innocent victim. He was enraged at others for their part in his self-destruction. This rage reflected the extreme harshness of his *Inner Critic*, which held him to stiflingly high standards and shamed him when he did not meet them. This part of him also lashed out toward others in equally hypercritical ways and regularly beat him up verbally. Following in its footsteps, he did the same with others, often without even realizing he was doing it.

Dean eventually met with a degree of career success as an adult. He made millions but then lost them — several times. The rules he played by were so close to the edge that he was always at risk of getting in trouble. That and a trail of failed relationships combined to serve as his wakeup call.

Dean began his journey of outgrowing his childhood survival plan and his adulthood *Redemption Plan*. His life now revolves around his business, his loved ones and his service work. His business thrives. It is more stable and personally fulfilling to him than ever. He treasures each moment he has with his daughters and loves nourishing and teaching them. His service work involves assisting men in developing integrity through becoming more authentic, caring and socially responsible.

As you explore your relationship with each of the five elements that survival plans contain, keep in mind the stories you read in this chapter.

CHAPTER 8

DISCOVERING THE ANATOMY OF YOUR SURVIVAL PLAN

"How can I discover why my past is limiting my present without having to go through years of soul searching or psychotherapy?"

Your childhood survival plan contains five key elements:

1. You developed a **Happy Ending Fantasy**. It is unbearable for most children to live without hope. Your happy ending fantasy gave you hope that there was more *connection, validation and/or safety* available than whatever amount you were receiving as a child. It kept you motivated when the going got tough and it shielded you from completely self-destructing as a child.

2. You developed a set of **Rules** you believed could make your happy ending fantasy come true. Your job was to figure out what those rules were and to follow them consistently. There were two sets of rules you needed to discover. The first set was about *your authenticity*, rules about what to change, cover up, over-emphasize in yourself to get more of the *connection, validation and/or safety* you needed. The second set was about *how to deal with others*. These were your rules for how to make things easier to compensate for, to contain, or to manipulate *others* in order to get more of the *connection, validation and/or safety* you needed.

3. You developed a **Pandora's box.** This metaphorical holding tank is your inner treasure chest that holds in safekeeping whatever you felt you could not show to the world. It includes the aspects of your authenticity you felt you needed to cover up in order to get more *connection, validation and/or*

safety. It also includes your undigested life experiences that are waiting for you to properly digest. Paradoxically, you are forbidden from opening this box. You know the box I'm talking about: it contains the "don't go there" experiences you have buried somewhere within you. It's the "don't mess with what isn't broken" story you tell yourself, even as you hide aspects of yourself from others because you secretly know that something is broken.

4. You developed a **Mask** that presents the public self you believe the world needs to see in order for you to be *lovable, accepted and/or safe*. Its job is to make you look like you're following the rules and also to hide from others the contents of your Pandora's box.

5. You developed **Anesthesias** to numb your emotional pain. This pain came from three primary sources: a) not experiencing sufficient connection with others when you most needed it; b) carrying a growing backlog of undigested life experiences; and c) failing to make your happy ending fantasy come true no matter how hard you tried to follow the rules, hide parts of yourself in your Pandora's box, and pretend you were your mask. Your first two sources of pain caused you to develop your survival plan to begin with. Your survival plan itself produced your third source of pain. The first things you turned into anesthesias may have been your greatest strengths, such as Dean's gift at science and invention.

Let's now take a look at your childhood survival plan one element at a time.

Discovering Why
You Developed a Survival Plan to Begin With

The following questions can help you clarify why you developed a survival plan in the first place. If you are uncertain about your answers to these questions, referring back to Chapter Five should help.

How often did you experience each of the four forms of disconnection as a child?

Violation:
❏ Rarely ❏ Sometimes ❏ Frequently ❏ Chronically
Abandonment:
❏ Rarely ❏ Sometimes ❏ Frequently ❏ Chronically
Indulgence:
❏ Rarely ❏ Sometimes ❏ Frequently ❏ Chronically
Stealing the Attention:
❏ Rarely ❏ Sometimes ❏ Frequently ❏ Chronically

With whom did you most often experience these forms of disconnection as a child?

Violation: _____

Abandonment: _____

Indulgence: _____

Stealing the Attention: _____

What did you learn about your Core Drives and about Life Experience Digestion as a child?

Authenticity: _____

Connection: _____

Impact: _____

Life Experiences Digestion: _____

Discovering Your Happy Ending Fantasy

What is a child to do in the face of unbearable fear, emotional pain, confusing life experiences, or an insufficiency of *connection, validation and/or safety*? Is s/he supposed to simply roll over, curl up and die? Let's hope not. If this were what was supposed to happen, very few of us would make it to adulthood intact.

Rather, we are called upon to instinctively construct false hope. Such a brilliant version, in fact, that we don't realize the hope is false until much later. This is the equivalent of falling under a spell, as in fairy tales such as the Hans Christian Anderson story of *The Emperor's New Clothes*. In this story, the Emperor is obsessed with clothes. He is talked into parting with a huge sum of money in return for what is to be the most extraordinary clothing ever created. He is told that the clothes are invisible to anyone who is unfit to fill their post or is unpardonably stupid. When the Emperor receives his clothes, he cannot see them. Not wanting to admit this because of what he was told about them, he decides to parade in them through the village. The citizens have heard about the extraordinary power of the garments the Emperor has purchased. They lavishly praise the magnificence of the Emperor's new clothes until a child points out that he is in reality naked. This story is a profound parable about the power of propaganda. The first propaganda we often fall prey to as children is our own: it is called a happy ending fantasy.

As children, we do our best to cloak whichever caregivers are the most important to us in the psychological equivalent of gorgeous and majestic robes. We see them as being more loving or capable or giving than they really are. This delusion serves a crucially life-preserving purpose for a young child. If we were to accurately see, at such a tender age, all of our caregivers' deficits, we would lose all hope that our needs for *connection, validation and/or safety* would ever be met. No young child can survive knowing that kind of stark truth without paying a huge price psychologically and/or spiritually.

There are those who don't live past childhood because they cannot develop a convincing happy ending fantasy and some children even commit suicide because they somehow cannot invent the false hope they would have needed in order to survive: the naked truth is too much for them to bear.

Children who somehow manage to remain alive without inventing false hope tend to end up feeling profoundly unworthy and empty. At best, they become the living dead (like the story about my mom); at worst, they become extremely harmful to themselves, to those around them or to society. In other words, they become big problems.

My natural developer clients didn't slip down the rabbit hole of despair that my mom lived in as a child. They invented and believed in hope that wasn't there when they were children. They found a way to harness the extraordinary power of hope — even false hope when needed.

Natural developers taught me the purpose a happy ending fantasy serves for all of us: it enables us to believe we have the *power* to get more *connection, validation and/or safety* than we are receiving, perhaps from our principal caregivers, or perhaps from some other adult in our life.

Our happy ending fantasy is the most brilliant childhood empowerment strategy ever created. Our core drive to have impact (i.e., make a difference) gives us the motivation to keep trying as children. Not only as children but also throughout our lives in all we do. This is why our childhood survival plan survives childhood to become our adulthood redemption plan, which you'll learn more about in the next chapter.

Psychologist Robert Firestone first articulated the dynamics of what I call the happy ending fantasy. In his groundbreaking book, *The Fantasy Bond* (which I consider mandatory reading for all mental health professionals), Dr. Firestone reveals what occurs when an adult caregiver falls significantly short of being able to meet a child's emotional needs: the child bonds with her/his fantasy of what they need an adult caregiver to be — what s/he believes the caregiver's potential is. This begins the child's quest to figure out how to bring out that potential.

The formula for doing that is the survival plan. The first ingredient in our childhood survival plan is our happy ending fantasy. It simply says, *"There is more connection, validation and/or safety available to me from (an important caregiver or substitute) than I am currently getting — and I can figure out a way to get it."*

What was your happy ending fantasy? "_____ can give me more ❑ Connection ❑ Validation ❑ Protection (Safety) than I'm getting from him/her."

As you got older, did you replace false hope with hopelessness?

❑ Yes ❑ No ❑ Mixture

Did you transfer your happy ending fantasy from caregivers to personal or career success, relationships with lovers or children, or with creating change in the world?

❑ Yes ❑ Never gave up on my parents ❑ Don't Know

Most likely, your childhood survival plan morphed into your redemption plan as you moved toward adulthood. Adulthood redemption plans are just as imprisoning as childhood survival plans.

Discovering the Rules You Used to
Try to Make Your Happy Ending Fantasy Come True

Hatching your happy ending fantasy started you on a quest that was to discover the rules you had to follow in order to make your happy ending fantasy come true.

Think of rules as prerequisites for deserving to feel worthy of love, connection, validation or being kept safe.

There are two sets of rules my clients taught me that we set out to discover and obey as children:

1. What we needed to change or cover up in ourselves in order to make our happy ending fantasy come true (that is, to get more of the *connection, validation and/or safety* we needed).

2. What we needed to do to make things easier for, compensate for, contain, or even manipulate our caregivers so that our happy ending fantasy had a better chance of coming true.

For instance, Isabel covered up her inner knowing, her intuition, and her yearning for spiritual connection, as part of trying to make her happy ending fantasy come true with her father. By agreeing to become a tomboy and be her father's escort as a prematurely "adultified" child, Isabel succeeded at preserving enough connection with her father so she could survive until adulthood in a relatively intact way.

Dean developed an extremely harsh inner critic. This part of him held his feet to the fire with his rules. It required him to meet stiflingly high standards. It shamed him when he did not meet them. It also lashed out toward others in equally hypercritical ways.

Shame largely stems from believing as children that the reason we are not getting the *connection, validation and/or safety* we seek is because there is something fundamentally wrong with us. Shame causes us to cover up or change who we are in order to hopefully get more *connection, validation and/or safety.* In other words, shame is paradoxically part of our attempts to empower ourselves as children. Unfortunately, shame is also at the root of why we sacrifice our authenticity and integrity beginning as children.

The development of an inner critic is one byproduct of the rules of the childhood survival plan. As you figured out the rules you had to follow as a child, you also developed a mechanism to make sure that you remembered and obeyed them. This mechanism probably became your inner critic.

The inner critic begins as the keeper of an inner file cabinet that contains the list of rules we are discovering. Before long, this part of us starts viewing itself as the most dependable guide and adviser we have and begins to shame us when we forget or don't follow the rules it is responsible for overseeing. It is also not beyond lashing out at others in equally harsh ways, especially when they do not respond to us in the ways our happy ending fantasy tells us they should if we are following the rules.

Most people bring their inner critics with them into their adult lives, along with the rest of their survival plans.

Life is structured so that very few of us experience as much connection, validation or safety as we need in order to thrive. Survival is our prime directive as children and our happy ending fantasy makes survival possible. Figuring out and following some set of rules is supposed to make it possible for our happy ending fantasy to come true. Our inner critic helps us follow those rules. We need a harsh taskmaster like an inner critic when the rules we are following require that we give up substantial parts of our integrity and authenticity.

This underlines one of the most important things to understand about your survival plan. For a child younger than early to middle adolescence, survival trumps integrity. As children, we will sacrifice however much authenticity and integrity as our survival requires. Why? Because we can regain these qualities as adults. Every one of my natural developer and successful deliberate developer clients can attest to this.

On the other hand, if we stop believing that we can get the *connection, validation and/or safety* we need to develop as a child, something far more devastating can occur. If we make it to adulthood, we may arrive with a significant amount of pessimism, hopelessness, emptiness or lifelessness. These feelings can challenge our ability to regain our authentic self and integrity at all. This is what happened to my mother despite her many efforts to heal herself as an adult.

As teens we may have sacrificed our security for the sake of our integrity by separating ourselves from our family or our environment sooner than would have been ideal. Those who do this sometimes preserve portions of their integrity that might otherwise have become more compromised. But, as you will see, virtually none of us escapes the process of our childhood survival plan morphing into an adulthood redemption plan.

From a reverse engineering perspective, our survival plan provides us with invaluable gifts as adults. Our happy ending fantasy teaches us precious lessons about the power of hope. The rules aspect of our survival plan teaches us valuable lessons about observation and discernment. From our attempts to discover the rules we begin learning about the law of cause and effect. Even though we will have to revise some of our faulty cause-effect ideas in adulthood, we at least learn to do our best to observe cause and effect. From faithfully enacting the rules we discover, the gift we gain is the ability to strive and persist against all odds.

What rules did you try to follow as a child to make your happy ending fantasy come true?

I can get the love/validation/safety I need if I do the following with my authenticity:

❑ Change, Cover Up or Tone Down

_____ in me

❑ Over-Emphasize This Ability of Mine:

_____

❑ Achieve This Goal or Standard:

_____

I can get the love/validation/safety I need if I do the following with key adults:

❑ Contain or Control These Qualities: _____

_____ in _____ (whom)

❑ Draw Out These Qualities: _____

_____ in _____ (whom)

Which of your three core drives became distorted as part of enacting the rules you developed?

❑ Rebellion is a distortion of your *Authenticity* core drive

❑ Compliance is a distortion of your *Connection* core drive

❑ Becoming a Savior is a distortion of your *Impact* core drive

As valuable as they were when we were children, devotion to these rules as an adult carries a big price tag. Following our survival plan-based rules hides our authenticity and is a substitute for integrity.

Discovering Your Pandora's Box

Pandora in Greek literally means "all gifts." The gods gave Pandora the box but forbade her to ever open it, supposedly because they would ruin the world.

We all have a metaphorical container within us that contains "all gifts," and we act as though we have been forbidden from ever opening it, for fear that if we do they will ruin our world. Our Pandora's box contains what we believe are harmful gifts from the "gods." We decided as children that parts of what we were endowed with were liabilities. Metaphorically speaking, surely God played a cruel trick on us to have given us certain emotions, thoughts, impulses, and even talents that cannot be used, because those who are important to us cannot bear us having them.

And God's trickery or punishment or ill will did not stop there. God also gave us life experiences that we could not digest. These too are locked in our box.

Worst of all, God placed in our box hope, and it was our hope of getting love that got us trapped in our survival plan in the first place. "How cruel is that?" we may be tempted to think.

In truth, our Pandora's box is a major miracle; it is a precious component of our childhood survival plan. This inner psychological holding tank contains the aspects of our authenticity that we needed to cover up in order to follow the rules. It contains the undigested life experiences we accumulated from our *disconnection, invalidation and/or lack of safety* experiences. These are the life experiences that never became teachable moments, meaning that we never harvested the true gifts they hold for us.

Our Pandora's box contains:

1. **Gold:** Our gifts, talents and dreams that we believed we had to hide as children. We were criticized or undermined for having them. For some reason, they felt too danger-ous to others for us to have, or they were simply ignored by others and we decided therefore that these gifts were unimportant.

2. **Lead:** Dark, seemingly unacceptable parts, emotions, faults, urges and temperament qualities we believed we had to hide in order to get love, or at least acceptance, as children, including undigested life experiences that were too painful, scary or confusing for us to face as children.

Thank goodness for your Pandora's box. For all these years, it has preserved for you all of your forbidden aspects, gifts and talents that are part of who you are. It has preserved for you the prior life experiences you still need to digest so you can harvest the gifts they wait to offer you. All you need to do is to set up the inner conditions that will allow you to access your Pandora's box, and to then learn how to effectively reclaim, transform and utilize what is inside your Pandora's box.

All successful developers I have worked with through the years developed a conscious relationship with their Pandora's box. They found, frequently to their surprise, that it contained crucial keys to restoring aspects of themselves.

Contrary to what ancient myth and some modern advice says about not opening it, this amazing inner box is well worth opening. In fact, if you are serious about becoming more fully in integrity, you have no choice but to open your box and harvest its gifts.

Only by dealing with what you hid within you for safekeeping can you truly claim these hidden gifts and put your past behind you.

> *In addition to what you hid, distorted or over-emphasized as part of following your Rules, what did you place in your Pandora's box as a child and teenager?*
>
> Undigested Life Experiences: _____
> Gifts and talents I have: _____
> "Negative" aspects of myself: _____

Discovering Your Mask

A Mask is a partly accurate version of your self that you show in public. That is why this aspect of your survival plan is often called your "Public Self." The technical name for your mask is your persona. Your persona is how you want to be seen. This, of course, implies that who you authentically are is somehow different from how you want others to see you. A persona serves a protective function. It is a mechanism through which you attempt to prevent others from seeing what you have placed in shadow, in your Pandora's box.

You are capable of developing multiple masks. Consider the masks you wore as a child and currently wear as an adult in the following contexts: with parents and other relatives, at school or work, with acquaintances, at your house of worship, in your civic activities, and with strangers such as store clerks.

My father was a master mask-user. His public self was one of competence, humility, amiability, kindness, devotion and ethics. My father indeed had all of these traits and I loved him for them. Dad's mask was quite consistent throughout his public life: at work, in the community and with our extended family. Yet, behind closed doors in the privacy of our little family of four, my father's mask dropped away: his competence often became stridence; his humility, arrogance; his amiability, tyranny; his kindness, rage; his devotion, emotional unavailability; and his ethics, dogma.

My father taught me huge lessons, some for better and some for worse, about the art of the mask. He taught me how common it is for people to look one way in public and sometimes behave in the mirror opposite fashion in private. Dad showed me more dramatically than anyone in my life how people create a mask to try to hide from others the content of their Pandora's box.

My clients discovered that the less they acknowledged and dealt with what was in their Pandora's box, the more their shadow side leaked out in private and, frequently enough in public, much to their chagrin. They also discovered that the more they acknowledged and dealt with what was in their Pandora's box, the smaller the gap became between their public mask and their private self.

Our mask is a mechanism for effectively dealing with unsafe, damaged, hostile or ill-willed people.

One important part of adult development involves transforming your mask from a hiding strategy into this kind of valued self-protection mechanism. Another important part of adult development is learning how to be with most people without a mask. The more you befriend what awaits you in your Pandora's box, the more you will become able to do this.

How were your parents' public masks different from how they behaved behind closed doors in the privacy of your immediate family?

_____

_____

What qualities did your public mask convey as a child and teenager? _____

What qualities of yours did your public mask hide as an adult?

_____

How is your mask different from how you behave behind closed doors in the privacy of your immediate family? _____

_____

Discovering Your Anesthesias

Survival plan anesthesias are the activities, substances, dreams or people you use for the purpose of numbing the pain you feel because of:

❑ Failing to get the *connection, validation or/or safety* you seek, no matter how much you follow the rules that were supposed to obtain these things for you.

❑ Being less than fully yourself because you sacrificed aspects of your integrity in order to make your survival plan work.

Survival plan anesthesias relieve the pain of:

❑ Having distorted or covered up or abandoned parts of your authentic self as part of your survival plan.

❑ Discovering that your survival plan is not making your happy ending fantasy come true no matter how hard you try to figure out and follow the rules.

❑ Carrying an ever-growing backlog of undigested life experiences because you did not learn how to fully digest them.

Your survival plan anesthesias shield you in two ways: they numb you from the pain you feel; and they distract you from this pain by getting you high instead of dealing with the issues.

What activities did you lose yourself in as a child? Drawing, building model planes, reading, imagination, dancing, music, acting, sports, eating candy?

These activities are *not necessarily* anesthesias because everyone needs time out to recharge their batteries as part of good self-care. Nearly everyone can lose himself or herself when they are in a delicious state of flow doing something they feel passionate about.

At the same time, virtually *anything* can be used as anesthesia, even otherwise healthy pursuits such as reading, eating, sleeping, computers, sexuality, watching television, clothes...well, you get the idea.

For instance, an indulgent relationship with self-soothing leads to lethargy, apathy, irresponsibility, self-sabotage and depression, among other symptoms. Overwork, too much stress, and being run by your to-do list and calendar eventually leads to an equal and opposite compensation: an indulgent relationship with self-soothing. That is simply a euphemistic way of referring to anesthetizing.

There are three important clues to the difference between using something as a survival plan anesthesia and using it as part of living a fulfilling integrity-based life which have to do with: 1) the intention why you are doing or utilizing this thing; 2) the function that it serves for you; and 3) the effect it has on your life. More specifically:

If something helps you clear your head or discharge and resolve strong feelings, you are most likely NOT using it as an anesthesia. If something helps you recharge your batteries so you can live your life with greater effectiveness, vitality and 3D Integrity, it is likely not an anesthesia. If something helps you become more able and willing to deal assertively and compassionately with the people in your life, it's most likely NOT an anesthesia.

If something helps you sidestep dealing with strong feelings you don't know how to handle, such as grief or fear or anger, you ARE likely using it as an anesthesia. If your family consistently complains about the amount of time or money you spend in your recharging or creative pursuits, you ARE likely using it as an anesthesia. If something you use to comfort you causes problems for you in school, at work or in your relationships, you probably ARE using it as an anesthesia.

Anesthesias have been used throughout history in all cultures. There is evidence that the brain is attracted to anesthesias; in fact, our body has a natural and valuable capacity to create opiates. In other words, we are biologically wired to anesthetize ourselves when that would be useful to do. So, most of us are unlikely to be able to get rid of our inclination to anesthetize.

Our natural inclination toward using anesthesia becomes particularly heightened during times of extreme pain, stress or trauma. On the other hand, as you hopefully now see that when survival plan anesthesia use remains a habit in adulthood, this takes us far beyond our body's natural and beneficial capacity to manufacture opiates.

That said, if your survival plan anesthesias are physically addictive substances, watch out — you are at grave risk of gradually losing your ability to choose whether you use them or they use you.

These include alcohol, cocaine, caffeine, marijuana, nicotine, heroin, amphetamines, and sugar (to name a few). All of these substances eventually tend to take control on a biochemical level.

Survival plan anesthesias also go far beyond chemicals and include things like excessive reading, or TV watching, or talking on the phone, or time spent on your computer, or on the Internet, or compulsive shopping, or gambling, or other forms of spending, or excessive or anesthesia-motivated sex, etc. Again, anything, including the loveliest things in the world, can be used as a survival plan anesthesia if that is the intention.

The trap built into anesthesias is that they can be quite effective at keeping you from feeling the pain that your survival plan is not working. However, in order to become motivated to outgrow your survival plan, you *need* to feel the pains of your survival plan not working. As long as you remain anesthetized this will not happen. Like a gangster who offers protection from his own violence, an anesthesia exacts a steep price for its services.

Here is the gift you can gain as an adult from your childhood attraction to survival plan anesthesias: learn to use any attraction you might feel toward anesthetizing as a wakeup call. You can recognize this attraction as your inner wisdom trying to tell you that you are going overboard with your self-soothing, or with the pace at which you are living your life.

What anesthesias did you use as a child to numb the pain you felt because your Rules weren't working to make your Happy Ending Fantasy come true?

_____

What are your favorite adulthood Anesthesias?

_____

Survival Plan Summary

Your survival plan is an amazing invention. It is the pinnacle of childhood genius. It contains the following ingredients:

1. **Happy ending fantasy:** there *must* be more love (*connection, validation, safety*) possible than I am currently getting (and that is actually available).

2. **Rules:** I can get that additional love if I cover up or change the right things in me and figure out ways to help or contain you. My inner critic's job is to enforce these rules by shaming and blaming whenever necessary to make sure I (or others) obey them.

3. **Pandora's box:** I do my best to hide my supposedly unacceptable aspects and distance myself from my undigested life experiences. I do this by creating a secret inner hiding place to hold these things for me so that they do not interfere with my survival.

4. **Mask:** I develop a public self (a persona), so you will believe that when I am following the rules I am being who I really am. My mask is the self I think I need to be to get your love. I depend upon my mask to hide from you the aspects of me that I decided must be unacceptable for me to show.

5. **Anesthesias:** I find effective ways to numb the pain I feel. My pain is from three sources. The first is the fact that I have become out of integrity in order to make my happy ending fantasy succeed. The second is because I am storing so many of my life experiences in an undigested form. The third is because, despite all the ways I have adapted in order to make my happy ending fantasy succeed, I am still failing to get the *connection, validation and/or safety* I need in order to develop properly.

Even though your survival plan is the pinnacle of childhood genius, I am confident that you can now see that it is also the foundation upon which lack of integrity is built.

Survival Plan Automation

As you now can see, everyone develops a survival plan to one extent or another, beginning in childhood. Our survival plan stifles and distorts our relationship with one or more of our three core drives.

In order for it to do its magic, your survival plan became unconscious and automated way back in childhood. Had it not, it would not have done you much good as a child. That would be like having to consciously think through the mechanics of walking each time you tried to walk. A survival plan is not useful if you need to consciously think it through each time you need it.

Because your survival plan became unconscious and automated, you entered adulthood wrongly believing that your survival plan is who you are. An extremely large part of adult development revolves around learning who you really are and living in accord with your true authenticity. You accomplish this through gradually freeing yourself from your survival plan's control. The key to accomplishing this is reclaiming from your Pandora's box that which you put into safekeeping, beginning way back in childhood.

If you completed the exercises in this chapter and also the more expanded ones in the *Workbook*, you now have a pretty good portrait of your personal survival plan. If you were unable to fully answer the questions, this means you need some assistance. There is no shame in that. Seek help from friends, mentors or professionals. The more you understand about your survival plan, the clearer you will be about what you need to outgrow as an adult in order to move into integrity among your three core drives (authenticity, connection and impact).

The next step in the "integrity makeover" that I am walking you through in this book is to become just as clear about the redemption plan your survival plan morphs into as you head toward adulthood. This plan too needs to be outgrown and this is what you will do in the next chapter.

In order to become fully authentic, in order to live in 3D Integrity, you must free yourself from your survival and redemption plans. Your relationships need you to be free from them, as does the world.

CHAPTER 9

How Our Childhood Survival Plan Morphs into Something That Compromises Our Integrity in Adulthood

"What prerequisites must I meet as an adult in order to feel lovable, worthy and safe?"

Your Survival Plan Was Designed to Be Temporary

You are not meant to be run by your survival plan throughout your life. You are meant to outgrow it as an adult.

Your happy ending fantasy was just that — a fantasy. If the adults in your life when you were a child had known how to connect with you in more nourishing ways, they would have done that. If they had known how to accept you more fully as you were, they would have done that. If they had known how to create the kinds of safety you needed as a child, they would have done that. Your happy ending fantasy was your brilliant way of empowering yourself to cope as a child with situations that would otherwise have devastated you at that point in your development.

Happy ending fantasies are for surviving not thriving. Natural developers know that thriving as an adult means learning how to digest life just as it is. They give up creating new happy ending fantasies to keep false hope alive that life will be different from how it is. They also avoid the downward spiral of false hopelessness that causes others to become jaded or to give up on life. Instead, they find the deep gifts hidden within all of their life experiences.

Creating a happy ending fantasy for the sake of your childhood survival was a marvelous thing. Your challenge as an adult is to outgrow your need for such a fantasy.

Why Your Survival Plan
Didn't Vanish When You Became an Adult

Even though our survival plan was meant to be temporary rather than permanent, it rarely works out that way. Why doesn't our survival plan simply disappear once we become an adult? It doesn't because it has become instantaneous, automatic and unconscious. It is kind of like only telling the punch line of a joke without the lead-up story.

Consider Joel's example. He remembers telling himself this as a teenager: "Screw Dad. Who cares what he thinks? I'll go over to Mike's and get stoned with him." When he did a slow-motion reconstruction of his internal conversation that led up to what he remembers telling himself, here is what he discovered:

> "Uh, let's see, I'm still looking for love from Dad. Yeah, I haven't given up on getting him to validate me for my talents and my good intentions and the good things that I do. I really want to get into a music conservatory after high school but I know what Dad thinks about musicians. I'd better hide from him how I spend three hours a day practicing my music. Even though my heart lives in music, I'll just tell him I'm still considering majoring in pre-law in college. Yeah, that'll make him happy. Maybe he'll break down and give me a little praise. I don't mind being out of integrity with him. What difference does it make anyway? It's just a little white lie. I'm not hurting anyone. Oh, wait. Now I feel that old familiar rage coming up inside me over Dad not encouraging me to be who I really am. Oh, wait. My inner critic is blasting me for hating him. I had better shove that hatred back into my Pandora's box. This is just exhausting. Screw it. I'll just tell Dad what he wants to hear. Then I'll go over to Mike's and get stoned with him."

A survival plan is like any other habit. In order for it to be effective, it must become instantaneous, automatic and unconscious. Joel saw that because his internal conversation occurred in a split second, he missed the fuller story that led up to the punch line: "Screw Dad. Who cares what he thinks? I'll go over to Mike's and get stoned with him."

Imagine how it might have been if you had to think through your survival plan each time you needed to use it as a child or teenager. Very few of us realize how out of integrity we became in order to make our survival plan work. As adults, very few of us realize the extent to which we are still living from our survival plan. Instead, most of us just think our survival plan is *"who I am"* rather than *"how I survived."*

Again, all of this is because our survival plan is like any other habit: instantaneous, automatic and thus unconscious. Habit is the reason we carry our survival plan into adulthood. However, our survival plan does morph in some important ways as we move toward and become adults.

The Birth of Your Ego's Redemption Plan: Old Theme, New Form

A time came when you were ready to face the fact that you failed to get what you most wanted from the caregiver(s) with whom you had your happy ending fantasy.

When did it come for you? ❑ While I was still a child ❑ During my teens ❑ As a younger adult.

When did you realize that no amount of covering up or changing yourself, or helping or containing them, would give the *connection, validation, and/or safety* you wanted?

That was an important turning point in your young life. It marked the first time you had enough inner strength to face that you wouldn't be getting what you wanted from the adults with whom you grew up.

Chances are that you were not conscious at that time of your survival plan or its particulars. Plain and simple, that's why you didn't decide to outgrow it then and there. Instead, you transferred your happy ending fantasy to someone or something else.

Which new person or goal did you believe would give you the *connection, validation and/or safety* you had always needed but never gotten enough of?

(Not sure? No problem. Consider Isabel and Dean's examples below. If they don't ring some bells, read the descriptions later in this chapter of the various forms redemption plans take.)

Isabel tried three ways to prove that she was a valid adult. One was to parent her children far better than her parents parented her. Even though she succeeded, one of them still didn't turn out the way she wanted. She became almost frantic trying to change that because her own validity hinged on her success. Another way she tried was to become a psychotherapist and despite becoming quite talented, her career never blossomed to the extent it should have. Isabel also tried a third more unconscious way: she got into relationships with broken men who had lots of potential and tried to bring them around. This was her unconscious plan for proving to herself that she was lovable after all. It backfired each time.

Dean made millions. This was his plan for proving he was safe and valid as an adult. He also lost millions, so money failed to prove to him that he was safe or valid as an adult. None of Dean's love relationships turned out the way he wanted either. None became lifelong partnerships and thus he could not prove he was lovable as an adult.

These are examples of how our childhood survival plan morphs when we become adults. These are also examples of how the form they morph into also fails. One way or another, our childhood survival plan morphs into an adulthood redemption plan.

At the point that our survival plan fails, we have two choices: either we can give up trying, or we can transfer our happy ending fantasy to someone or something else.

If we give up trying, life becomes a dreary empty journey and we become a hollow empty shell. If we can make our happy ending fantasy come true with other people or accomplishments, we will be redeemed from having failed with our caregivers.

Your ego's redemption plan originates in your own pain, guilt and unmet needs.

It is identical in structure to your survival plan as it contains a version of your happy ending fantasy, rules, Pandora's box, a mask, and anesthesias. There are two main differences between your survival plan and your redemption plan:

1. Your redemption plan's happy ending fantasy usually focuses less on your childhood caregivers and more on accomplishments or other people. (However, some people never quite get over trying to make their happy ending fantasy come true with their childhood caregivers, even as adults.)

2. Your redemption plan is an attempt to absolve you for having failed to make your happy ending fantasy come true with your childhood caregivers.

The problem with this is that no amount of trying to redeem yourself as an adult can absolve you of something that was not your fault as a child. Your redemption plan therefore cannot succeed any more than your survival plan did, no matter how hard you try.

We have made up lots of attractive euphemisms for our redemption plan: ambition, drive, single-mindedness, etc. But what my clients taught me, and what I have also had to face in myself, is that what we call ambition and drive is far too often more about redemption than about passion. Because of this, I suggest that survival and redemption plan failure is the root of almost all self-esteem problems.

Redemption Plan
Variations on the Happy Ending Fantasy

Most adults transfer their unquenched happy ending fantasy from their childhood caregivers to other people or accomplishments.

Your redemption plan was probably your first adult "success formula." Its function is to redeem you as an adult for having failed to make your happy ending fantasy come true with your caregivers as a child. Its purpose is to prove to both yourself and others that you are lovable, valid and/or safe after all, despite your childhood failure to prove this.

Your redemption plan may include accomplishing things about which you have authentic passion and which could include accomplishing what your childhood caregivers would approve of.

Two things in particular degrade passion into a redemption plan:

1. Your redemption plan's excessive focus on absolution at the expense of what you really need in order to feel whole, happy and fulfilled.

2. Your redemption plan's assumption that your wellbeing, self-esteem, lovability or fundamental legitimacy as a human being depends on you being successful with what you are passionate about (or what you believe will cause your childhood caregivers to finally bless you).

The next section explains what I mean.

Six Common Types of Redemption Plans

All redemption plans have one thing in common: they overemphasize passion or other lovely qualities for the purpose of absolution. This obsession with absolution (being released from prior mistakes or failures) is one of the hallmarks of redemption plans. As you read these six types of redemption plans, look for clues about the structure of yours. You will have a chance to describe your own redemption plan later in this chapter. Just remember that this is meant to be a personal discovery process and not a way of labeling yourself or others in a judgmental or shaming way. Also bear in mind that most people combine more than one of these redemption plan styles.

1. **Succeeders:** These folks believe that outward accomplishments will redeem them. These accomplishments may include achievement, money, power, social standing, image or lifestyle. It is wonderful to have success goals. When in service of a redemption plan, however, attaining success becomes all-consuming. Succeeders tend to be greedy, self-centered, overly ambitious, and obsessed. This is because they tend to feel they must become truly extraordinary in order to be marginally acceptable. Virtually anyone or anything that stands in the way of a success goal is dispensable.

Because of this, succeeders tend to have a particularly difficult time with relationships. Their *connection* core drive takes a back seat to outward success. No amount of outer success ever quenches a succeeder's thirst for redemption. Can you think of any succeeders you have known or read about? Are there aspects of this that are part of your own redemption plan? If so, what form does this style take in you?

2. **Self-Reliers:** Fierce independence is the trademark of these folks and personal freedom is their prime directive. Anything that stands in the way of personal freedom must be eliminated from their life. Self-reliers tend to have little interest in introspection or personal development. They tend to be driven to prove they can take care of themselves without anyone else's help. To prove this, they will sacrifice their personal growth, close relationships and most kinds of community involvement. I say "most" because some extreme self-reliers are survivalists. Their version of community involvement is to get others to join them in arming for whatever they believe will be the next holocaust. But, garden-variety self-reliers simply tend to be "counterdependent." They are highly reluctant to get deeply involved with others. They do not learn the art of synergy and co-creation. They neglect their *connection* and *authenticity* core drives. Usually they also neglect their *impact* core drive too. Can you think of any self-reliers you have known or read about? Are there aspects of this that are part of your own redemption plan? If so, what form does this style take in you?

3. **Over-Connectors:** In contrast to the self-reliers, there are those who feel connection-starved. Their *connection* core drive is so unquenched and so deep that they will give up just about anything in order to be in relationship. They are the black-belt relationship addicts of the world. Their focus may be on friends, a primary relationship, children, and/or being part of a community. Over-connectors come in two main forms: dependents and fixers. Those who are dependent simply give up themselves in order to not be alone. Fixers most often attract self-centered people or those who are stuck in their own woundedness. They tend to befriend

or fall in love with the human equivalent of wounded puppies who don't really want to be healed. They also tend to stay in relationships long after the wounded puppy has turned vicious. Redemption connectors tend to turn people into projects. Because of this, those they care about tend to resent them for trying to turn them into something they are not. People under the spell of a *connection* redemption plan are baffled by this resentment. They swear that all they are doing is trying to love or support or help the person by bringing out all they can be. Over-connectors tend to neglect their authenticity and impact core drives. Can you think of over-connectors you have known or read about? Are there aspects of this that are part of your own redemption plan? If so, what form does this style take in you?

4. **Self-Expressers:** These are the folks who live for the sake of creativity, whether in the form of art, music, acting or dance, etc. When I say "live" I mean that these folks feel like there is no room in their life for any person, cause, or goal except their creativity. They are similar to succeeders in this way: succeeders tend to be outwardly and materially focused whereas self-expressers tend to be more inwardly and artistically focused. Self-expressers tend to cherish their neuroses and they believe that their creative gifts stem from their suffering and pain. They therefore tend to cherish the contents of their Pandora's box. This leads them to fear healing what is in there. They believe that if this were to happen, their creative edge would become forever dulled. Self-expressers' primary relationship tends to be with their creativity rather than with other people. Other than steamy, passionate and short-lived affairs, self-expressers tend to neglect their *connection* core drive. Similarly, their creativity is the primary way they express their *authenticity* core drive. And, unless their creativity takes the form of contributing to the world, they also tend to neglect their *impact* core drive. Can you think of any self-expressers you have known or read about? Are there aspects of this that are part of your own redemption plan? If so, what form does this style take in you?

5. **Over-Improvers:** An over-improver's *life* revolves around personal development. This might include healing their wounds, or mastering the power of intention, or developing themselves physically, emotionally, mentally, or spiritually. Self-Improvement as a redemption plan is actually a hiding strategy. Over-improvers tend to hide from relationships and/or from social responsibility. Some hide out in gyms, wanting to build the perfect body while others hide out in spiritual retreat after spiritual retreat, trying to make sure that come hell or high water this is their last lifetime here on earth. Some hide out in therapists' offices or self-development seminars, lost in a parade of wound after wound that needs to be addressed and still others try to master the art of positive thinking as a way of side stepping the baggage they carry. No matter what the form, over-improvers become so self-absorbed in their self-improvement that life passes them by without them even noticing. They never fully express any of their three core drives. Can you think of any over-improvers you have known or read about? Are there aspects of this that are part of your own redemption plan? If so, what form does this style take in you?

6. **Crusaders:** This redemption plan is an extreme and misguided form of being a do-gooder. Crusaders believe that in order to redeem themselves they must save the world. Crusaders believe it is their job to figure out what is best for others and they feel they must become indispensable in order to be valid. They tirelessly try to bring their message to anyone who will listen and frequently view themselves as having an almost divine responsibility to enforce their ideas of right and wrong onto others. They fear that the world will go to hell in a handbasket unless they devote all of their life energy to whatever cause for which they have decided to crusade. Because of this, crusaders are particularly at risk for developing Fanaticism Disorder. Some go even further and become terrorists. Crusaders believe that only through people's (or God's) deep gratitude for their selfless martyrdom will they finally get the emotional nurturance and validation they so desperately lacked as children. I am

not speaking here about religiously devout people who seek to attract others to their religious path. Crusaders are those who allow their cherished relationships and their self-care and their creative self-expression to fall by the wayside. Their crusading obsession eclipses their *authenticity* and *connection* core drives. Can you think of any crusaders you have known or read about? Are there aspects of this that are part of your own redemption plan? If so, what form does this style take in you?

Redemption plans can:

❑ Require us to become codependent, covertly manipulative, needy, or dependent.

❑ Turn us into martyrs who give up ourselves for the sake of others.

❑ Make us overly sensitive or susceptible to being easily manipulated.

❑ Cause us to seek more closeness than is healthy.

❑ Result in our developing an over-active or under-active conscience.

❑ Turn us into passive victims who feel dominated and controlled by others.

❑ Result in our never having enough money or enough of anything.

❑ Cause us to remain loyal in relationships that are harmful to us while we think we are being ultra-ethical by staying.

❑ Give rise to being counterdependent, ruthless, dominating, overtly manipulative, sadistic, or a user of others.

❑ Turn us hard or harsh or cold.

❑ Cause us to avoid closeness.

❑ Motivate us to seek power, domination and control over others.

❑ Cause us to seek huge amounts of wealth at the expense sacrificing our own ethics or wellbeing, or our most precious relationships, in order to succeed.

Can you see why the things our redemption plans require of us cause us to continue to sacrifice our integrity as adults?

False Hopelessness
Variations on the Redemption Plan

Some people have difficulty generating one of the redemption plan versions because they don't have sufficient hope for a better future for themselves to make any of those hope-based versions work.

These folks tend to go in one of two directions. Some live high risk lives because they don't feel like they have anything larger to live for. Life is about surviving between periodic thrills. Others live caved-in lives in which life is about deprivation. Some who feel caved-in believe they truly are worthless and therefore deserve to fail as an adult. Others believe they are not worthless but that they need to be absolved for being a failure because the damage that was done to them is too severe to recover from.

Even these variations of the Redemption Plan sidestep the real issue: we are proving something rather than living our passion (life mission, calling) simply because it is our passion. Regardless of whether we try to prove our worth or prove how damaged we are, we are still proving a point rather than living our life. This is a cornerstone of any redemption plan regardless of whether it based on hope or hopelessness.

Three Redemption Plan Examples

Remember Carl the do-gooder from an earlier chapter? He was the millionaire business executive who came to me in profound pain because his wife and children left him. One of the things he faced was just what his drive for success attempted to redeem. He had been trying to redeem himself for not having succeeded in his countless attempts to get his father to bless and honor his fundamentally sensitive and loving nature.

Three things freed Carl to love like he had never loved before: forgiving himself for having failed to obtain his father's blessing; inwardly blessing his father for the gifts his lack of acceptance of him had brought Carl; and forgiving his father for being a flawed human being like the rest of us.

As a result of this, he took up painting, and his passion and creativity opened wide. He began approaching his business life with more of an orientation to serving highest good. He finally became capable of learning the joys of synergy and co-creation in his relationship with his children and a wonderful woman who would become his second wife. He was also able to make amends with his former wife and they developed an amicable post-divorce friendship. He said, "I never knew before now how incredibly liberating it is to live in integrity in my relationships. To be honest, I had never known what relationship integrity was." These were the deeper riches this financially wealthy man gained from surrendering his ego's redemption plan in favor of the Seven WisePassions of 3D Living that you will learn about later in this book.

What about Melissa the connector? She had come to me for psychospiritual support to assist her in recovering from the cancer she was convinced she had developed because she had spent her life nurturing others while neglecting herself. Melissa realized she had failed to save her mom from being swallowed by chronic depression. When she finally gave up trying to save her mom, she had to prove to herself that she could save *someone* in order to redeem herself for having failed with her mom. She was shocked to find that as she learned to care for herself with as much love and compassion as she had offered to her husband, children and church, they all loved her even more. Not only that, but for the first time in her life she actually experienced the joys of being truly respected by people for who she really was. It was finally okay for her to live in integrity with her personal boundaries.

And then there's Sam the self-improver. He came to realize that a large part of why he had become so focused on creative self-expression was that he had given up on finding love. He discovered that he had come to believe that the only way he could make a difference in the world was to bring beauty to it through his art and music. He had felt he could never contribute to the world the way he felt his parents had through their careers in the diplomatic corps. As his ego's redemption plan began to crumble, he became terrified that he would lose his connection to his creativity. But by then he had become so painfully aware of the ways he had been out of integrity in his life, this was a risk he felt ready to take.

As his adult development process evolved, Sam noticed four major shifts that propelled him into deep gratitude. The first was that the theme of some of his artwork shifted toward representing important social issues. In turn, his new creations started to attract the attention of buyers that had never before been interested in him. The second was that he found he had more time for his own self-care and relationships without having to sacrifice his passion for creating art. The third was that, as a result of this, he entered into a sustained relationship for the first time in years. Better still, his partner appreciated him for how attentive he was. That was new for him. The fourth was that he became far less interested in all those self-improvement books and workshops because he started to feel like he was now truly living his life.

Huge pieces of their authenticity were embedded within Carl, Melissa and Sam's redemption plans. They each suffered in their own way because they did not recognize how damaged their authentic passion had become by their unconscious belief that if only they achieved or loved or created enough they would be redeemed. *Redemption plans are bottomless pits.* One's calling is simply one's calling and is never meant to be embodied at the expense of the rest of what makes us whole people.

Your Redemption Plan

My redemption plan was a combination of success, self-reliance, self-improvement and crusading. My contribution to the demise of my first marriage grew from having unconsciously reverted into being controlled by my old redemption plan. Digesting this experience gifted me, among many other things, with a far deeper respect for how important it is for us to understand our redemption plan and outgrow our need for one.

With that in mind, allow yourself to move past any initial reactions of "that can't be me — it can't be that bad." In your heart of hearts you know which of the above redemption plans you adopted. It could be more than one. As you search for your favorite redemption plans, keep in mind a special thought: the focuses that became part of your redemption plan may well have been things you have authentic passion about.

If after reviewing the six common redemption plans you are still unsure what your redemption plan looks like, review the anesthesias you used as a child as they might give you some clues. Above all else, remember that there is absolutely no shame in having developed a redemption plan. Graduating from a survival plan to a redemption plan is part of life. From the perspective of reverse engineering adult development, it is all part of our soul's growth. There is a wealth of gold to be found in your redemption plan, once your integrated adult development moves into full swing. In fact, a significant part of adult development is about placing the gold in your redemption plan in service of fulfilling all three of your core drives.

A particularly quick and easy way to begin identifying the core of your ego's adulthood redemption plan is to identify the prerequisites your programming tells you that you must meet in order to be lovable, worthy or safe.

> *What rules do you follow as an adult that keep you loyal to your Survival Plan?* (If you are not sure, think about the rules your Inner Critic berates you or others for not obeying.)
>
> *I will be* ❏ lovable ❏ worthy (valid) ❏ safe if I cover up, change or over-emphasize _____ _____ in me and/or if I achieve _____ _____ in the world, and/or if I contain, control or draw out _____ _____ qualities or behaviors in the following people: _____ _____

Your Redemption Plan Symptoms

The more your survival plan ran your life as a child, the more it is likely your redemption plan continued running your life as you became an adult. The more you do the kind of work on yourself that you will read about later in this book, the freer from your redemption plan you will become. If you come to this book relatively inexperienced in doing this sort of inner work, it is possible you have been living predominantly from your redemption plan in most if not all aspects of your life.

If you have already done some effective inner work as an adult, or if your survival plan did not dominate your life as a child, one of the following three possibilities is likely to be true for you:

1. You could be living primarily from your redemption plan in some aspects of your life but not others. For instance, you might be relatively free of your redemption plan in your career but not in your romantic life, or vice versa.

2. You might be living from a mixture of your redemption plan and true authenticity and integrity.

3. You have become authentic and in integrity much of the time, but when you become self-neglectful or extremely stressed you revert back into your redemption plan in some significant ways.

> *How much is your Redemption Plan currently affecting your life?*
>
> ❑ My redemption plan currently pervades most aspects of my life.
>
> ❑ My redemption plan currently pervades some aspects of my life but not others. (If so, specify which aspects of your life your redemption plan dominates, such as your health, self-expression, career, relationships, community involvement, etc): _____
>
> ❑ I currently live from a mixture of my redemption plan and being authentic and in integrity.
>
> ❑ I am currently authentic and in integrity much of the time but when I become self-neglectful or extremely stressed I still revert back into my redemption plan.

The clearer you are about the extent to which you are living your life from your redemption plan, the more motivated you will be to free yourself from it. The more you know your own redemption plan symptoms, the clearer it will be when you have some more inner transformation to do. (See my website for a free quiz: *Your Redemption Plan Symptoms Checklist*.)

Why is learning this information about yourself important? The more your redemption plan controls you, the more your integrity, authenticity, relationships and ability to serve highest good will be compromised.

The Price and Gift of Your Ego's Redemption Plan

The reason people follow their redemption plan's rules rather than be authentic is that they secretly believe there are prerequisites to deserving to feel lovable, valid or safe. This is also why people over-achieve rather than finding fulfillment in their lives in ways that are fully harmonious with their personal integrity, their relationship integrity and their integrity with the collective.

So, I ask you now: What are the prerequisites to deserving to feel love? Consider this question carefully before you continue reading.

The answer is "None." Until you know that, not just in your head but in the cells of your being, you will have a very difficult time outgrowing your ego's redemption plan. Yet, outgrowing your survival and redemption plans is a cornerstone of integrated adult development.

SECTION THREE

DEMYSTIFYING THE RHYTHM
OF ADULT LIFE

CHAPTER 10

THE FOUR LifeZones THAT RULE ADULT DEVELOPMENT

"Is there a predictable rhythm to my development that I should know about?"

Section Two painted a portrait of the "why" and "how" of what you developed in childhood and brought into your adult life. The question in your mind at this point in the book is probably, "What do I do about all this?" The answer is to outgrow the aspects of your survival and redemption plans that still influence you and to upgrade the skill sets that are meant to replace our survival plan skills when we are adults: the Seven WisePassions. This is precisely what we will focus on in Sections Three and Four.

Integrated adult development is about experiencing ever-increasing amounts of inner fulfillment by moving into full integrity with all three of your core drives.

Integrated adult development is about:

1. **Soul Learning:** Harvesting from all of your life experiences deep learnings about your spirit and heart.

2. **Service Mission:** Making a positive difference in the world through embodying these learnings.

3. **Personal Mission:** Experiencing ever-expanding love, joy, abundance and fulfillment along the way.

One interesting way to view life is as a symphony that includes a prelude and four movements: the prelude is the "music" of your childhood, including your survival plan and the ensuing four movements in your symphony of life are composed and continually upgraded throughout your adult life.

The four recurring adulthood movements in your life symphony provide the structure through which your development occurs ...or doesn't occur. I call them LifeZones, and they are: Wakeup Calls, Survival Plan Attachment, Transformation Chapters and Consolidation Periods. Mastering your LifeZones is one of the keys to adult development. Each chapter in Section Three discusses a LifeZone in detail.

The diagram below summarizes the flow of life from childhood through adulthood that this book describes.

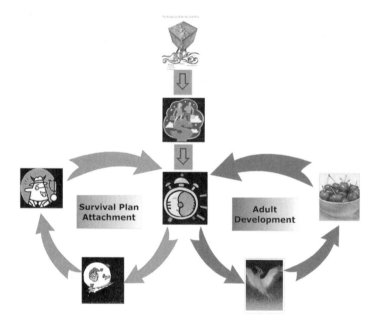

- The top icon represents our childhood *survival plan.*

- At some point in adolescence or early adulthood, this morphs into a *redemption plan*, which is represented by the icon beneath the survival plan icon.

- Life events called *wakeup calls* invite us to emerge from the hypnotic trance created because our survival and redemption plans have become habitual, automatic and unconscious. The wakeup calls' icon is the alarm clock.

- We respond to each wakeup call either by strengthening our attachment to our survival and redemption plan (the cycle on the left) or by choosing a transformation chapter (the cycle on the right) during which we outgrow portions of our survival plan and upgrade our seven WisePassions.

- If we respond to a wakeup call with *survival plan attachment,* our life continues on a downward spiral that pushes us further out of integrity and further from true fulfillment. This causes our next wakeup call to be more intense. Future wakeup calls inevitably occur at increasing levels of intensity until we either finally choose a transformation chapter rather than survival plan attachment, or until we die, whichever comes first.

- If we surrender into a *transformation chapter* in response to a wakeup call, this is ideally followed by a *consolidation period* during which we integrate our gains until our next major wakeup call occurs.

CHAPTER 11

LifeZone #1:
Wakeup Calls

"What is life's way of inviting me into deeper integrity, fuller authenticity, more effective and fulfilling connection with others, and greater contributions to the world?"

The pivotal LifeZone around which the other three revolve is a wakeup call.

Life, in its infinite wisdom, tries to help us reclaim our true identity by offering us repeated opportunities to awaken from the slumber into which we hardly know we have fallen.

- *A wakeup call is any life circumstance that exceeds your current ability to respond to it with centeredness, compassion, integrity, collaboration and life balance.*

There are only two ways you can respond to your wakeup calls: reinforce your survival and redemption plan or you can begin to replace it with the skill sets of integrated adult development (the WisePassions). Replacing your survival and redemption plans with the Seven WisePassions will restore or upgrade your 3D Integrity and fulfillment. Integrated adult development revolves around this restoration and upgrading process. Cycling among wakeup calls, transformation chapters and consolidation periods enables you to continue developing throughout your life.

Wakeup Call Profile

We all have an inner thermostat that regulates our psychological and spiritual comfort levels. When our emotional pain exceeds what we are used to tolerating, our inner thermostat turns on the equivalent of "air conditioning." It tries to cool down our pain so that it moves back down into the range we have learned to tolerate.

Similarly, when our happiness levels rise above what we are used to tolerating, our inner thermostat brings us back into the lower happiness range to which we have become accustomed.

The original "temperature" of your inner psychospiritual thermostat was set by your survival plan. By the time you graduated to your redemption plan, you were able to tolerate being out of integrity and having an unbalanced relationship with your three core drives. As the saying goes, "It may be hell but it's home."

From the perspective of reverse engineering, our development as adults requires that our inner thermostat settings be challenged. This is why we are periodically gifted with wakeup calls. These are the life experiences with the most potential to wake us up from our unconscious tolerance of the temperature at which our psychospiritual thermostat is set.

Wakeup calls are designed to be doorways to your next development cycle. Nothing more, nothing less.

A wakeup call is any situation or event, usually unexpected or unasked-for that substantially rocks your expectations, beliefs, routines, lifestyle or identity. A wakeup call is anything that exceeds your current ability to navigate your way through life with centeredness, compassion, integrity, collaboration and balance.

Wakeup calls are invitations to upgrade your life, your integrity and your relationship with your three core drives (authenticity, connection and impact). From a reverse engineering perspective, they are neither awful events (like losing your job) nor dreams-come-true (like unexpectedly coming into a substantial inheritance).

Wakeup calls can be dramatic or subtle. Obvious wakeup calls include:

1. Major life transitions such as marriages, divorces, deaths, births, empty nest syndrome, moves, job changes, etc.

2. Traumatic events such as serious illness, injury, being raped, etc.

Experiences not commonly recognized for the wakeup calls that they are, include:

1. Transcendent experiences, such as a deep spiritual experience unlike anything that you have previously encountered.

2. Being in a relationship in which there is deeper love than you have ever before experienced.

3. Sudden extreme good fortune, such as landing a dream job, coming into a significant amount of money, and the like.

Experiencing deeper love than she had ever experienced before was Isabel's first wakeup call. It came in her late teens. She didn't answer it and spent her entire adult life regretting it. Only after multiple subsequent relationship breakups did one finally become intense enough to wake her from the spell of her redemption plan, and by then she was in her early sixties. This is the price we pay when we ignore our wakeup calls.

The following symptoms are clues that you are being gifted with a wakeup call:

❑ Your life circumstances exceed your life skills.

❑ Your pain levels exceed your pain tolerance.

❑ Your happiness levels exceed your happiness tolerance.

❑ An outside-the-box life experience challenges your pre-existing ideas and beliefs. These may be about you, another person, spirit, relationships, how development works, how the world works, or how the universe works.

All of these situations are the adult equivalent of what is called, in some child-raising literature, a "Teachable Moment."

What wakeup calls have you experienced as an adult? Which did you try to ignore? Which did you respond to by trying to build a better survival or redemption plan? Which did you intuitively respond to by surrendering into a transformation chapter?

Responding Effectively to Your Wakeup Calls

This means that there are only two ways you can deal with a wakeup call:

1. Twist the experience however you need to so that it does not challenge or threaten your pre-existing beliefs. This means allowing your psychospiritual thermostat's temperature settings to be in charge. When you select this strategy, you distort the wakeup call experience so that it no longer threatens your pre-existing beliefs. This reinforces your survival plan attachment. When people use this strategy, they decide they imagined the experience, or they decide they made a bigger deal of it than it really was, or they decide that what happened was a one-in-a-million fluke.

2. Allow the wakeup call to revise your pre-existing beliefs about yourself, others, spirit and/or life. When you use this strategy you start a process in which you change the temperature at which your psychospiritual thermostat is set. This is what invokes a transformation chapter. Successful transformation chapters require a very different set of skills from your survival and redemption plan skills: the Seven WisePassions.

Here are the most common ways I have seen people respond to wakeup calls:

1. **Resistance:** Fight the experience, resist it, or try to put off dealing with it.

2. **Overwhelm:** Feel like you are being drowned by the experience.

3. **Teflon:** React to the experience by pretending it isn't a big deal and trying to let it roll off your back without it expanding your beliefs or upgrading your WisePassions.

4. **Transformation:** Allowing the experience to transform you for the better (allowing it to propel you further along in your integrated adult development).

People frequently warm up to a wakeup call rather than immediately surrender to it. Their initial reaction might be *shock* —

feeling horrified, overwhelmed and/or self-pity. This is often followed by *resistance* — denying the possibility that this wakeup call is inviting you into a transformation chapter. Resistance gives way to *unraveling* — beginning to feel like you are coming apart because of the wakeup call, gradually becoming aware that resistance is futile, and ultimately realizing that you have an important choice to make about how you will respond to this wakeup call. Hopefully this one invokes the beginning of a transformation chapter rather than a retreat into deeper survival plan attachment.

Tips for Successfully Navigating Your Wakeup Calls

- **Recognition:** Learn how to recognize wakeup calls at lower and lower levels of intensity. This will reduce how often you need really intense life upheavals to become willing to enter a transformation chapter.

- **Compassion:** Be compassionate with yourself as you travel through the four-step sequence of warming up to a wakeup call. Try not to give in to the temptation to fight the wakeup call, feel swallowed by the life experience creating it, or react to that experience like you're Teflon.

- **Acceptance:** The laws of cause and effect will have their way with you so you might as well accept them. You can choose to delay responding to a wakeup call. You can choose to respond to one by reinforcing your survival plan attachment. These choices simply mean that you are choosing for your next wakeup call regarding this adult development issue to be more intense than the current one. No harm, no fault, your choice. This is simply the way development works. You cannot rewrite the rules; you can only pretend you are exempt from them; or you can accept them.

- **Choice:** Look closely at the risks and benefits of waiting until your next wakeup call regarding this adult development issue versus the risks and benefits of the surrendering into a transformation chapter now. The choice of which way to go is always yours, so it's best to make it with your eyes open.

- **Competence:** The more comfortable you become at moving through transformation chapters, the easier they will be for you to choose as your response to wakeup calls. The more well developed your Seven WisePassions are, the more comfortable you will become with going through transformation chapters. The WisePassions will help you get greater value from your transformation chapters in less time.

- **Levity:** Do your best to approach wakeup calls with a sense of reverential light-heartedness. When in the midst of a life upheaval, try to remember — if the world did not suck, we would all fall off. Or, as a friend said to me many years ago, "It's all much too serious to be serious about." A little levity can go a long way, particularly when you are in the midst of deciding whether to respond to a wakeup call by allowing it to lead you into a transformation chapter.

- **Sacredness:** Do your best to approach your wakeup calls, especially the more dramatic and unasked-for ones, as sacred struggles are meant to bring you closer to Source or God and are a part of life. The more intense a wakeup call is, the more gold you can be certain it contains. Viewing an event as a tragedy can block you from harvesting its gifts.

- **Delaying:** If you choose not to respond to wakeup call to enter a transformation chapter, forgive yourself for choosing a more intense wakeup call later. You are welcome to continue trying to make your redemption plan work, for however long you need in order to become satisfied that it will not bring you the fulfillment you seek. Press the snooze button on your wakeup call alarm clock all you like — it will still be there for you later.

Assistance: If you need assistance navigating the wakeup call LifeZone, select a helping professional who will do the following three things. First, they need to be comfortable with your being in emotional pain while you are deciding how you will answer your wakeup call. If they want to help you make that pain go away before you have made your decision, run from them as fast as you can. Second, they need to know how to help you find the courage to answer your wakeup call by surrendering into a transformation chapter. Third, they need to be unattached to whether you will do this. It's your life. You get to answer your wakeup calls when you decide to do that. It's not a helping professional's job to decide this for you unless you are being so harmful to yourself or others that the helping professional is required by law to take action.

CHAPTER 12

LifeZone #2:
Survival Plan Attachment

"How do we deal with life until we know how to do what natural developers do?"

Survival plan attachment is responding to a wakeup call through our survival and redemption plans rather than choosing to outgrow these strategies, by replacing them with the Seven WisePassions.

It seems as though most of the world lives in a state of survival plan attachment without knowing it. For many people life is largely about bearing up or coping while trying to take as many breaks as possible from the pain or deadness; or it is about finally redeeming themselves through making their redemption plan version of their happy ending fantasy come true. Some might pursue their redemption through a lover or a child, some through career or other personal achievements, and some through trying to create change in the world.

I believe "Survival Plan Attachment Disorder" is so prevalent because most adults don't realize they are living their life using the same basic formula they originated during childhood for survival purposes. They do not recognize that this formula will never enable them to become fully authentic, loving, and of service in the world. They do not realize how out-of-integrity they are. This is because most people confuse their survival and redemption plans with their true identity. This is because our childhood survival plan has become unconscious and automatic by the time we are adults.

We move into survival plan attachment whenever we don't believe there is another way to live. We select survival plan attachment when we don't believe that being fully authentic in the world will actually help us thrive more fully than our survival and redemption plans will ever allow. We select survival plan attachment when we are unaware of much our survival and redemption plans prevent us from building and sustaining the truly co-creative relationships most of us genuinely long for. We select survival plan attachment when we are oblivious to the extent of the harmful impact we have on ourselves, or our world, because of how lacking in integrity we are because our survival and redemption plans are running our lives. We select survival plan attachment when we do not realize how important it is for us to live in integrity with all three of our core drives.

I believe it is vital that all of us develop deep compassion for the part of ourselves that is still attached to our own survival and redemption plans. It is similarly vital that we remain compassionate when other people's actions reveal how attached they are to their survival and redemption plans. Just keep in mind that compassion does not mean allowing unacceptable behavior; on the contrary, it means doing whatever is necessary to contain it. Compassion, however, does this as an act of love rather than revenge; as an act of humanity rather than hatred.

Survival Plan Attachment Profile

Remember the inner psychological thermostat I talked about in the last chapter?

In place of the *Teachability* WisePassion, the thermostat setting of our survival and redemption plans allows us to misuse willpower or tolerate feeling like a victim.

In place of the *Self-Care* WisePassion, the thermostat setting of our survival and redemption plans allows us to tolerate self-neglect and self-indulgence, and to use anesthesias in place of self-care.

In place of the *Discernment* WisePassion, the thermostat setting of our survival and redemption plans allows us to tolerate their rules as well as the resulting disconnection from self, higher wisdom, and others these rules cause.

In place of the *Harvesting* WisePassion, the thermostat setting of our survival and redemption plans allows us to tolerate an ever-growing Pandora's box of denied aspects of self and undigested life experiences. It prevents us from reclaiming our full self and gathering the gifts our undigested life experiences have been waiting to offer us, so we can put an end to our happy ending fantasy once and for all.

In place of the *Authenticity* WisePassion, the thermostat setting of our survival and redemption plans allows us to tolerate living through our mask as a false self. This creates in us needless fear, anger, and unfulfillment.

In place of the *Synergy* WisePassion, the thermostat setting our survival and redemption plans use allows us to tolerate impaired relationships.

In place of the *Stewardship* WisePassion, the thermostat setting of our survival and redemption plans allows us to tolerate distorted notions of what serves highest good, or enables us to serve highest good at the expense of ourselves and our most precious relationships.

These inferior alternatives to our WisePassions lead to a downward spiral of deterioration.

How You Can Break Free of Survival Plan Attachment

Being in the survival plan attachment LifeZone does not readily lend itself to introspection and because of this, the best therapist for those who do not understand the nature and prices of survival plan attachment is life. However, you can save yourself a lot of heartache by learning to recognize when you are in this LifeZone and by realizing that there is far better alternative.

Remember that the universe is both accommodating and firm and it is only a matter of time before it sends you a more intense, dramatic, painful or costly wakeup call than your last one. How intense, dramatic, painful or costly a wakeup call needs to be is always in direct proportion to your level of attachment to your survival or redemption plan. It will try to offer you pain that is greater than whatever fear or objections you have to surrendering into a transformation chapter.

If you are currently in this LifeZone, bless you for reading this book. Hopefully you now understand that there is an alternative to your survival plan attachment. The most useful thing you can do next is the equivalent of what a doctor tells you before prescribing a medication or performing a surgery. It is called "informed consent." Either on your own with the help of the exercises in this book, or with trusted friends, or a seasoned helping professional, map out the details of your childhood survival plan and subsequent adulthood redemption plan. Then, list the benefits your survival and redemption plans provide you and the costs they charge you for these benefits. Doing this will put you in the best possible position to make an informed consent choice. Your choice will be about whether you will decide to wait for a yet more intense wakeup call before surrendering into your first (or next) transformation chapter. I trust that this informed consent process will itself be enough of a wakeup call for you to select a transformation chapter beginning now.

If you decide it would be helpful for you to get assistance in moving out of survival plan attachment, seek a helping professional to help you:

- Understand the origins of your survival plan and assist you in identifying the form your particular survival and redemption plans take.

- Appreciate that delaying the shift into a transformation chapter will only invite your next wakeup call to be more intense, dramatic, painful or costly than your last one.

- Do a survival plan attachment risk-benefit analysis and a similar analysis of the risks and benefits of initiating a transformation chapter. You may be concerned about family, friends or business associates whom you believe are in grave danger because of being in a severe state of survival plan attachment. This might include alcoholism, drug addiction, untreated biochemical imbalances such as Bipolar Disorder, etc. If so, contact a local treatment center for a referral to an Intervention Specialist. If your concerns are not quite this severe, try to resist the temptation to force this book in their face. There is a huge difference between making someone aware of a resource and forcing them to use it. Do your best to bear in mind that mostly people change not because they see the light but because they feel the heat.

LifeZone #3:
Transformation Chapters

*"Isn't there an easier way to develop than by doing
deep inner work on ourselves all the time?"*

A *transformation chapter* is your alternative to survival plan attachment. It is the second of two possible ways of responding to a wakeup call.

A transformation chapter is a period of intensive focus on inner work. While transformation chapters are part of the fabric of integrated adult development, you are not meant to live the bulk of your life in them. Life is much too precious to spend any more time in transformation chapters than is absolutely necessary. At the same time, life is much too precious not to harvest the profoundly sacred gifts that these periods are designed to yield to others, the world and ourselves.

Transformation Chapter Profile

The engine that runs transformation chapters is the Seven WisePassions. Transformation chapters tend to upgrade your WisePassions in a specific sequence:

1. First comes *teachability*. Without it transformation cannot occur.

2. Second comes *self-care*. It is impossible to undertake a successful transformational journey if you are in a depleted or anesthetized state.

3. Third comes *discernment*. Unless you are able to recognize useful input from sources wiser than your survival and

redemption plans' rules, you will not be able to transform the contents of your Pandora's box into gifts. Doing this is what makes transformation chapters worth going through.

4. Fourth comes *harvesting*. You venture into your Pandora's box to retrieve, heal, or upgrade the contents your wakeup call invited you to finally address. This is what gives meaning and purpose to your wakeup call. Successful harvesting ultimately allows you to become truly grateful for even the most unpleasant of wakeup calls.

5. Fifth, having harvested deep inner gifts, you grow into an expanded appreciation of your true authenticity and personal *power*. You explore new expansions in your ability to be effective in manifesting your intentions that become available to you as a result of your harvesting.

6. Sixth, from a place of greater inner wholeness and solidness, you become able to expand your capacity for *synergy* with others. You move beyond coercion or capitulation, or even compromise, in your relationships; this enables you to co-create better personal and work relationships than you ever thought possible.

7. Seventh, your capacity for wise *stewardship* leaps forward as the gifts you have harvested through this transformation chapter enable you to become better at discerning and serving highest good; this lets you lead more effectively than ever before.

Your Seven WisePassions make it possible for you to simultaneously enhance your personal, relationship and leadership development. They enable you to upgrade and coordinate how you express all three of your core drives. This is how you harness the power of The Integrity Effect. This is what integrated adult development is all about.

Tips for Getting the Most from Your Transformation Chapters

Transformation chapters are generally best navigated with professional assistance.

The shortest possible route through most transformation chapters (except the rare ones that can be moved through in only a few days) is to move through all Seven WisePassions in a developmental sequence; doing this also produces the best possible results. The WisePassions you develop and upgrade during successive transformation chapters are all absolutely vital to your ability to honor all three of your core drives. (You will find greater detail about the Seven WisePassions in Section Four of the book.)

Beware of what I call "Windows of Willingness," as they can be quite seductive. When we are in a window of willingness we are definitely looking for help. But, the help we seek is often to just make the symptoms go away, not to turn a wakeup call into a transformation chapter. Our motivation is to learn how to decrease the amount of pain we can tolerate. Many people, including psychotherapists, are often seduced into confusing a window of willingness with a transformation chapter. This is because people who are in a window of willingness often initially believe they will do anything necessary to deal with the dilemma they are facing. In truth, they want to be out of pain or to stop feeling so disoriented by an outside-the-box life experience. Someone in a window of willingness will have one of the following three priorities: a) to bring their pain levels down below their pain tolerance levels; b) to bring their happiness levels down below their happiness tolerances; or c) to bring their disorientation levels down below their disorientation tolerances. These intentions are the cornerstones of survival plan attachment. When someone is truly committed to going through a transformation chapter, they surrender into the heart of their disorientation.

How long any specific transformation chapter may take to complete will vary depending on how much life reconstruction is required. Most take anywhere from a few weeks to a few months to complete, but some take longer. For instance, the transformation chapter my divorce led me into lasted for nearly three years, since I needed to completely rebuild my inner and outer life. It was worth every moment. *It all depends on how much repair work, upgrading and life reorganization needs to occur.* How long a transformation chapter will take you to complete will depend on: a) how pervasive the life upheaval was that initiated your transformation chapter; b) how much of your Pandora's box was stirred up by your latest wakeup call; c) the extent to which you treat your transformation chapter as your top life priority; and d) how well you select and utilize the resources you use to assist you with each of your Seven WisePassions.

Individual and/or group coaching or therapy can be extremely helpful during transformation chapters. If you do choose to work with a helping professional, select one who is already familiar with the material in this book — or who is willing to read it. Also make sure they feel confident about their ability to facilitate you through the process I have described. Be aware, though, that they may be trained in methods for doing this that I don't cover. The methods do not matter. What matters is that the method fits the need, that the facilitator is skilled at using the method, and that you both are using the method to accomplish what is described in this book.

Willingness.com contains more tips to assist you with your transformation chapters.

CHAPTER 14

LifeZone #4:
Consolidation Periods

"Isn't it normal to just want to take a break sometimes?"

Consolidation periods are the luscious times that follow a transformation chapter. During these periods you integrate your latest transformation chapter's gifts into the fabric of your identity, your life, your relationships, and your way of helping to make the world a better place. Consolidation periods are not times of intensive development. They are relatively relaxed periods of celebration and joy, heightened well-being and love, particularly high productivity and worldly effectiveness. Enjoy these delightful life oases; they are periods for enjoying the fruits of your labor during a transformation chapter.

Profile

Personal, relationship and leadership development continues during consolidation periods, but at a much more leisurely pace. The primary development focus during a consolidation period is on fun, love, productivity and integration.

Integration during consolidation periods centers on synergizing your three core drives in order to live in greater personal, relationship and stewardship integrity.

Getting the Most from Your Consolidation Periods

I could usually tell when one of my psychotherapy or executive coaching clients had moved into a consolidation period. They would start talking in a particular way about wanting to take a break. They reported feeling as though they had just finished coming through a long tunnel. They felt they were now out in the sunshine, feeling deep gratitude for what they had just come through. They were beginning to bask in the light of their accomplishments. They wanted to take a well-deserved rest from doing intensive inner work.

These people weren't looking to take a break in order to avoid their development. They were immersed in celebrating the completion of a significant chunk of work well done. They wanted time to allow it to filter into all aspects of their life.

By and large, consolidation periods are not times of intensive coaching or therapy. While periodic check-ins or tune-ups can be useful at any point in the adult development process, deep development work is not the purview of consolidation periods. That's what transformation chapters are for.

Despite being in a consolidation period, some people still find themselves drawn to reading a book or attending a workshop on a personal, relationship or leadership development topic. If you find yourself so inclined, make sure you are truly doing it just for fun or because you feel some genuine passion about the topic. Remember: we all need breaks.

Consolidation periods are most of all about integrating into your daily life the gifts you obtained and the WisePassions you upgraded during your last transformation chapter. So, if you find yourself inclined to do any development work during a consolidation period, do things that will help you integrate your gains into your daily life. Don't go starting a new chapter of deep personal, relationship or leadership work right away. If you do, you will deprive yourself of the well-earned and very necessary benefits a consolidation period can provide to you.

Tips for Navigating
Consolidation Periods More Gracefully

When you're in a consolidation period, reading the WisePassions chapters will help you identify any WisePassions you feel passionate about focusing on in a leisurely way. Only do this, though, if you believe it will assist you in expanding your integrity and synergizing your three core drives. Reading the final chapter of this book might also give you some clues about what you might want to do during a consolidation period. The chapters on WisePassions #5–7 (power, synergy and stewardship) may provide you with other clues. You may also find value in the daily practices provided in the *Workbook*.

Focus primarily on integrating, coordinating and balancing among your three core drives during consolidation periods. Focus on aligning and rising to new levels of personal, relationship and leadership integrity in your daily life.

Remember that consolidation periods are not intensive periods of inner work. They are times when life goes relatively smoothly and you can experience satisfying joy, well-being and productivity.

If you choose to utilize resources during a consolidation period, select ones that support you in integrating the gifts that came from your latest transformation chapter. Select resources that help you expand your integrity and effectiveness in your personal, relationship and leadership life. Select ones that can help solidify your new level of 3D Living.

Now that you understand what each Adult Development LifeZone is about, you will likely have little difficulty determining which one you are predominantly in at the present time. As you consider this, bear in mind that even if you are currently in more than one LifeZone, only one is most primary at any given time. You will find a simple quiz to help you pinpoint your current primary LifeZone in the *Workbook*.

SECTION FOUR

THE SEVEN KEY LIFE SKILLS
NATURAL DEVELOPERS DEVELOP...
AND HOW YOU CAN DEVELOP
THEM TOO

CHAPTER 15

A CLOSER LOOK AT
THE SEVEN WISEPASSIONS:
THE ALL-PURPOSE LIFE SKILLS

"Is there a single set of core life skills that personal,
relationship, leadership and integrity
development all depend upon?"

The Seven WisePassions may well be the master key to integrated adult development. No one should be without them. You need them for the sake of your personal well-being, freedom and self-expression. You need them in order to connect, collaborate and co-create well with others. You need them in order to be an effective leader. You need them in order to serve highest collective good. Now, that's efficiency.

Why Developing the Seven WisePassions is So Vital: The Kaiser ACE Study

There is a saying that you can't afford the luxury of a negative thought. I believe a much more accurate statement would be that you can't afford the luxury of an undigested life experience.

The Adverse Childhood Experiences (ACE) Study is a landmark research study that posed the question of whether, and how, childhood experiences affect adult health decades later. To answer this question, Kaiser Permanente, a large U.S. Health Maintenance Organization (HMO), in conjunction with Robert Anda, M.D., of the Centers for Disease Control, studied 14,421 adults. The answers they discovered were stunning and conclusive. (For more information about the ACE Study, visit www.acestudy.org)

The researchers found that:

- ACEs (Adverse Childhood Experiences — their name for undigested life experiences) are surprisingly common, happen in even the best of families and are simply part of the fabric of life.

- ACEs do indeed have quite dramatic long-term consequences on our physical and mental health.

- ACEs disrupt our neurological development, which leads to social, emotional and cognitive impairment. This, in turn, causes us to develop "health-risk behaviors" that create disease, disability and social problems, and which ultimately results in early death.

The ACE Study revealed a powerful relationship between our emotional experiences as children and our physical and mental health as adults, as well as the major causes of adult mortality. It documented the conversion of traumatic emotional experiences in childhood into organic disease later in life. This study makes unequivocally clear the importance of you learning how to properly digest your life experiences.

The ACE Study also found that time, in and of itself, does *not* heal Adverse Childhood Experiences. One does not just get over some things — not even fifty years later and this is why I stress the importance of understanding the anatomy of your own childhood survival plan and subsequent redemption plan, and of freeing yourself from their control.

The findings from the ACE Study provide remarkable insights into how we become what we are as individuals and as a collective. The findings are vitally important medically, socially, and economically. In other words, ACEs affect all three of our core drives, and hence our integrity.

Natural developers and successful deliberate developers provide a valuable model for how all of us can prevent ACEs from damaging our wellbeing as adults. The Seven WisePassions they use are the secret formula for digesting our life experiences, freeing ourselves from the control of our survival and redemption plans and moving into integrity with all three of our core drives. This is the essence of integrated adult development and the WisePassions that you will continue to learn about in this section are your keys to doing your integrated adult development in the most efficient ways possible.

The Health Insurance Company Trap

Unfortunately, many insurance companies have not yet recognized how important it is that they support clients in doing this. They may, in fact, try to resist supporting you in outgrowing your survival and redemption plans and upgrading your WisePassions.

This is because the ACE study findings have not yet been embraced by all health insurance companies. This may be because if they did they would have to change one of their primary treatment directives.

You see, the health insurance industry mandates that the role of a helping professional is to restore the client or patient to their "prior level of functioning." What this phrase means is: "Treat the symptoms so that the client's life works the way it did before the symptoms became unbearable, or so the patient's health is like it was before they became overtly ill."

Most health insurance and managed care companies don't seem to realize that the "previous level of functioning" got the client into the problem in the first place. They do not seem to understand they are requiring helping professionals to reinforce survival plan attachment rather than encouraging them to teach their clients how to upgrade their Seven WisePassions!

The ACE Study convincingly illustrates the insanity of this mandate to restore people to their prior level of physical or psychological functioning. This mandate prevents our underlying problems from being addressed, virtually guaranteeing that another new problem will eventually come along to take the place of the current problem. The ACE Study makes it clear beyond a shadow of a doubt that living life from our survival and redemption plans astronomically increases the likelihood of severe adult illness and even premature death. This isn't good for us or for those who love and work with us. It's also awful for the collective because of the huge financial and other societal costs it creates.

If your insurance covers psychotherapy, your therapist is authorized to work with you for only so many sessions. If your insurance doesn't cover psychotherapy, or if you choose another modality such as life coaching, you are most likely not going to want to be paying for sessions with no end in sight.

Either way, using the material in this book can enable you to get the most you possibly can out of the limited number of sessions you have. In fact, if you are working with a helping professional, you may find it quite worthwhile to ask her/him to read this in order to better support you in your development process. If you are a helping professional, you will find information on my website about how you can learn to provide ten-session Integrity Makeovers that revolve around helping clients upgrade their Seven WisePassions.

The Seven WisePassions

You likely will appreciate the purpose and importance of each WisePassion almost instantly. Your reaction will typically be, "I knew this but I didn't know enough about these skill sets to fully harness their power in my life."

As it has been a while since I first introduced them earlier in the book, here in greater detail, is a list of the Seven WisePassions:

1. **Teachability:** Your willingness to respond to wakeup calls with self-responsibility, humility and receptivity, so they can be transformed into blessings instead of baggage.

2. **Self-Care:** Maintaining the abundance of life energy you need for authenticity, connection and service (i.e., your three core drives) as well as for completing transformation chapters as rapidly and efficiently as possible.

3. **Discernment:** Your ability to recognize and utilize useful input from inner and outer sources that are wiser than the rules your inner critic tries to enforce; your capacity to distinguish between what fits and doesn't fit for you; and your ability to tell the difference between truth, partial-truths and lies.

4. **Harvesting:** Your capacity to properly digest your life experiences in order to extract unexpected gifts from unexpected, unasked-for or undesired experiences. This prevents life experience indigestion that creates more baggage that impairs your integrity and your ability to honor your three core drives.

5. **Power:** Expressing your inner light, gifts, deepest truths and creativity without holding back, and remaining true to the boundaries you must honor in order to do that, is the core of personal integrity.

6. **Synergy:** Co-creating more fulfilling, collaboration-based, effective and resilient relationships than you ever thought possible, through synchronizing your intentions, boundaries, energy and manifestation abilities with others to create results that are even more wonderful than you can create by yourself. This is the core of relationship integrity.

7. **Stewardship:** Your capacity to synergize with others, as your truest self, and to accurately co-discover and serve collective highest good. Stewardship includes leading with impeccable integrity in the forms and contexts that are authentic for you and without doing so at your own expense or the expense of those who are precious to you. This is the core of leadership integrity.

The first four WisePassions (Teachability, Self-Care, Discernment and Harvesting) provide the foundation for personal, relationship, leadership and integrity development. The last three (Power,

Synergy and Stewardship) are the core aspects of 3D Integrity. Together, all Seven WisePassions are the ingredients required for building a life of fulfillment and integrity that I refer to as 3D Living.

Each WisePassion builds on the ones that come before it. The natural developers and successful deliberate developers I have worked with create successful transformation chapters (periods of particularly intensive integrated development) by building these WisePassions in sequence, as developmental stages.

One WisePassion is not a substitute for the others. All are equally important and all are necessary; there is no fluff or filler here. The WisePassions collectively provide the antidote to the toxic effects of adverse childhood experiences (as documented by the ACE Study).

This section of the book acquaints you with your Seven WisePassions and how you can rapidly and effectively upgrade each of them. Resources now exist that can help virtually anyone develop or upgrade any of their Seven WisePassions. (The exceptions to this are those who are significantly developmentally disabled, mentally ill, brain damaged and the criminally insane.) I cannot put into words how excited and gratified I am that the human development field is finally at a point where virtually no one need be left behind ever again.

At the same time, so many resources are now available that selecting the right one at the right time can be quite a challenge, even for helping professionals. Just take a peek in the self-improvement, relationships or leadership section of any bookstore, or look at the articles and advertisements in development-oriented magazines; the choices are staggering and the marketing for each one screams out as if it were saying "Pick me, pick me!"

This is what I call "resource overwhelm." How are you to choose the right ones for you each step of the way? You are in the midst of learning a complete road map for efficiently developing all three of your core drives in ways that can elevate your integrity and deepen your fulfillment. The LifeZones and WisePassions sections of the book offer you an antidote to resource overwhelm. The more accurately you can pinpoint where you are in your development, and the more you understand what to focus on in that location, the easier it will be for you to narrow down your prospects.

My search for the world's best resources has resulted in a list of far too many to include in this book. Because I am constantly refining and adding to my list of "finds," the most practical place to maintain them is on my website.

Length limitations also precluded the inclusion of all the self-assessments and exercises that accompany the material in this book. The *Workbook* contains all of them and more.

For additional information, read the "Going Further" section in the Appendix.

There is one all-purpose resource I do want to mention here. Some truly exciting new upgrades in the field of psychology have been unfolding over the last decade. These advances are finally beginning to align psychology with the stunning discoveries that have been made over the past 75 years in the field of quantum physics. Energy Psychology, in my opinion, is leading the way with these innovations. Following some rather hefty initial skepticism, I have become persuaded that these methods are leading the way into twenty-first century psychotherapy and coaching. Energy Psychology methods appear to provide rapid, reliable and lasting assistance with a broad range of baggage removal and peak performance challenges, through utilizing some of the principles of quantum physics and the new biology. This recently emerging family of methods appears to provide an all-purpose way to upgrade each of your Seven WisePassions. You will find references to Energy Psychology methods in many of the upcoming WisePassions chapters. For information about these easy-to-use methods, read the "Going Further" section of the Appendix.

CHAPTER 16

WISEPASSION #1:
TEACHABILITY

"Why do I need to respond to everything life throws at me with self-responsibility, humility and receptivity?"

Teachability is authentic openness to new ways of understanding and acting that are substantially different from your pre-existing beliefs and habits.

My father was repeatedly physically abused by his father and he never dealt with these traumas. When he became a father he made a vow to himself that he would never abuse his children the way he was abused. He remained true to his vow: he never physically abused his children. It was not until my brother and I were adults that he realized he had done the same thing to us that his father had done to him, only in a different form. He had repeatedly verbally abused us with his chronic rages and shaming.

Despite my father having far more IQ points than I, he never became truly teachable. In fact, one of my father's favorite phrases was, "You can't teach an old dog new tricks." This was how he justified never dealing with his considerable baggage from childhood and young adulthood. By the time he was in his fifties, Dad was already referring to himself as an old dog. He rarely learned any new tricks. His aphorism became a self-fulfilling prophecy. He was dead before he reached seventy.

My father was a classic illustration of the ACE study's findings. The old dog's dedication to not learning new tricks led him to becoming a rageoholic, a heavy smoker, and to dying young. His undigested Adverse Childhood Experiences damaged him, his relationship with his wife and children and all of his closest friends, and diminished his ability to have positive impact in the world.

Teachability is the foundation of our ability to digest our life experiences in ways that enhance our personal authenticity, our capacity for connection with others and our ability to make a positive difference in the world. Yet, what teachability really is is widely misunderstood.

The Grazer and the Know-it-all

By the time Jeanne arrived at my office, she had already been through therapy with three prior therapists, had attended almost as many personal development workshops as I had and was always reading at least three self-help books at the same time. She told me that the reason for all this was that she was thirsty to grow and there was no time to waste. Jeanne had a long list of things she wanted me to teach her.

As I inquired about the fabric of her life, it became clear that Jeanne was frightened to be fully herself in the world and that she felt almost desperately alone. She also believed there really wasn't much she could do to help make the world a better place.

Another client, George, made it clear to me in the first session that he was dragged there by his wife. He wasn't interested in "some snooty professional telling me what to do." He could figure things out quite well on his own, thank you very much. His idea of being teachable was that his own best thinking could reveal to him everything he needed to know.

Interestingly, both Jeanne and George viewed themselves as being teachable. However, Jeanne quickly revealed herself to be a New Age dilettante, searching and flitting from one learning experience to the next, while never aligning her three core drives. No wonder this chronic self-improver felt so unfulfilled despite all her "inner work." George just as quickly revealed himself to be a know-it-all, believing he could teach himself all he needed to know. Clients like Jeanne and George taught me how many people do not recognize when they are not in a state of teachability.

The Positive Thinking Addict

I have had quite a few clients over the years who have unintentionally tried to use positive thinking as a substitute for teachability. These folks adopted a belief that says, "If I simply stay motivated and think positive thoughts, my baggage will go away on its own." It was a very painful lesson for each of these clients to recognize that they had been using motivational techniques, positive affirmations and inspirational slogans as anesthesias.

The popularity of the movie and book *The Secret* has brought about a resurgence in this kind of false thinking. I do not say this as an indictment of *The Secret*, because I actually like it very much and recommend it highly. The techniques offered in *The Secret* are, however, a trap when used in the way that I just described. They are powerful, so it can look for a while as though they are being used in service of transformation even when they aren't.

What too often occurs is that people unintentionally use these techniques to develop a more sophisticated survival and redemption plan. There is no substitute for removing blocks when that is what's called for. Placing positive thoughts on top of crap does nothing more than create sweet-smelling crap.

I point this out with deep compassion, born of personal experience. In the late 1970s, I dove headfirst into metaphysical thinking, Eastern philosophies and altered states of consciousness. Meditation got me higher than any drug could have. Thinking I was profoundly wise, I spouted metaphysical drivel that made even my sympathetic friends retch. I continually disregarded my friends' feedback no matter how often they told me, "Beam back down to earth, David."

It wasn't until years later, after I started to discover and outgrow my survival plan, that I understood what my friends had been trying to tell me. As the baggage beneath my survival plan healed, I became able to put the wisdom of the principles spoken of in *The Secret* to good use. In hindsight, the real lesson for me from this experience was that there is no substitute for fully developing all Seven WisePassions.

The Manager and the Avoider

Other clients came to me realizing they had problems becoming teachable. These clients tended to fall into two groups: the Managers and the Avoiders.

Barbara managed everything. As a single working mom, she had to, because if she didn't do it, it wouldn't get done. She felt as though she had no time for the luxury of being teachable...until she became so ill that she had to go on disability. That wakeup call motivated her to become teachable.

Anthony, on the other hand, characterized himself more as an ostrich. His primary goal had simply been to figure out a way to survive each day. His motto was: "Don't make waves — do as little as possible to keep your head above water." By the time he reached my office, it had begun to dawn on him that there was a connection between his "avoidance" approach to living and the fact that he increasingly felt like a hollow shell of a human being.

Sometimes the Manager and the Avoider are the same person, as was the case with me just before and after the turn of the millennium. My wife had developed a life-threatening illness. I focused my life energy on holding our business together without her help, while also being her caregiver. At the same time, I searched inwardly for the spiritual gifts embedded within this difficult life experience. I was not saying to myself, "I didn't sign up for this awful experience." Rather, I was consistently asking myself, "For what soul growth reasons had I been given this experience?" Because this was my attitude, I sincerely believed that I was in a state of teachability.

However, I also told myself that there was too much to manage for me to focus on myself and that I would wait to focus wholeheartedly on my own growth until after the crisis passed. As a result of not seeking help to do my own inner work during this profoundly stressful period, I isolated and neglected myself. So, in truth, my style of "managing" was to be an avoider who acted like a know-it-all. Meanwhile, I would have sworn that I was teachable.

After four years of living with this major life upheaval and a number of other significant upheavals that surrounded it, I had deteriorated into a kind of zombie. Even though most of the world still saw me as highly functional and something of a hero, the secret truth was that I had become a hollow shell. I had lost touch with my heart and thus with my capacity to love. It was not until my wife healed and subsequently told me she wanted a divorce that I actually became teachable.

My delayed teachability came at a substantial cost. My restored teachability ultimately yielded utterly extraordinary and priceless gifts. Life can be messy. I truly hope yours will be less messy from now on because of what you are learning in this book.

What Teachability Is and Isn't

We have three choices for responding to a life experience: try to avoid it, try to "manage" it, or allow ourselves to be transformed by it. When we try to avoid or manage a life experience, we might decide to learn new skills to accomplish this. Wanting to learn these things is the opposite of teachability. It is the desire to develop new and better ways to protect ourselves. Teachability means allowing ourselves to be transformed by a life experience.

Margaret and Jordan Paul, in their classic relationships book, *Do I Have to Give Up Me to Be Loved by You?* proposed that there are two fundamental intentions: the intent to protect and the intent to learn. I agree with them. (This book and its companion *Workbook* provide some of the best self-assessments available for identifying your self-protections.) While there are many forms of self-protection, I believe they all boil down to avoidance or coping. The problem with both of these self-protection strategies is that they are ways of coping with the Adverse Childhood Experiences studied in the Kaiser ACE study but are not ways of digesting those experiences. Self-protection strategies erode our integrity rather than expand it. You will learn more about how to effectively digest your life experiences in the "Harvesting WisePassion" chapter.

Movies like *The Karate Kid* accurately portray the importance of true Teachability. This classic movie is about a bullied teenage boy, Daniel, who wants to learn how to fight. Daniel's mentor is Mr. Miyagi, a Karate master, but before Mr. Miyagi agrees to take him under his wing, he requires Daniel to do a series of tasks that seem meaningless, menial and even demeaning to Daniel. Daniel thinks

Mr. Miyagi is trying to turn him into his slave. He does not realize that Mr. Miyagi is testing him to see if he truly teachable. A wise teacher does not begin working with the student until she or he is satisfied that the student has first become teachable.

Wakeup calls are the universe's best way of inducing teachability. The more teachable we become, the gentler our future wakeup calls will tend to be. Even when a future wakeup call is particularly intense, the habit of Teachability makes it far easier to surrender into a transformation chapter so we can harvest its gifts as rapidly and effectively as possible.

Teachability is the starting place for any kind of personal, relationship or leadership development. Teachability is the first step in becoming the leader of our own life; nothing new can happen until we become teachable. Until then, the results we will continue to get will be the same unsatisfactory results we have gotten before. You may have heard the saying that insanity is doing the same thing over and over again expecting different results. It's true.

3D Teachability is the willingness to discover in unexpected, unasked-for and undesired experiences, pearls of great value about personal authenticity, connection with others and serving highest good. It is the willingness to learn things you did not know about the part you play — and don't play — in various life situations, through opening to ways of understanding that stretch beyond the assumptions you make and the beliefs you hold. You might not harvest the gifts themselves until you focus on WisePassion #4, but teachability is the first building block all of us need in order for harvesting to occur.

Wakeup calls are Teachability devices; and may, in fact, be the most powerful vehicles for opening us into Teachability. (The best therapy for the unwilling is real life, not therapy!)

Assessing Your Teachability

Think about a pain or desire you have today that you know in your heart is very important to deal with, but which you *haven't* yet decided what to do about. Which statement most accurately reflects what is most true for you at this time regarding your issue?

❏ I am mostly trying my best to avoid dealing with this issue.

❏ I am mostly trying to figure out how to cope with this issue or how to control the unpleasant symptoms this issue is causing.

❏ I am considering the possibility of treating this situation as a wakeup call that is trying to invite me into a transformation chapter (review the "Four LifeZones" section if you need to refresh your memory of what these are).

Regarding what issues in your current life are you being arrogant instead of teachable at the moment? What are your symptoms of being arrogant instead of teachable? How do (or could) these symptoms damage your integrity?

Regarding what issues in your current life are you being a victim instead of teachable at the moment? What are your symptoms of being a victim rather than teachable? How do (or could) these symptoms damage your integrity?

What Happens to Your Integrity When You are Unteachable

Take a moment now to briefly review the times in your past when you were unteachable. What was the situation? How did your unteachability damage your integrity with yourself? How did it damage your relationship with others, and with whom? How did it limit your capacity to have a positive impact in the world or to serve collective highest good?

The point of this brief exercise is to embed in you a deeper respect for the importance of Teachability and the prices of unteachability.

The Task and Key Ingredients of 3D Teachability

The **Task** of teachability is to replace your survival and redemption plan strategies of willpower, victimhood and arrogance with the integrated adult development skills of willingness, self-responsibility and surrender.

Willingness is receptivity to finding a way to live, love and lead that is better than anything your survival and redemption plans can provide; it is openness to learning. Willingness is your best anti-dote to wrong use or over-use of willpower and defensiveness.

Self-responsibility means accepting that your intentions, inter-pretations and choices determine how you attract, understand and respond to life events. Self-responsibility is your best antidote to victimhood, blame and making excuses. (A victim is someone who believes that her or his happiness, integrity or capacity to love is in the hands of another person or situation.)

Spiritual Surrender means opening your heart to input that is wiser, more loving and more helpful than your own best think-ing. Surrender is your best antidote to arrogance and to the self-destructively high pain tolerance that our survival and redemption plans require.

WisePassion #1: *Teachability*

Willingness

Receptivity to finding a way
to live, love and lead
that is better than what
your Survival Plan can provide
*(vs. using willpower
to force outcomes)*

Self-Responsibility

Accepting accountability
for how your
intentions, interpretations
and choices affect the
life situations you attract,
and determine how you
understand and respond
to them
(vs. entitlement)

Spiritual Surrender

Opening your heart to a
wiser and more helpful
source of input
than your own best thinking
(i.e., your ego)
*(vs. humiliation because of
not being able to
solve everything yourself)*

How Teachability Amplifies the Integrity Effect

Imagine responding to your everyday life experiences with curi-osity rather than defensiveness. Imagine how your life might be dif-ferent if you were more devoted to self-responsibility than to being a victim. Imagine how your life would be different if you sought inner and outer input that is wiser than your own ego, rather than remaining in a state of arrogance. Imagine how you would feel if you didn't have to expend so much life energy on acts of willpower, but could instead open yourself into a state of willingness.

How would living these ways more of the time help you move into fuller integrity with yourself, with your relationships and with the collective? Can you see that without consistent teachability, integrity is impossible, and also that teachability is the doorway into personal, relationship and leadership development and integrity?

Remaining in a state of Willingness, Self-Responsibility and Spiritual Surrender is a matter of daily intention, monitoring and practice. 3D Teachability is a discipline that becomes more natural the more you practice it.

The simplest practice I have found for building teachability is a method used by indigenous Hawaiian healers. *Ho'oponopono* is a four-sentence process that is inwardly repeated over and over throughout each day. In my experience the Ho'oponopono sentences feel soothing to those of just about any faith, and even to those who are not faith-based:

"I'm sorry. Please forgive me. Thank you. I love you."

These sentences are inwardly directed, not toward another person, but toward the representation of Source or Spirit or universal wisdom you choose. It is especially useful when having a distressing, judgmental or attacking thought. You will find complete instructions for this practice in the *Workbook*.

Remember:
Being teachable makes you reachable.

181

CHAPTER 17

WISEPASSION #2:
SELF-CARE

*"How can I maintain the abundance of life energy I need
for authenticity, connection, and service?"*

Self-care provides you with the life energy you need to honor all three of your core drives. In addition, self-care is an important part of personal integrity. The more you neglect the various aspects of self-care, the more you are giving yourself the message that you don't matter. If you do this long enough, your body will ultimately get the message and give up on you too. That is, you will become ill.

For all of us, well-rounded self-care is unavoidably a daily practice. It may be tempting to think that exercise and nutrition can compensate for chronic lack of sleep, or that a beautiful home and living within your means can compensate for ignoring your physical health. The human organism is a complex machine that is part physical, part spiritual, part psychological, and part energetic. No one part can ever be a substitute for the rest and no amount of passion about what you do as creative expression, in your career, or as acts of service, can be a substitute for self-care.

I am one of those people with a tendency to forget myself. It has taken me a very long time to truly accept that the less I take care of myself, the more emotionally unavailable I am to others, and the less centered I am when being of service in the world. For this reason, this chapter, as important as it is, is both my least and most favorite in the book.

How about you? How good are you with your self-care during a typical week? Take the following self-assessment and find out. Rate how much of the following you experience in your life right now on a scale of 0–10 (0 means not at all and 10 means an extreme amount):

- Exhaustion: _____
- Irritability: _____
- Weight problems (overweight or underweight): _____
- Chronic stress: _____
- Psychological or emotional distress: _____
- Physical imbalances, distress or illnesses: _____
- Self-indulgence or gluttony in general: _____
- Tolerating home or work ambiences that drain you rather than feed you: _____
- Tolerating being close to people who undermine your well-being, self esteem or growth: _____
- Tolerating being close to people for whom crisis and melo-drama is a lifestyle: _____
- Making commitments to other people that you can't keep: _____
- Tolerating being chronically disorganized: _____
- Tolerating being chronically stretched too thin: _____
- Tolerating an improper balance between work and play: _____
- Tolerating an improper balance between spending and sav-ing: _____
- Tolerating being chronically behind with home mainte-nance or errands: _____
- Not having enough time for the creative activities you most love to do: _____
- Not having enough time to make a positive difference in the world in the ways you most love to do: _____

If you like to do scoring, add up your totals (if you don't like to do scoring, just take note of items you scored 4 or higher, because these indicate self-care areas most in need of upgrading):

36 points or less: your self-care is better than most but you probably still have a couple of areas that could benefit from strengthening — put an asterisk (*) next to specific items that you scored 4 or higher because those are the ones on which to focus.

37–90 points: your self-care is suffering even though you're in a range where you've got a lot of company.

90 points or more: your self-care needs some serious focused attention sooner than later

(More will be revealed later in this chapter about identifying the specific self-care areas you may benefit most from strengthening.)

Self-Indulgence and Self-Neglect

Joe just couldn't get enough exercise. Whether it was a run in the park, a workout at the gym, kayaking, skiing or whatever, Joe lived to move. He had a difficult time pinning down exactly why he came to see me. He viewed himself as a physically fit specimen who had a great job in the computer industry that paid him good money, while leaving him with lots of free time as well. It bothered him that he didn't have many buddies outside the gym and that he couldn't keep a relationship for more than a couple of months at a time. In his mind, he was a pretty good catch and he didn't understand why it seemed that others didn't agree with him.

In time, Joe came to see that what he viewed as self-care was actually a form of self-indulgence. He gradually discovered that he had been using exercise as an anesthesia and that there was far more to self-care than only exercise, nutrition and sleep.

Sue never got enough sleep; there was just too much to do and not enough hours in the day to do it all. Lack of sleep turned out to be the tip of the iceberg for Sue. In time she confessed that her home was so full of clutter she was embarrassed to invite friends or dates to visit. Virtually every available wall in her executive office suite had stacks of papers, files and books propped up against it, always on the verge of teetering over. Similarly, her mind felt like it was bulging at the seams. Her internal chatter was incessant and this, in part, was why Sue never got enough sleep.

Sue's redemption plan was focused on getting validation; her strategy involved busy-ness and productivity. It did not matter to her how many work hours she had to put in, whether in the office or at home, Sue was always drained, perpetually scattered and alone. Her social and love life were nearly nonexistent. She had no time for the jewelry and macramé she so dearly loved to create. Nor did she have time for the social causes that were close to her heart. She had resorted to making sizable donations, but as guilt offerings rather than love offerings. Speaking of money, her bank accounts were a mess, and as a result she was regularly bouncing checks despite having enough money to cover her expenses.

Sue had an under-energized, self-neglectful relationship with self-care, while Joe had an over-energized, self-indulgent relationship with self-care. Both self-neglect and self-indulgence mean that too little life energy is left over for self-expression, relationships and service.

What Self-Care Is and Isn't

3D Integrity begins with teachability, but teachability means nothing if you don't have the life energy to do something useful with it. At the same time, it is quite difficult to be Discerning (WisePassion #3) if you are either anesthetized or in a state of self-neglect or self-indulgence, rather than doing good self-care. That's why self-care comes second in the Seven WisePassions.

The **Task** of self-care is to replace your survival and redemption plan strategies of anesthesia, self-neglect and self-indulgence with the integrated adult development skills of creating effective internal, environmental and logistical self-care "climates."

Self-care is the habit that maintains the abundance of centeredness and life energy you need for authentic self-expression, connection with others and being of service in the world (in others words, your three core drives).

Self-care is about:
- ❑ Keeping your energy strong and balanced.
- ❑ Keeping your mind calm yet alert.
- ❑ Keeping your body capable of supporting you in all areas of your life.

❑ Keeping your environment nourishing.

❑ Keeping your life logistics under control and in service of all three of your core drives.

One area of self-care is not a substitute for the others. Integrity requires having them all.

The Key Ingredients of 3D Self-Care

Inner Self-Care includes daily habits for keeping your energy field strong, developing a caring and nourishing relationship with your body, and learning to quiet your over-active mind.

- **Basic Physical Health Habits** include enough good quality sleep for your body's needs, movement, high-quality nutrition and energy system balancing. (See the Glossary for a definition of "energy system." Basic energy system balancing exercises are included in the *Workbook*.)

- **Soothing, Recharging and Play Habits:** Soothing habits are anything that makes you purr, such as a massage or a bath. Recharging habits are anything (not anesthesias) that restores your inner juice, such as watching your favorite sitcom, gardening, or just about any truly creative endeavor that gives you energy rather than takes energy from you. Play habits are anything (again not anesthesias) that brings out the kid in you. Anything that is not an anesthesia but calms you down is a soothing habit. Anything that is not an anesthesia but gives you energy rather than takes energy from you is a recharging habit. Anything that is not an anesthesia but brings out the kid in you is a play habit. You may find that some of the things that soothe you are also recharging and/or feel playful to you and vice versa, but that some are only one or the other.

- **Internal Quieting Habits** are practices that enable you to enter inner silence so you can take vacations from constant mind chatter. Some people use prayer to quiet their mind. Others use one form of meditation or another. Yet others use physical disciplines such as Tai Chi, Qigong or Yoga, enabling them to simultaneously take care of both their daily need for physical movement and internal quieting. Some people find that their internal quieting habit is also soothing and recharging.

🖋 **The survival/redemption plan version of Inner Self-Care** is exhaustion, irritability, weight problems, chronic stress or psychological symptoms, physical imbalance or illness, and gluttony.

Environmental Self-Care includes arranging your surroundings so that they most deeply nurture you. This includes not only your physical environments but your people environments as well.

- **Physical Environments** include home and work, as well as regularly spending time in the natural settings that most nourish you.

- **People Environments** include not only who you regularly spend time with but knowing what your optimal blend is of one-on-one time, small group time and large social setting time. It also includes knowing your optimal blend between "alone time" and "people time."

🖋 **The survival/redemption plan version of environmental Self-Care** is tolerating home or work ambiences that drain you rather than feed you, and people who undermine your well-being, self esteem or growth, or for whom crisis and melodrama is a lifestyle.

Logistical Self-Care includes keeping your stress levels low through making sure that tasks (such as chores, errands and finances) are handled as efficiently as possible so that your life logistics support your 3D Living rather than keeping you from it. This includes:

- **Details Management:** mastering goal setting, implementation planning, time management, file management and money management.

- **Streamlining** your chores and tasks, including home maintenance and errands.

- **Choices Management:** balancing work with play, spending with saving, and making sure that your job and financial choices support your needs for creative self-expression and your ability to spend quality time with those you love, while still having energy left over to be of service in the world in ways that call to you.

💣 **The survival/redemption plan version of logistical Self-Care** is tolerating being disorganized or stretched too thin, being imbalanced between work and play, or between spending and saving, and falling behind with home maintenance or errands.

WisePassion #2: *Self-Care*

Internal

Basic physical health and soothing, recharging and internal quieting habits

Environmental

Creating nourishing living and work environments; surrounding yourself most closely with people who support your 3D Development/Integrity

Logistical

Simplifying your commitments and tasks, and organizing your life logistics, in ways that best support your 3D Development/Integrity

Assessing Your Self-Care Habits

Most people have never really thought about all the different aspects of self-care. As a result, most people have never really taken stock of their relationship with all of the necessary self-care habits. Here is your chance to do this, perhaps for the first time.

Grab a piece of paper and go back and review the items listed in each of the sections and subsections in the 3D self-care description above. Rate your strength and weakness with each one.

As you do this, please keep in mind that if you find you are weak in a number of self-care areas, this is not at all unusual. What is important is that you discover how much your capacity for 3D Integrity and 3D Living depends on the extent to which you utilize *all* of these self-care habits. If you make the link strongly enough inside you, this will help motivate you to upgrade your self-care habits.

After you have completed this self-assessment, review where you are strongest and weakest, which self-care dimensions are natural for you to do and which feel less natural. Select no more than one or two weak areas to upgrade at a time. You will find a much more extensive self-care self-assessment in the *Workbook* and extensive resource recommendations for upgrading various aspects of your self-care WisePassion on my website.

If you notice that you have a large number of areas that need upgrading, this WisePassion may well be your top priority to upgrade at this time. Should this be true for you but you find you have inner objections blocking you from doing this, I encourage you to learn self-help methods for overcoming objections to success. Energy Psychology methods provide some of the most promising new ways to achieve this. *The New IQ Integrity Makeover Workbook* includes Energy Psychology basic balancing exercises as well as Energy Psychology Self-Help instructions. Should whatever self-help methods you select to overcome your success objections not work for you, I strongly encourage you to seek professional assistance.

What Happens to Your Integrity When You Are Self-Neglectful or Self-Indulgent

Since self-care is about making sure you have sufficient life energy for living, developing right relationship with all aspects of 3D Self-care is absolutely crucial to your capacity for authenticity, connection and service. Anesthesias, self-neglect and self-indulgence make it impossible to maintain sufficient life energy to maintain and coordinate your three core drives. If you're not clear about how this is so, take another look at your first self-assessment responses at the beginning of this chapter.

How Self-Care Amplifies the Integrity Effect

Self-care is the foundation of personal, relationship and leadership integrity. It is your most fundamental way of demonstrating to yourself and others that you truly do matter. Self-care also provides the foundation that makes it possible for you to express all three of your core drives. You might be someone who, like me, is blessed with a strong stamina. I have learned the hard way that no matter how productive I am able to remain, even when I am neglecting my own self-care, in the end my self-neglect always ends up doing harm.

How does your relationship with yourself suffer when you are out of integrity with your self-care needs? How does your relationship with others suffer? How does your ability to lead or to serve collective highest good suffer? If you're not sure, get some help with this before your denial catches up with you. I offer this as someone who paid a high price for neglecting my own self-care simply because I thought I had enough stamina to get away with it.

Four Keys to Knowing When Your Self-Care System is Doing What It's Supposed to Do

How do you know when your self-care system is working for you? When:

❑ You score 36 or less on the first self-assessment toward the beginning of this chapter.

❑ You spend the bulk of your days feeling a vibrant sense of well-being and having the life energy you need for creative self-expression, connection with others and being of service in the ways that call to you.

❑ Everything you need to get done logistically takes as little time and effort as you think it can, either because you're using great systems and/or because you have hired others to assist with some of your life logistics.

❑ You feel like there are indeed enough hours in the day and there is enough money to pay your expenses.

If, despite your best efforts, you find that you just can't get it together to care for yourself in the ways described in this chapter, you likely have some significant self-sabotage programs going. Consider doing some Energy Psychology Self-Help treatments on yourself, focusing on removing whatever blocks are in the way. If that does not do the trick, or doesn't resonate with you, please get professional help to remove your blocks. Your self-care is simply too foundational to the rest of your WisePassions, to your integrity, and to 3D Living, for you to have the luxury of neglecting it.

Remember:
*Your Self-Care should never be rare since
Self-Care is the hardware of 3D Living.*

CHAPTER 18

WISEPASSION #3:
DISCERNMENT

*"How can I become better at telling the difference
between truth, partial-truths, and lies?"*

Discernment is a combination of keen insight and good judgment. Discernment means having right relationship with input. Even great listeners don't necessarily don't know what to do with what they hear. And far too few of us have right relationship with the input that comes from our bodies, our emotions, aspects of our intuition and ourselves. Right relationship means not only knowing how to pay attention to input but knowing how to determine which input fits, which doesn't fit and which will fit only if it is revised in some way.

- How frequently do you feel controlled by your inner critic?

- How frequently do you feel susceptible to being manipulated by other people?

- How often do you accept as fact what you read in the newspaper, a magazine or on the Internet, or what you hear on the radio or television?

- There are spin-doctors everywhere today, for all causes, and across the entire range of the political spectrum. How good are you at sorting out truth from partial truths from spin doctoring?

- When you are not quite sure what you feel inside or are faced with making a decision, how often do you explore your subtle inner felt sense for its input? How often do you get useful input from this source of internal information?

● How often do you find it difficult to access and keep company with your full range of emotions? Which emotions do you tend to shut down the most? Which ones do you push too far away for you to learn from them? Which ones tend to engulf and overwhelm you if you start feeling them? Which emotions are you particularly good at feeling and learning from without becoming engulfed or overwhelmed by them?

● How frequently do you intuit the right thing to do in a particular situation? How frequently do you then ignore your intuition?

● How frequently do you get in trouble because you intuited that a situation was dangerous but you ignored your intuition? How often do you give in to your fear when it is coming from your old programming rather than from your intuition? How often do your trust your fear when it is coming from your intuition? (An extremely important book about learning to trust your intuition-based fear is *The Gift of Fear,* by Gavin De Becker.)

Your answers to these questions can offer you some initial clues about how well-developed your Discernment WisePassion is. If you had chronic or significant disconnection experiences as a child (refer back to Section Two), chances are that aspects of your discernment skills did not develop properly.

Co-opted from the Inside, Co-opted from the Outside

Gina came in because she was all tied up in knots over whether to say yes to a job opportunity that had come her way. Part of her said this was a great opportunity while another part of her insisted that she would be in way over her head if she took the new job. Compounding matters further was a third inner message criticizing her for not making a decision. As if all of that wasn't enough, her boss was pleading with her not to take the job and continue working for him, while her boss's boss was really leaning on her to take the job.

She had tried to be logical and rational, carefully weighing the pros and cons of saying yes and saying no. She reviewed the potential risks and potential benefits. She dejectedly told me that this had gotten her nowhere. She had talked with friends and loved ones, only to end up feeling even more confused about what to do.

Remember George, the guy from the WisePassion #1 chapter who "could figure things out quite well on his own, thank you very much"? This attitude of his turned out to have been the reason his wife dragged him in to therapy in the first place. It seems that poor old George was a stone wall, not only with his wife but with everyone. George was in the habit of dismissing everyone's opinion and everyone's input, as well as dismissing his own feelings and intuitions.

Gina felt as though everywhere she turned, both inwardly and outwardly, someone or something was trying to co-opt her. She was trying to figure out the rules for making a good decision, but the more input she got the more confused she felt. Gina's response to the pressure she felt was to feel paralyzed. When I asked her what paralyzed her the most, she said it was that inner critical "voice" that kept blasting her for not making a decision.

George taught me that he too had felt similarly to Gina, once upon a time. His solution was to cut himself off from all outer and inner input except for one part of him: his inner critic. George had long ago decided that the only reliable friend he had, the only thing that had never ever abandoned him in his life, was his inner critic. His inner critic had thus gained his undying loyalty, and one of the things this loyalty led to was that he became impervious to input from other parts of himself and from other people.

Being co-opted and being impervious is the same thing in opposite forms, and both are part of the inner critic's territory.

Welcome to the World of the Inner Critic

You discovered that one of the legs of the survival plan is rules. As we start stringing together the rules we believe we need to follow in order to get the *connection, validation and/or safety* we seek as children, a new part of us develops: an inner rules-keeper. As this part of us develops over time, it takes on the responsibility of trying to make sure that we follow the rules it is keeping for us. When we don't follow those rules, this part of us tends to criticize us. When we do follow those rules but others don't do what our happy ending fantasy promises us will happen, this part of us tends to criticize those other people.

Almost all of us have an inner critic and some of us have an inner critic that pushes us mercilessly and/or shames us dreadfully. Yet, few of us think of this as simply one part of us. More commonly, we think there is no difference between "me" and these inner critical messages; even fewer of us have developed effective strategies for getting the upper hand on our inner critic.

What Discernment Is and Isn't

For many of us who are somewhat like George, our inner critic is our substitute for discernment. For those of us who are like Gina in some ways, other people's input is our substitute for discernment …as long as what they say matches what our inner critic believes.

There is a world of difference between the rules that groups, communities and countries need in order to strike a balance between individual freedom and collective highest good, and being a slave to our inner critic's rules.

WisePassion #3 is about outgrowing our inner critic's childhood rules and replacing them with principles that empower us to discover what does and does not "fit" for us, moment after moment, day after day as adults. The more we learn to trust our inner sense of what "fits" for us, the more receptive to input we can become, because we know how to discern what is of value to us.

Star Trek's Captain Kirk is an excellent example of what I mean. Whenever Kirk was faced with making a major command decision, he sought out the perspectives of his key crewmembers. He especially sought input from two senior officers he knew almost always had diametrically opposing points of view: Mr. Spock and Dr. McCoy. He would listen carefully to their input, asking questions to draw them out and posing possibilities to see what they said about them. In the end, after appreciatively weighing the input he received, Kirk acted like the Captain that he was and did what he believed best served collective highest good. This is discernment. Each of us is the Captain of our Self. Not enough of us act that way, in part because our discernment skills are not sufficiently developed.

Natural developers have a natural passion to listen. They take their truth wherever they can find it. They also reserve the right to determine what fits and doesn't fit for them — to separate the wheat from the chaff. This is discernment: a crucial step beyond listening, the capacity to distinguish between what fits and doesn't fit, to distinguish between truths, partial-truths and lies. The TV show "24" provides a wonderful example of this in President Palmer, and Jack Bauer is also an amazing embodiment of The Integrity Effect.

Without being teachable, listening is impossible. Discernment is quite difficult to maintain when we are anesthetized or in a state of self-neglect or self-indulgence. This is why discernment development comes after self-care development. In addition, a well-developed capacity for discernment is a crucial prerequisite for effective harvesting (WisePassion #4).

The Key Ingredients of 3D Discernment

3D Discernment is your ability to recognize useful input from sources wiser than the rules your inner critic tries to enforce on behalf of your survival or redemption plan. The three varieties of 3D Discernment are: internal, intuitive and external.

Internal Discernment is your capacity to accurately understand input being offered to you from your body sensations, your emotions and the parts of you that comprise your community of self. Surprisingly few people know how to pay attention to, let alone accurately discern, messages from their own internal cues. However, the capacity to do this is the doorway into the 85 percent of who we are that is *not* readily available to our conscious mind.

Intuitive Discernment is your capacity to accurately register input from a wiser and more loving source than your ego or your inner critic. Different people call this source by different names. For some, this is their Higher Self. For others, it is the Holy Spirit, their "spirit guides," or whatever representation of highest wisdom and love their spiritual or religious beliefs teach them to connect with for higher guidance. And for yet others, it is simply Source or even the Wisdom of the Universe. Whatever you call it, it's definitely wiser than your inner critic/ego.

External Discernment is your capacity to distinguish between when you are being told the truth and lied to by others, and when you are being told something about yourself that you didn't know versus being told an inaccurate interpretation of who you really are. One of the most common reasons people are so easily manipulated by politicians, advertisements, certain members of the media and some charismatic figures is that few of us possess sufficiently developed critical thinking skills to be immune to the effects of propaganda.

These three aspects of 3D Discernment are significantly different from the rules leg of the survival plan that they replace. The more we are a prisoner of our survival plan, the more disconnected we become from our inner cues, higher wisdom and the wisdom in others. Instead, we become highly susceptible to being rigid and/or gullible. The more attached we are to our survival/redemption plan, the more we will tend to go back and forth between swallowing input indiscriminately and being impervious to influence. In other words, the less discerning we are, the more easily others, and our inner critic, can co-opt us.

Assessing Your Discernment Skills

Here is a quick way to get a feel for how well developed your discernment skills are at the present time. Think about a decision you are currently struggling with making.

❑ What has your own bodily felt sense revealed to you concerning this decision?

❑ What are the various parts of your "community of self," including but not limited to your inner critic, saying regarding this decision?

❑ What has your "higher guidance" (intuition, spirit, etc.) offered to you about this decision?

❑ What parts of the input you have received from other people about this decision fully fits, partly fits or doesn't fit at all for you?

Now, consider your responses to the above questions:

❑ To what extent do you understand what each question is referring to?

❑ How good are you at accessing each source of input?

❑ What is the extent to which you are able to gather useful input from each of the above sources?

Your answers to these questions can point out which aspects of your discernment WisePassion you may be most in need of developing or upgrading.

WisePassion #3: *Discernment*

Internal
Capacity to accurately understand input from your body sensations, emotions, and "parts" of your "community of self"

Intuitive
Capacity to accurately register input from a "higher" source that is wiser and more loving than your ego (the "still, small voice within" vs. your Inner Critic)

External
Capacity to distinguish between when you are being told the truth and when you are being lied to, and to allow in influence from others that "fits" to accept, while leaving behind the rest (Critical Thinking)

What Happens to Your Integrity When Your Discernment Skills Need Upgrading?

It should be clear at this point that lack of discernment can get us into an awful lot of trouble in our relationship with ourselves, our relationships with our friends and loved ones, our relationships at work, our relationships with those with whom we do business, and our relationship with the mass media. Without a doubt, discernment is as much an all-purpose tool as teachability and self-care.

How Discernment Amplifies the Integrity Effect

Imagine being good at recognizing your inner critic's messages and not being manipulated by them. Imagine being good at spotting spin doctoring and being able to get to the bottom of what the truth really is. Imagine being able to access and learn from both your inner cues and your intuition. Can you see how huge an impact these abilities can have on your integrity?

The good news is that each one of these skills is eminently learnable. You will find discernment-development exercises in the *Workbook* and extensive resource recommendations for upgrading specific aspects of your discernment WisePassion on my website.

Remember:
The secret to learning is great discerning.

CHAPTER 19

WISEPASSION #4:
HARVESTING

"How can I become really good at turning difficult life experiences into blessings rather than baggage?"

The philosopher Jean-Paul Sartre said, "Freedom is what you do with what's been done to you." The single greatest thing that keeps us out of integrity with ourselves, others and the collective is our undigested life experiences.

The idea that you can put your past behind you simply because it is in the past is an utter and total lie. So is the idea that you can merely affirm your way out of your past. Not harvesting the gifts embedded within your undigested life experiences makes them worthless. And, I assure you both personally and professionally that there is no such thing as a worthless experience.

Harvesting is the high art of freedom. *Harvesting is your capacity to transform your life experiences into gifts of love to yourself, to those around you and to humanity.*

- How often do you forget that "there is no such thing as life experience without a gift for you in its hands?"

- How quickly do you recognize when you have a life experience that needs further digestion?

- How readily do you recognize when you have had a traumatic experience?

- How acquainted are you with the anatomy of your unique version of the survival plan and redemption plan?

- How good are you at recognizing when something in your Pandora's box is erupting?

- Are you proficient at using at least one method that enables you to fully digest your life experiences?

- How clearly can you recognize when you have properly digested a life experience?

- Do you know when to get professional assistance when you are having difficulty digesting a life experience on your own?

Your answers to these questions can offer you some initial clues about how well-developed your harvesting WisePassion is. As crucial a life skill as harvesting is, not enough of us are proficient at it.

Misusing New Thought as a Hiding Strategy

Al felt an almost overwhelming drive to be of service in the world. He had been a dedicated minister in a New Thought church for decades. He faithfully used positive thinking, affirmations and prayer, just as he encouraged and facilitated his congregants to do as well.

He began to lose faith in these methods as his own twenty-year marriage started deteriorating. In his most private moments, he began to question the usefulness and effectiveness of these methods. Soon, he doubted both his personal faith and his church.

When the movie *What the Bleep Do We Know?!* was released, Al set aside his misgivings in favor of believing that he just wasn't using these New Thought methods well enough. When *The Secret* later became the rage, this renewed his optimism and faith in these methods. He dared to once again hope that his marriage could be saved through them.

His optimism proved short-lived when his wife announced that she had given up once and for all on their marriage and filed for divorce. It seemed as though none of the methods that his church encouraged, that *What the Bleep* expanded upon and that *The Secret* drove home, were sufficient to save Al's marriage after all.

Not until after his wife left did Al start to recognize and free himself from the unknown bondage his survival and redemption plans had kept him in. Through doing that, he began to put the wisdom of *The Secret* into perspective for the first time. "I believed that focusing on my positive intentions would take care of everything. I was so focused on amplifying my positive intentions that I did not realize how much I was hiding from the substantial blocks I had been carrying. I genuinely had no idea how much they were sabotaging my positive intentions from working."

Now that Al knows how to recognize and clear away his blocks, his positive intentions are manifesting more easily and consistently than ever. He is more passionate and devoted to his ministry than ever before. Yet, he also no longer feels controlled or driven to be of service now that he realizes what caused him to be so neglectful of his wife that she finally gave up and left. He has done a wonderful job of fully grieving the end of his marriage, instead of pushing his grief beneath his positive intentions. Now, not a day goes by during which Al doesn't experience waves of gratitude flowing through him because of the profound gifts he has harvested…despite the sad demise of his marriage.

Being a Perpetual Victim as a Hiding Strategy

Jennifer had no use for New Age philosophies. She was a traditional mainstream Presbyterian who believed in prayer, family, hard work and community service. Even though she was firmly convinced that she was doing all the right things, she had been unable to shake a chronic depression she had lived with for many years. She first tried antidepressants but they didn't seem to do much for her and she didn't like the side effects. At her minister's urging, she finally entered into conventional long-term psychoanalytically oriented psychotherapy.

Twice a week, session after session, year after year she talked and talked and talked and about all the problems that she had, the injustices in the world, and how unfair it was that any essentially good person like her should be plagued by an ever-deepening depression. Her well-meaning therapist tried to help her see that her victim mentality was causing her depression and that her Adverse Childhood Experiences had brought about this mentality.

Jennifer dug in her heels. She believed that her therapist was trying to get her to go against her religion, which required her to obey the commandment that said she must honor her father and her mother. Even though she sought her minister's counsel on this question, she didn't believe him when he told her that doing inner healing does not violate that biblical commandment.

Eventually, Jennifer began to wonder why God was punishing her despite her good values, her devotion to prayer and her willingness to follow her minister's advice to be in psychotherapy. Despite believing she was doing all the right things, Jennifer found herself trapped in a downward spiral of what Caroline Myss aptly terms "woundology."

What Jennifer did not realize was that "talk therapy" by itself is inefficient at best and ineffective at worst in helping people digest their life experiences in ways that turn them into gifts. What her psychotherapist didn't realize was that he was inadvertently helping Jennifer hide rather than heal. His devotion to the time-honored psychotherapy methods in which he was trained blinded him in ways that are quite parallel to how Al had been blinded because of his devotion to his church's incomplete teachings.

Being an Obsessive Crusader as a Hiding Strategy

Hank was a retired professional athlete whose daughter had been killed by a hit-and-run drunk driver. Overcome by rage and grief, Hank vowed to do whatever it took to find the driver and bring him to justice. He believed that only this could provide him with the resolution he felt he needed in order to put this behind him. However, after the driver was apprehended, convicted and imprisoned, Hank was surprised that this did not bring him the inner resolution he sought. Relatives and friends urged Hank to join a grief recovery group. Hank shrugged them off, saying, "I don't believe in that psycho-bullshit; I believe in action."

With that, Hank turned into a crusader against drunk driving, using his status as a retired professional athlete to speak to as many groups as he could. Hank truly believed that he was being of service in the world. Meanwhile, his family and friends felt more and more neglected by him. Where Hank saw himself doing good in the world, those who loved him most saw him as an increasingly self-righteous, obsessed crusader who was sacrificing his own well-being and his relationships with those he loved in order to avoid digesting the painful life experience he had gone through.

New Age Denial, Being a Perpetual Victim and Being an Obsessive Crusader are All Forms of "Harvesting Avoidance"

What Al, Jennifer and Hank had in common was that they did not know how to turn unasked-for and unacceptable life experiences into gifts. Harvesting is sheer bliss compared to the purgatory in which each of them was living.

The ability to turn adversity into gifts is one that I have observed with 100% consistency in all of the natural developers with whom I have been privileged to work. I have come to refer to these as "Awe-full Gifts." Yes, they are awful to go through in the beginning, but we are meant to eventually become awed by and grateful for these experiences nonetheless. Harvesting is the art of doing precisely this.

What Harvesting Is and Isn't

"It happened. It's in the past. I'm over it." Lots of people try to tell themselves that because a life experience is done and over with, that automatically means they can put it behind them. That is an attempt to use willpower to do something that willpower is incapable of doing. Remember the phrase, "It's not over until the fat lady sings?" Well, a life experience is not "over" until its gifts sing in your soul. In fact, harvesting is not about trying to get over an experience as much as it is about getting gifted by it.

Bestselling author Dr. Stephen Covey captures the essence of harvesting in this quote: "Effective people are not problem-minded; they are opportunity-minded. They feed opportunities and starve problems." However, in their quest to be opportunity-minded, too many people unintentionally make the mistake of skipping over the need to turn blocks into blessings. This capacity to properly digest our life experiences is the heart of the harvesting WisePassion.

Harvesting is the ability to turn lemons into lemonade. The task of harvesting is to gather deep gifts from every life experience you ever had, are now having and will ever go through, no matter how unexpected, unasked-for, unacceptable, traumatic or outside the box that experience might be. This ability frees you once and for all from bondage to your survival and redemption plans. It frees you to be more of who you truly are rather than less. It frees you to be more loving rather than less. It expands rather than contracts your vision of and devotion to highest collective good.

In this way, harvesting is true psycho-spiritual alchemy. It is the process through which you turn your leaden life experiences into golden gifts of great value.

Harvesting is the heart of the transformation process. It includes digesting all your life experiences: the seemingly positive and the seemingly negative from both your past and your present. This is the key to restoring crucial aspects of your integrity and authenticity, and to upgrading your capacity to love and lead.

Harvesting may take work, and gifts don't often appear overnight. But, the results are more than worth the effort and in the long run the work involved is far less than the ongoing pain that comes from being perpetually imprisoned by undigested life experiences.

When harvesting prior undigested life experiences, you unlock your survival plan's Pandora's box and retrieve, heal, and transform into gifts the contents that are relevant to the current life experience you are going through. This is the secret to enabling your past and present life experiences to expand your wisdom and compassion about yourself, others, and life in general. It is the key to becoming more fully yourself, becoming more collaborative with others, and being of service in the world in the clearest and most effective ways possible.

Rightness Addiction:
The Secret Reason People Avoid Harvesting

The common denominator I have seen among my clients who had avoided harvesting is what I call Rightness Addiction. *Rightness* is a frozen belief that a particular perception or interpretation is the "truth" or "reality." It means being closed to evidence that does not support that belief. Rightness addiction is an unswerving conviction, sometimes approaching delusional intensity, that your fundamental beliefs about yourself and the world are correct and unchangeable.

Rightness addiction in its extreme forms the foundation upon which fanaticism is built. Fanaticism is an illness not a blessing; it is one of the panoply of potential consequences of allowing undigested life experiences to remain undigested. The current worldwide pandemic of what I call Fanaticism Disorder is a source of far more conflict and damage than most people realize.

Rightness addiction takes two forms: blame and shame. Blame means proving how right you are about how wrong someone else is, and that their wrongness is preventing you from having the life experiences you want to have. Shame means proving how wrong (damaged beyond hope) you yourself are because you are not having the life experiences you want.

Rightness addiction makes being right more important than healing. It is, in fact, the heart of what makes people unteachable. Rightness addiction thus blocks us from harvesting gifts from our life experiences. Review Jennifer and Al's stories from earlier in this chapter and see if you can spot the rightness addiction that was blocking them from harvesting.

Harvesting is a narrow path forward, surrounded by various forms of rightness addiction on all sides. On one side of the harvesting path is Woundology Swamp, in which you become a victim trapped in the mud of your own baggage. On the other side is Crusading Cliff from which you can holler out your crusading messages to all who will listen. Behind you is Avoidance Cave, where you can retreat into all the glorious forms of denial that are available to you. Are you ready to give up rightness addiction and master the art of harvesting?

The Key Ingredients of 3D Harvesting

3D Harvesting includes the following elements that are implemented in this sequence: digestion ➜ meaning ➜ gratitude. Any other sequence results, at best, in discovering gifts that may be intellectually true but aren't fully embraced in the heart.

Digestion means putting unresolved life experiences to rest once and for all through integrating them into the larger fabric of your authentic self. Recall a time when you ate something that sat like a lump in your stomach. How did you feel? Nauseated?

Bloated? Constipated? It was definitely there inside you, but the nutrients it contained were not being absorbed to feed your body, nor were the rest of the contents being eliminated. That is what an undigested life experience is: you carry the experience within you but it's as though it's sitting like a lump in your "psychological stomach." The gifts the experience contains have not been put to good use and the rest has not been eliminated from your system once and for all. Instead, the experience is just sitting there within you, undigested, uncomfortable and toxifying you. Highly effective methods now exist that can help you do your digestion work more rapidly than ever. The "Going Further" section of the Appendix tells you how to locate them on my website.

Meaning is the deeper understanding that naturally begins to reveal itself as you complete a life experience digestion process. "Deeper understanding" means discovering specific gifts within a life experience. These gifts contain three core qualities: 1) expanding your heart — your love and compassion toward yourself, others and humanity in general; 2) enriching your joyous connection with Spirit or the Universe; and 3) deepening your sense of life purpose and sparking your passion to fulfill it with love, wisdom and impeccable integrity. In fact, if this kind of meaning does not emerge – or if you understand the gifts in your head but your heart has not fully embraced them — this means that your digestion process is not yet complete.

Gratitude is the deep, bodily felt awe that emerges within you in response to embracing in your deepest being the precious gifts you have harvested from a life experience. This enables your spirit to soar, like the phoenix rising from the ashes of the life experience you have just digested. If you do not experience, deep within your body, this flavor of gratitude, it means your gift-gathering process is not yet complete.

The more you practice digestion, meaning and gratitude, in that order, the greater your harvesting powers will grow. The greater your harvesting powers grow, the freer you will become from your survival and redemption plans, and the more authentic, empowered, loving and of service you will therefore become.

WisePassion #4: *Harvesting*

Digestion

Putting unresolved
life experiences to rest and
reclaiming hidden
parts of yourself,
including your disowned gifts
(all of which have been
kept safely for you
in your Pandora's box)

Meaning

Finding gifts within your
life experiences that expand
your heart and your
joyous connection with Spirit,
deepen your sense of purpose
and spark your
passion to fulfill it

Gratitude

Deep bodily-felt awe,
especially regarding your
most difficult life experiences,
because of the gifts
they brought you,
enabling your spirit to soar,
like a phoenix rising
from the ashes

In addition to these three elements, your harvesting ability also depends on how well developed your first three WisePassions are.

Unless you're teachable you won't think there is any harvesting needing to be done and/or you won't be willing to discover your role in your own suffering.

Harvesting work can sometimes be emotionally taxing and/or time consuming, since it can involve dealing with issues that were buried alive long ago. So unless your self-care habits are strong, your own self-protection mechanisms will rightly block you from doing harvesting work until you are sufficiently ready to do it.

Effective harvesting builds upon every one of your discernment skills as well: in order to heal what needs healing and gather gifts waiting to be harvested, you must first know how to listen below the surface and discern the sometimes subtle messages that live there.

On the other hand, the quality of your personal power (WisePassion #5), synergy capabilities (WisePassion #6) and stewardship skills (WisePassion #7) can only be as good as the extent to which you have properly digested your life experiences.

That's why harvesting comes fourth in the WisePassions sequence.

A Rather Dramatic Personal Example
of All Three Harvesting Elements

Three weeks had passed since I had been able to stay out of bed for more than a few minutes. I had spent my days writhing in a darkened room, in deep emotional pain, in overwhelming self-pity, in unbearable humiliation and in utter confusion. I had been through some pretty intense upheavals during my lifetime, but all of them paled in comparison to how unbearable this one felt.

On a cloudy, sad-looking morning, I finally forced myself to roll out of bed and onto the cold floor so I could literally get on my knees to pray. As I called out with all of my heart to all of my spiritual resources, what emerged from my mouth was not a prayer in the usual sense of the word. It was a demand and an ultimatum that came from the very cells of my being. *"I demand that gifts ultimately come from this experience that are far more profound than my pain is deep."* And then I proclaimed the unspeakable: *"Unless this occurs I will kill myself."*

I had finally arrived at teachability, albeit in a rather unorthodox way. A response to my prayer began to unfold almost instantly. Through my drawn blinds, I could see the sun beginning to burn through the clouds. I became aware that for the first time in three weeks I finally had enough energy to get out of the house.

Putting on my rollerblades, I slowly began skating on a paved path surrounding a nearby bay. Oh, the joy of finally feeling my body move through a gentle breeze as the sun soothingly beamed down on me and the water glistened before me. I was maybe 10 or 15 minutes into my skate when, from out of nowhere, a vision started unfolding within me that was so powerful I immediately had to stop skating and lie down. Fortunately, at that moment, I was skating beside a grassy area where I could flop down as the vision unfolded.

I quickly realized that I was being shown the history of my arrogance. I had been transported back in time to my childhood. Life experiences flashed before me that revealed the important life-saving and family-saving reasons my arrogance first emerged. As the vision unfolded, I gradually moved forward in time, being shown incident after incident through adolescence and adulthood in which I had been arrogant, and the impact of that arrogance on myself and those around me.

What amazed me most about this experience, other than the fact that I am not given to having visions like this, is that even though I was reviewing life experiences I found quite embarrassing, I did not feel an ounce of shame. It was as though my inner critic had been told to take a temporary vacation. Instead, as the vision ended, I felt strangely elated and had a very distinct experience of being surrounded and cradled by a profoundly deep Love.

The vision ended with the day I had become bedridden three weeks earlier. That was the day my wife packed up and left after telling me she had fallen in love with the woman who had helped her heal from a life-threatening illness. She wanted a divorce. Her final request to me was that I solemnly promise not to try to win her back because for her there was no going back. I felt the depth of her sincerity — that she had deeply and carefully considered this for a long time. It was neither a manipulation nor a temporary whim. I therefore felt like the only loving and honorable thing I could do was to make that promise and honor it. I could hear within me the old phrase about how one of the tests of loving someone is whether you can love them enough to let them go.

That was the day my life as I had known it for nearly two decades came to an end. We had been the couple that other couples looked to, personally and professionally, as a role model for a happy, healthy relationship. Our lives have been intertwined in every possible way because we had also been business partners. Now all of that was at an end. I felt profoundly abandoned, humiliated and lost.

The vision I had that day was but the first step in a healing process that took years to complete. There is a saying that you can estimate how long it will take to recover from a divorce by dividing the number of years you were married by four. That meant it might take me four years. It took me three to do the bulk of my recovery work. During the first year of my journey, my primary focus was on digestion, not meaning and certainly not gratitude. My digestion involved quite a bit of anger completion work, grief work, Energy Psychology treatments, intensive psychotherapy, and a huge amount of soul-searching to uncover my part in what had happened.

It wasn't a lot of fun, but, the more digestion I did, the more meaning emerged and gradually meaning gave way to gratitude. The demand I had made from the core of my being on my knees that cloudy morning had at last come to pass. I was now living each day in gratitude, feeling more deeply and consistently connected with my spiritual resources than ever before. The fabric of my life was more balanced among my three core drives that it had ever been. Wonderful new directions emerged for me that I found extremely enlivening and fulfilling. And I, who have always deeply valued integrity, and have always been seen by others as a pillar of integrity, felt as though I was discovering what integrity really is for the first time in my life.

A year and a half before the first edition of this book was published, I remarried. I could not be the husband that I am to Laurie had I not gone through the upheavals I experienced and had I not fully harvested the profound gifts they contained. I adore Laurie and I adore our marriage. It makes my first marriage, which everyone thought at the time was truly extraordinary, pale in comparison. I will be eternally grateful to my first wife and my first marriage, but what amazes me is that I — an "until-death-do-you-part" kind of guy — now live in daily gratitude that my first wife had the good sense to end our marriage.

The gifts I harvested through this dramatic life upheaval are now your gifts through this book. Without the benefit of all that my natural developer and successful deliberate developer clients taught me about the adult development process, I could not have reached the point I am at in my own development. Without having gone through — and fully digested — the life upheaval I just shared with you, as well as many others, I could not have written this book. And I know deep within me that I was very much meant to write this book. All is as it needed to be and I am profoundly grateful.

You will find a harvesting skills assessment and upgrading exercises in the *Workbook*. Extensive resource recommendations for upgrading various aspects of your harvesting WisePassion are available on my website.

What Happens to Your Integrity When Your Harvesting Skills Need Upgrading?

As I wrote at the beginning of the chapter, the single greatest thing that keeps us out of integrity with ourselves, others and the collective is our undigested life experiences. Harvesting is the mechanism that enables us to digest those experiences.

How Harvesting Amplifies the Integrity Effect

Everything our survival requires us to hide about ourselves, both gold and lead, gets placed inside a Pandora's box for safekeeping until we become ready to retrieve those aspects of ourselves and use them for higher good. Harvesting enables this to occur. The doorway to this harvesting is your wakeup calls and your undigested life experiences. The more harvesting you do with the contents of your Pandora's box, the more authentic you will become, the more you will move into right relationship with your personal power, the greater your relationship synergy skills will become and the more solid your stewardship will be. Well, that covers personal, relationship and collective integrity. The more you harvest, the more the Integrity Effect in you will grow.

The good news is that the art of harvesting is learnable. When I co-wrote *Sensible Self-Help* in the mid-1990s, people were already doing deep inner healing work more rapidly than they had before that time. Now it is more rapid still, thanks in part to newer innovations such as Energy Psychology methods.

Even though some life experiences take years to fully sort out, it is now possible to digest all life experiences far more fully and rapidly than ever before. The secret to this is understanding what needs to be done and knowing the best resources to do it.

So far, this chapter has focused on providing you with a portrait of what harvesting is and isn't. In the remainder of this chapter I will share with you the most effective harvesting strategies and resources I have found.

Ways to Identify Your Undigested Life Experiences and Digesting Them So You Can Harvest Their Gifts

Energy Psychology methods can be extremely helpful in digesting life experiences and harvesting their gifts. The *Workbook* contains an exercise to help you illuminate undigested life experiences that may be the most liberating way for you to do some harvesting work. It also includes a particularly powerful adaptation of Energy Psychology self-help methods to help you digest the life experiences you decide most need further digestion and harvesting.

How to Know When You Are Finished Harvesting a Life Experience's Gifts

Harvesting is a lifelong process and people frequently uncover additional gifts from earlier life experiences many years after their initial harvesting work. This is because as we mature our perspectives evolve, opening us up to new frames of reference for reformulating old experiences. These additional gifts are precious and usually unexpected bonuses.

What I mean by "finished" here is more about how to know when your harvesting process with a particular life experience has contributed in a meaningful way to your journey toward 3D Integrity and 3D Living.

Very few helping professionals check in detail to see how finished a client is with harvesting gifts from their life experiences. Yet, I believe that harvesting is the most important and sacred reason to be doing deep inner work in the first place. Feeling better is, of course, great; but when you stop merely with feeling better, you sell yourself and those around you far short.

After you have completed a piece of harvesting work, use my Gifts Harvesting Assessment in the *Workbook* to determine how successful your harvesting was. You can also use this to determine the extent to which you have already done successful harvesting with other prior life experiences that you believe you have put behind you.

How to Tell If You Are Making
Progress in Mastering the Art of Harvesting

The following are a few of the symptoms that you are making progress in mastering the art of harvesting:

- ❑ Enhanced authenticity and right use of personal power.

- ❑ Greater ability to manifest (bring about) your intentions and goals more easily.

- ❑ Deeper compassion-based love.

- ❑ Expanded openness to life on its own terms.

- ❑ Greater resilience when the unexpected and unasked-for come along.

- ❑ A decreased need to be right and a corresponding increased desire to be happy.

- ❑ Finding forgiveness not only easier to do but more enjoyable to seek. Here are two definitions that convey what I mean by the word forgiveness. *"Forgiveness is the ability to make peace with your own life by no longer arguing with or objecting to the way it unfolds."* — Fred Luskin, Former Director of the Stanford Forgiveness Project (www.forgiveness.org). The following is my own definition: *"Forgiveness is demonstrating in the present that I am no longer harmed by the unacceptable that occurred in the past."*

Visit my website for links to new and proven harvesting skills resources.

Remember:
To reduce your strife harvest gifts from your life.

CHAPTER 20

WISEPASSION #5:
POWER

"How can I express my inner light, gifts, deepest truths, and creativity without self-censoring and holding back?"

You may have previously read the following quote from Marianne Williamson, which appears in her book *A Return to Love*:

> Our deepest fear is not that we are inadequate. Our deepest fear is that we are powerful beyond measure. It is our light, not our darkness that most frightens us. We ask ourselves, Who am I to be brilliant, gorgeous, talented, fabulous? Actually, who are you *not* to be? You are a child of God. Your playing small does not serve the world. There is nothing enlightened about shrinking so that other people won't feel insecure around you. We are all meant to shine, as children do. We were born to make manifest the glory of God that is within us. It's not just in some of us; it's in everyone. And as we let our own light shine, we unconsciously give other people permission to do the same. As we are liberated from our own fear, our presence automatically liberates others.

This quote is custom-made for WisePassion #5. Some people shrink away from their personal power. Others misuse or indulge their personal power, often without knowing it. Because the issue of power is huge for so many people, the most appropriate name for the fifth WisePassion is...well...power.

Power is your ability to use your capacities to effectively manifest your intentions. This chapter will show you how power is the heart of authenticity and personal integrity, and how it forms the foundation of relationship and leadership integrity. You will also discover how healthy power depends on how well you have developed your first four WisePassions.

- ◈ In what situations are you able to embrace your personal power without embarrassment and yet with deep humility? In which situations are you reluctant to embrace and express your personal power?

- ◈ Do you tend toward self-absorption or entitlement, or to be self-forgetting or codependent with others?

- ◈ Do you tend to use your personal power at the expense of others or at the expense of your own life balance?

- ◈ Do you tend to tolerate living in fear or anger, or with a sense of unfulfillment?

- ◈ How well do you know what your strengths are, as an individual and as a man or woman?

- ◈ Which strengths of yours do you hide? From whom?

- ◈ Which strengths of yours do you misuse? Under what circumstances?

- ◈ How much do you unabashedly utilize your strengths on behalf of your own authentic self-expression, love and being of service?

- ◈ Are you clear about which ways of expressing your creativity nourish you the most? How frequently do you need time for your creative outlets in order to maintain your inner well-being? How consistent are you in giving yourself that amount of time?

- ◈ How happy are you with your career?

- ◈ How happy are you with your relationship with money?

- ◈ To what extent have you mastered the art of compassionate self-disclosure? To what extent do you instead wear a mask with others? With whom? Can you describe your mask? What aspects of your authenticity does it hide?

- ◈ How aware of your own boundaries do you tend to be? How upset do you need to get before you even realize you have a boundary? How effective are you at compassionately disclosing and respectfully honoring your boundaries with others?

🔸 How much of a procrastinator are you? How free are you from being under the shadow of incomplete projects and commitments?

🔸 How consistent are you in your ability to manifest your intentions? In which aspects of your life are you best and weakest at manifesting your intentions?

Your answers to these questions can offer you some initial clues about how well-developed your power WisePassion is.

Why Call This WisePassion "Power" and Not "Self-Esteem"?

This is a question I have been asked, and it deserves an answer in this book. I view the self-esteem movement as having unwittingly played an extremely significant role in helping to create a culture of entitlement and greed. Many do-gooders I have known hold a particular animosity toward the self-esteem movement for precisely this reason.

I do not believe most self-esteem advocates meant to foster self-indulgence and abdication of social responsibility, but this is what I believe happened despite better intentions. (The classic self-esteem books by Nathaniel Brandon are a notable exception to this.)

Right use of our power WisePassion goes to the heart of what natural developers focus on upgrading. They did not strike me as being terribly concerned with developing their self-esteem. My hunch is that this is because truly healthy self-esteem is the natural outgrowth of 3D Integrity. It does not seem to need to be intended or willpowered.

Ms. Boundary-less and Mr. Entitlement

Everyone knew Jim as a driver. He did everything with a level of intensity that most people found exhausting just to watch. And not just at work and sports. His kids had to be better than any of his friends' kids; the social gatherings he and his wife Sally had at their house had to be better than anyone else's. He tried his best to be amiable about this, at least on the surface, but almost everyone saw through his mask.

Jim's unaddressed redemption plan was success. Achievement, money, being in control and being a socialite were Jim's unconscious recipe for getting the love and validation he had not experienced nearly enough of as a child. He had never done any harvesting work around the Adverse Childhood Experiences that birthed the childhood survival plan that eventually evolved into his adulthood redemption plan.

The darker shadow beneath Jim's achievement-oriented redemption plan, the one he hoped no one would see, was that he felt a deep sense of entitlement. Jim felt that the world owed him big time for his having gotten such a raw deal as a child. You see, he grew up in a poor family on the wrong side of town, with an abusive, alcoholic father and a frightened, dependent mother. As an adult, whenever things didn't go the way he wanted them to, Jim would go into an indignant, self-righteous rage.

He tried his best to keep his rightness addiction hidden, but he could not hide it at home. Sally and their two children knew his shadow side all too well and they were terrified of it.

Sally had been attracted to what she saw as Jim's self-confidence. Her own father was the opposite of Jim's: well meaning and good-hearted but passive and lacking in ambition. As a result, her mother resentfully ruled the roost and Sally felt tyrannized by her. She grew up wanting to be taken care of, as she didn't want to be like her Mom.

Jim was going to be the man who would finally take care of Sally so she didn't have to become domineering like her mom. She in turn would need as little as possible and would make life as easy for Jim as possible because her redemption plan was the codependent version of connection.

Ms. Boundary-less and Mr. Entitlement Were Made for Each Other

Can you see how Jim had looked perfect to Sally? Can you see how Sally had looked perfect to Jim? Ms. Boundary-less was going to take good care of Mr. Entitlement and he loved that idea. Mr.

Entitlement would be in charge of providing for Ms. Boundary-less and she loved that idea.

Neither Jim nor Sally understood much about healthy personal power. Jim threw his power around as though he was the center of the universe and Sally happily hid hers in order to be taken care of. "So what if Sally is mousy," Jim thought. "I can always spice things up by having an affair. She'd forgive me." "So what if Jim throws a fit when he doesn't get his way," thought Sally. "That's just what real men do. I can take it. He's such a great provider."

Jim and Sally did not end up in therapy until both of their "perfect" children got into severe trouble within weeks of each other. The boy was arrested for stealing and the girl was caught smoking pot in the girls' bathroom at school. You might not be surprised to learn that, when therapy first began, neither Jim nor Sally had any idea that there was a connection between their children acting up and their own unaddressed redemption plans.

Happily, both of them ultimately did their harvesting work to digest the undigested life experiences that resulted in their respective redemption plans. Jim agreed to go to a ManKind Project weekend intensive called the New Warrior Training Adventure. He came back ready to do his harvesting work. Sally, in turn, agreed to go to one of the two parallel experiences for women. She selected the H.E.R weekend. She too came back ready to do her Harvesting work.

The more harvesting Jim did, the more his entitlement issues faded. The more those issues faded the more humble his relationship with his personal power became. This resulted in his losing most of his over-the-top need to be in control. The more harvesting Sally did, the more excited she became about exploring the kind of personal power that nourished her, without abandoning those she loved. This was a completely different version of power than she saw her mom express.

The relationship each of them had with their own personal power was now changing quite dramatically. Fortunately, the love between them was strong enough that they found ways to re-vision their marriage in light of their newfound relationship with their own personal power. Oh, and as they did this, the kids also turned around pretty quickly, thanks to their own responsiveness to therapy, combined with the son going to a Boys to Men weekend that is an offshoot of the ManKind Project.

What Power Is and Isn't

Power means being who you truly are when not imprisoned by your survival or redemption plans, or the undigested life experiences that caused them to develop. Power is a combination of self-knowledge, being self-revealing, manifesting your intentions and maintaining balance among your three core drives.

Stephen Covey defines power this way: "Power is the faculty or capacity to act, the strength and potency to accomplish something. It is the vital energy to make choices and decisions. It also includes the capacity to overcome deeply embedded habits and to cultivate higher, more effective ones."

Healthy power is thus the backbone of authenticity and integrity. It is the key to your wholeness and sovereignty (a blend of utmost character and superb effectiveness) as an individual. Power fills your cup with the vitality, wholeness, passion and aliveness, not only just for your own sake, but also for the sake of having successful personal and work relationships and making a positive difference in the world.

My natural developer clients taught me that our capacity for healthy power depends on the extent we are free from our survival and redemption plans. As successful deliberate developers, Jim and Sally reflected this principle perfectly.

The Key Ingredients of 3D Power

3D Power adds a fourth element to the three-step sequence you learned about in the harvesting WisePassion chapter: digestion ➔ meaning ➔ gratitude ➔ manifestation. The entire point of harvesting is to remove the blocks that stand between you and being effective at manifestation.

Growing into right relationship with your power can be boiled down to three core ingredients: 1) humbly embracing your strengths; 2) learning how to recognize and steadfastly but compassionately honor your boundaries (limits); and 3) becoming effective in manifesting your intentions without stepping on others. Let's explore each of these in a bit more detail.

Embracing Your Strengths means developing conscious relationship with your abilities, talents and creativity, and knowing how to use them on behalf of being authentic, connecting with others and making a positive difference in the world. It does not mean flaunting your strengths, talents or creativity, or using them to manipulate others.

Compassionate Boundaries means honoring your personal truth, your passions and your limits without manipulation or tyranny. Boundaries intelligence enables you to stay true to all three of your core drives in a coordinated and integrated way. When brought forward into relationships, boundaries intelligence becomes a primary vehicle for helping you build collaboration and synergy with others. (We will explore more about this aspect of boundaries intelligence in the next chapter about the synergy WisePassion.) When brought forward into stewardship (WisePassion #7), boundaries intelligence becomes one of the key means by which you help groups of people join together to discover what truly serves their collective highest good. A compassionate boundary does not mean bashing, intimidating or manipulating people.

Effectiveness With Your Intentions means channeling your life energy to manifest your highest desires, including creating a nourishing, fulfilling, joyous and fun life for yourself. When brought forward into your relationships and service work, it also means helping manifest your relationship's intentions and helping manifest collective highest good. Effectiveness with your own intentions does not mean using willpower to fulfill your narcissistic needs at the expense of others. Similarly, being effective in fulfilling a group's intentions does not mean making your group's needs more important than collective highest good.

The more you embrace your strengths, develop your boundaries intelligence and become effective at manifesting your intentions, the greater your power will grow. The greater these kinds of power grow in you, the more authentic, empowered, loving and of service you will become.

These three dimensions of power make "procreation" possible. Procreation is a word for the entire range of ways your creativity is capable of expressing itself, including career, parenting, and hobbies that give expression to your natural creative gifts. All of us have a deep urge and need to procreate, and as precious as having children is, raising children is but one form of procreation. Unless you give your procreative urge authentic ways to passionately express itself throughout all phases of your life, you will feel incomplete and unfulfilled. This is why finding an outlet for your creative juices is such an important outgrowth of your power WisePassion.

Power may have been a dirty word for you earlier in your life, either because you have misused it or because you have been at the receiving end of someone who has misused it. If so, now would be an excellent time to transform your understanding of what true power really is. If you find you have objections to doing this, consider trying the *Holding the Risks with Grace* exercise in the *Workbook* concerning these objections.

WisePassion #5: *Power*

Strengths

Humbly yet honestly
owning your
abilities, talents and creativity
and placing them
in service of your
3D Living/Integrity

Boundaries

Honoring your own limits
so you can
love and work with others
without resentment
and with integrity

Intentionality

Channeling your life energy
to manifest your
highest desires and
3D Living/Integrity,
rather than to serve your ego,
your Survival Plan
or your Redemption Plan
(Intentional
Effectiveness)

In addition to these three power elements of strength, boundaries and intentionality, healthy power also depends on how well developed your first four WisePassions are. My hope is that by this point in the book it is clear why neglecting any of your first four WisePassions will sabotage your capacity for healthy power.

On the other hand, the quality of your relationship synergy skills (WisePassion #6) and your stewardship skills (WisePassion #7) can only be as good as the extent to which you have right relationship with power.

That's why power comes fifth in the WisePassions sequence.

What Happens to Your Integrity When Your Power Needs Upgrading?

Here are five common symptoms indicating that your relationship with your power probably needs upgrading:

1. Self-absorption, self-centeredness or entitlement issues.

2. Indulging your personal power at the expense of others.

3. Being self-forgetting, overly deferential or codependent with others.

4. Tolerating living in fear, anger, or with a sense of unfulfillment.

5. Being over-attached to stability in your life, at the expense of your vitality.

If you find yourself reluctant to fully embrace or express aspects of your power, consider self-treating this using the *Ho'oponopono* exercise briefly described at the end of the teachability WisePassion chapter or the *Holding the Risks With Grace* exercise in the *Workbook*. Then upgrade your self-care WisePassion. I have found that the reason some people are out of integrity with their self-care is that this prevents them having sufficient life energy to fully move into their power. After all, you might upset certain people's apple carts if they are used to you abdicating your power and you suddenly start embodying it.

How Power Amplifies the Integrity Effect

Healthy power is one of the vital keys to wholeness and authenticity. Authenticity — being true to yourself in healthy ways — is the first of the three dimensions of 3D Integrity.

Have you ever tried to build connection with someone who either hid himself or herself from you or imposed themselves on you? Nourishing and durable relationships are only possible between two whole and authentic people. Synergy is only possible between or among people who have right relationship with their power. This is the second of the three dimensions of 3D Integrity.

Have you ever been exposed to someone who felt s/he was fully living their life purpose? These are the people who make profoundly positive contributions to the world as an expression of their deepest, most authentic self. Without proper power, truly serving collective highest good is impossible. This is the third of the three dimensions of 3D Integrity.

True power is not narcissism. It is the foundation from which synergy with others and high quality stewardship becomes possible.

Developing healthy power has never been easier. Absolutely wonderful strategies and resources now exist that can help you develop or upgrade each of the three key dimensions of your Power WisePassion. You will find key power self-assessment and upgrading exercises in the *Workbook* and resources for upgrading all the dimensions of your power WisePassion on my website.

Summary of Top Ten Power WisePassion Development Objectives

1. Identify and embrace your strengths.

2. Embrace and live from the high side of your maleness or femaleness.

3. Become good at self-disclosure and boundaries (replacing your survival plan's mask with adulthood authenticity and staying true to yourself).

4. Upgrade your manifestation skills (become highly effective at turning your intentions into results).

5. Regularly express your unique forms of creative self-expression.

6. Conquer procrastination and complete incompletes.

7. Develop impeccable personal integrity.

8. Articulate and embrace your life mission.

9. Upgrade your relationship with time, tasks, money and career through further strengthening these aspects of your self-care WisePassion.

10. Allow full expression of your life energy, aliveness and vitality.

Remember:
Embrace your Power and your life will flower.

CHAPTER 21

WISEPASSION #6:
SYNERGY

"How can I learn to co-create more fulfilling, collaboration-based, productive, and resilient personal and work relationships than I ever thought possible?"

I imagine you are familiar with the statement, "the whole is greater than the sum of its parts." This is synergy. Combine blue and yellow and you get something distinctly different from either called green. This is synergy. Combine hydrogen and oxygen and you get something distinctly different from both those gases called water. This also is *synergy: combining seemingly separate elements to create something that is greater than the parts.*

Your car is an example of synergy. The engine, fuel, drive train and you, as the driver, all magically synergize to enable a bunch of seemingly separate and independent parts to function as a whole. Your body is an example of synergy; your cells combine into organs and bones and muscles and systems. These systems almost magically synergize with each other to give you the illusion that you are a singular organism rather than a community of synergized organisms.

Our relationships are meant to work the same way. Synergy turns out to be the heart of healthy, happy, productive and durable relationships. However, far too often, relationships are run by coercion or compromise rather than by synergy. My natural developers showed me over and over again how synergy is the master skill of relationships.

Why then is synergy so uncommon? The answer becomes obvious once you understand the nature of survival and redemption plans and the ways in which our capacity for synergy depend upon our first five WisePassions being strong.

Inflicting His Will

An old college buddy of mine had been quite successful in business. He had risen through the ranks and had generated quite a significant income and nest egg for himself. He had done this through mastering the arts of coercion and compromise. He had also gone through three marriages and his adult children didn't speak to him. He did not understand how he could be so successful in business and yet such a miserable failure in his personal relationships. It turns out that he also didn't appreciate the extent to which those who worked for him complied with him out of resentful fear rather than motivated respect. He did not understand that coercion destroys connection.

Even though my old buddy had great interest in the latest management and leadership in skills, he had little interest in personal or relationship development. He had no appreciation of how inextricably connected personal, relationship and leadership development actually are. Business success was his redemption plan and his devotion to his redemption plan had cost him his most precious relationships. There he was, with all this money and no one to share it with. In fact, he had far less money than he otherwise might have because he was paying a hefty alimony to three ex-wives. Conducting relationships through imposing one's will on others is a costly way to be in relationship.

This college friend of mine was quite weak in teachability, favoring the over-use of willpower instead. He was reasonably good with self-care because he had realized how crucial that was to his ability to succeed in business. In terms of discernment, his critical thinking skills were quite developed but his internal discernment skills were not and he seemed to only use his intuitive discernment skills at work. When it came to harvesting, he knew how to turn what seemed like adverse business situations into opportunities. But he had never used his harvesting skills to digest any of his lifelong undigested life experiences. His version of power was to inflict his will on others while believing he was doing this for their own good.

This poor fellow provides a painful reminder that our capacity for synergy can only be as good as our first five WisePassions are strong.

Keeping the Peace

Remember Sally from the last chapter on the power WisePassion? She was married to Jim, another man who was good at "inflicting." If you recall, Sally was willing to defer to Jim because he was such a great provider, so they counterbalanced one another perfectly. While Jim saw Sally as being mousy before they began their transformation together, Sally saw herself as keeping the peace on behalf of the family. Keeping the peace was just a prettied-up euphemism for "submitting," which is the counterbalance to "inflicting."

Think about how often you have read about, seen or been in an "inflictor-submitter" situation. Tasks can get accomplished through the "inflictor-submitter" dance, but at what price?

Compromise is certainly a step better than the "inflictor-submitter" dance. In fact, most of the literature I am familiar with about relationships stresses the importance of learning how to compromise. However, the vast majority of couples I have ever worked with in psychotherapy ended up in my office precisely because each had compromised away more and more of their authenticity for the sake of the relationship.

When looked at objectively, compromise is about both people giving up equal amounts in order to create what seems like a mutual agreement. When viewed honestly, the best possible outcome available through a "compromise" strategy is that both people agree to a plan that leaves both of them feeling equally ripped off. No wonder people commonly don't make good on the commitments they make as a result of compromise.

Compromise and authenticity tend to conflict with each other. Far too often, compromise involves sacrificing a portion of one's integrity for the sake of a solution and far too often, compromise requires at least one person to dim her or his healthy Power for the sake of a solution.

A far better way to co-create agreements becomes possible when our first five WisePassions are well-developed and we are well on the way to freeing ourselves from our survival and redemption plans. The name of that far better way is synergy.

What We Do Instead of Synergy

Coercion means thinking you know what's best for another adult...or thinking that what you want is more important than what anyone else wants. Imposing or inflicting your will is one of the most reliable ways to create bad blood and conflict. Coercion is one of the traps which do-gooders are susceptible to falling into because of how deeply they believe in their causes. Coercion is also one of the key ingredients of tyranny. You may get what you think you want in the short term, but this will always be at the expense of having traded away long-term goodwill in order to get it. Only when we have not sufficiently dealt with our internal Pandora's box are we capable of this kind of arrogance.

Capitulation means submitting, the opposite of coercion and another word for this is being codependent. Capitulation is one of the traps into which connectors commonly fall. As you'll recall, connectors are those who make their *connection* core drive more important than either their *authenticity* or *impact* core drives. Connectors are so focused on relationship, and especially on taking care of the other person, that they tend to neglect themselves and cover up aspects of their own authenticity. Doing this makes true synergy impossible, since synergy requires two whole people who are in right relationship with their power.

Compromise, as popular as it is, is a dangerous tool that has been relied upon far too often in personal and business relationships of all kinds. Compromise should only be used as a desperate last resort, not as a way of life. This is because compromise creates deadness, resentment and non-compliance instead of the aliveness, passion, collaboration and durability that synergy creates. Add enough compromises together over the lifetime of a relationship and watch that relationship aliveness, vitality, productiveness and effectiveness die.

What Synergy Is and Isn't

Synergy is combining elements to create new solutions that are even more wonderful than each of the elements by themselves. Natural developers and successful deliberate developers know that they are not islands unto themselves and that they do not have all the answers. They relish opportunities to combine what they know and want with what others know and want, to create solutions that are far better than any one person can create alone. This is synergy and it is the most vital key to good relationships and conflict resolution.

Whereas authenticity is about creating internal coordination and unity so that you can be effective in the world at manifesting your intentions, synergy is about synchronizing your power, energy and manifestation abilities with others in order to love, co-create, collaborate, resolve conflict and spread kindness.

Synergy is a WisePassion to be used with loved ones, friends, co-workers and strangers; with individuals, groups and cultures. (It is also something to use within yourself to unify your "parts" – refer back to the internal discernment information in WisePassion #3 for more about this.) In other words, the synergy WisePassion is something to bring into all of your interactions every day of your life. It is a far better alternative than imposing your will, being codependent or compromising.

The Blind Men and the Elephant:
An Allegory About Synergy

Consider this version of an ancient teaching story about synergy.

One day, three blind men were spending some time together when their conversation turned to the topic of elephants. None of them had encountered one. "I wonder what this odd animal might be like," said the first one. The other two agreed that meeting an elephant would be a most interesting experience.

As fortune would have it, a peasant and his elephant just happened to be passing by at that moment. Overhearing the conversation among the three blind men he asked, "Would you fellows really like to feel an elephant?"

All three at once said excitedly, "Yes, please!" "Then follow me," said the peasant.

The three men formed a line, each holding the hand of the one in front of him, with the first one taking the peasant's hand. When they reached the elephant, the peasant carefully positioned each man around his elephant.

The first man was on the left side of the elephant. He reached out his hand and touched the elephant's front leg from top to bottom, and then her hind leg. When he was done, he said with a sense of satisfaction, "Ah, so that's an elephant. I understand!"

The second blind man was at the rear of the elephant. As he touched her tail, which was wagging back and forth, he proudly proclaimed, "Ah, so that's an elephant. I understand!"

The third blind man was in front of the elephant, touching her trunk, which was twisting and turning. He too exclaimed with excitement, "Ah, so that's an elephant. I understand!"

The three blind men thanked the peasant for this enlightening experience. He led them to a nearby shady tree where they could sit down and talk about their respective experiences.

The first man could hardly wait to share what he had experienced. "What an odd animal! It's like a tree but without branches."

The second jumped in saying, "No, that's not right at all. How could you possibly say that? This strange animal is like the straw fans we swing back and forth to get a breeze on a hot day, except it's not as big or well made. The main portion is actually kind of wispy."

"No, no, you're both wrong!" the third man impatiently interjected. "This queer, bizarre animal is more like a huge snake: long, round, swinging about and incredibly strong."

What an argument ensued among them as each insisted that he alone was correct! Eventually, each walked off in different directions, still convinced that only he was right and having lost respect for the other two because of how wrong they both had been.

The Key Ingredients of 3D Synergy

The three key ingredients of 3D Synergy are: treasuring differences, co-creating "us" and no residue.

Treasuring Differences means that you value the unique perspectives, talents, and quirks of each and every individual, rather than trying to turn others into another version of you. Treasuring differences is an expression of humility and an authentic desire to learn and expand, which thus requires teachability. Whenever you are building bridges, teamwork, agreements or deeper closeness with others, remember the Blind Men and the Elephant story. Treasuring differences is about trusting that the information you have is valuable and also trusting that you do not have all the information. It also means being willing to discover that you do not necessarily know how to best understand the information you do have in the context of a larger whole that you do not necessarily see.

Co-Creating "Us" means individuals or groups joining to create something greater than each can create alone. It means birthing and nourishing a larger whole that cherishes what each individual (or group) brings to the collective, and yet is far more than the sum those parts. The extent to which co-creation is possible depends upon how whole and authentic each participating individual is, and how developed their WisePassions of teachability, self-care, discernment, harvesting and power are. Co-creating "us" does require a fair amount of talking, but this should never be a replacement for being and doing together. The heart of connection lives *beyond* words, in sharing experiences together. At work that means doing projects together, not simply talking about them. In personal life it means having enjoyable and playful connection-creating experiences together.

No Residue means that disconnection experiences and other unfinished business or unresolved issues are not allowed to permanently remain unaddressed and unresolved. Disconnection experiences, unfinished business and unresolved issues occur in all relationships. Hurt, conflict and other relationship challenges are treated as opportunities to create greater synergy and connection, instead of allowing these experiences to add one more nail into the coffin of a relationship that will eventually become suffocated once enough residue has built up. This is harvesting in relationships and is another reason why developing your harvesting WisePassion is a prerequisite to being capable of synergy.

WisePassion #6: *Synergy*

Treasuring Differences

Valuing other people's uniqueness, sovereignty, perspectives and gifts so you are motivated to synergize with them

Co-Creating "Us"

Joining with others to discover mutually honorable clarity, solutions and joint procreation that neither you nor they would have been able to discover or create alone

No Residue

Addressing & resolving disconnection experiences (hurt, conflict, boundary violations, etc.) and other forms of "unfinished business" that will damage synergy if ignored, covered up or rolled over)

Your capacity to synergize depends on your inner wholeness, self-responsibility, integrity, accountability and vulnerability; neediness, manipulation, disrespect or blame sabotages synergy. Only those with high authenticity and personal integrity are capable of synergy and of being in integrity in their relationships with others. In other words, the foundation that makes synergy possible is the prior five WisePassions. Similarly, our capacity for stewardship (WisePassion #7) serving collective highest good depends very directly on our capacity for synergy, as you will see in the next chapter. All of this is why synergy comes sixth in the WisePassions sequence.

An Example of Synergizing Personal Boundaries

Remember that old college buddy I mentioned toward the beginning of this chapter? I was in Toronto for a week to give a number of presentations and workshops and, as he had moved there, he wanted to take me out for an evening to show me around. We had not seen each other for a number of years. When we were making final plans for the evening, after I was finished with my day he, not surprisingly, had already figured out what we were going to do. He was going to take me on a walking tour of the city followed by dinner at a restaurant he liked way out in the country.

I had been on my feet all day giving a workshop. Between standing in front of the room as I presented and circulating through the room while everyone was practicing, the last thing in the world my feet wanted to do was a walking tour.

As I mentioned earlier, my buddy was used to taking charge, making decisions and being followed. When I explained why a walking tour wouldn't work for me, he immediately launched into a sales pitch about why it would be good for me to do this anyway. I asked him what made our doing this walking tour so important to him. Ultimately, the intention beneath his position became clear: he had been cooped up in his office all day; he hadn't even gone out for lunch; and, after sitting in meetings and at his desk for the entire day, he needed to move his body and be outdoors.

I recognized and deeply appreciated his self-care motivation and I wanted to support it without my support coming at the expense of my own self-care. I first checked with him to make sure I accurately understood the intentions beneath his position. Then, in an intention to honor our differences, I pointed out that just as he had great reasons to need to move his body, I had great reasons to rest my feet. Finally, in an intention to honor our common ground, I told him how being outdoors would work very well for me too.

Knowing that he loved to work out, I proposed that he do that at the hotel's exercise room while I caught up with my daily barrage of e-mails and then we would meet afterwards for a Jacuzzi to refresh my weary feet before we went out for the evening. He liked that idea very much.

Apparently my desire to invite him into synergy was starting to work because he then suggested that there was a delightful cruise through the Toronto Islands that we could take. Since sunset comes fairly late in Toronto in the summertime, we would be able to enjoy the outdoors together on the cruise and then have dinner afterward. My friend's suggestion was a true synergy suggestion because it met his need to be outdoors and my need to not be walking around a lot after spending all day on my feet.

We had co-created a plan that honored our differing self-care needs, our shared desire to be outdoors, and our interest in doing something that would allow us to talk and catch up with one another. We had a delightful evening, during which you can bet that I didn't miss the opportunity to talk with him about the benefits of synergy over compromise.

How Synergy Amplifies the Integrity Effect

Relationship integrity is the second of the three dimensions of 3D Integrity. The more in integrity you are with your core drive for authentic self-expression through having a well-developed power WisePassion, the more capable you will be of co-creating synergy with others. The more synergy you build into your relationships, the closer, more productive and durable they will be. This is the heart of relationship integrity. The better you are at co-creating synergy in groups, the more effective you can be in discovering and facilitating what truly serves collective highest good. This is an important aspect of leadership integrity. You will learn more about collective highest good in the next chapter on the stewardship WisePassion, and you will find a synergy WisePassion self-assessment in the *Workbook*.

The Art of Synergy-Building

I think you will agree that the evening I spent with my college buddy is an example of converting a potential relationship problem into a synergy experience that brought us closer together, and of how synergy is far better for relationships than compromise.

The art of synergy-building has four underlying principles:

1. Personal Integrity comprises WisePassions #1–5. It includes teachability (especially self-responsibility), self-care, discernment (especially being appropriately open to influence), harvesting (especially to making the most of the situation) and power (especially boundaries intelligence).

2. The more two people are willing to bring their personal integrity into their interaction, the more capable they will be to co-create synergy between them.

3. The prerequisites for synergy are that both people have personal integrity and the desire to co-create through compassionately combining their vision, wisdom and intentions.

4. The formula for synergy is: Core Intentions Clarity + Treasuring Differences + Combining Perspectives.

These principles are embedded within a three-part synergy-building exercise you will find in the *Workbook*. That exercise will make these concepts clear and when you can master this one simple exercise, you will have mastered the heart of synergy. This exercise also serves as your mini-boot camp for learning how to discover what serves collective highest good. Mastering this core synergy skill lays the final part of the foundation needed for a fully developed stewardship WisePassion (see the next chapter).

What to Be Flexible With and What To Stick to Your Guns With: Three Guidelines for Creating Synergized Boundaries

The story about my old college buddy illustrates the importance of remaining true to your core intention while being flexible about the plan through which your core intention is honored. With that in mind I want to offer you three guidelines for creating Synergized Boundaries.

1. Don't be attached to your idea about the method or plan through which your intention will be honored. Be prepared to be *really* flexible about that.

2. As the two of you explore your respective core intentions, allow this discussion to reveal any needed clarifications or refinements about your own core intention. If this occurs, allow yourself to upgrade your understanding of your core intention accordingly.

3. The one and only thing to *not* compromise or abandon when you are co-creating synergized boundaries is your core intention. The penalties of doing that include resentment,

diminished aliveness, and an erosion of connection with the other person.

The better you want to become at co-creating synergized boundaries with others, the more worthwhile it will be for you to practice the exercises I have provided for you in the *Workbook*.

Synergy WisePassion Summary

1. Use your expanded authenticity and right relationship with your power WisePassion to join with others more deeply than ever before.

2. You have three basic choices about how to conduct your relationships: *coercion, capitulation* or *co-creation*. Coercion and capitulation dance perfectly with each other: Coercion seeks to figure out, "How can I get you to do what I want you to do, (or what I think you should do 'for your sake')?" Capitulation and compromise is the same thing. Capitulation seeks to figure out, "What can I get from you if I do what you want me to do?" Think about how these questions parallel the rules leg of our childhood survival plan. Coercion and capitulation are, in fact, adult versions of survival plan strategies. They are symptoms of lack of relationship integrity and have no place in mature adult relationships. The alternative to the coercion-capitulation dance is *co-creation*, which is the essence of synergy. Co-creation seeks to discover, "What is the authentic intersection between what you want and what I want?"

3. Learn to **Treasure Differences** between you and others so you can avoid the trap portrayed in the Blind Men and the Elephant story, and so you can expand your ability to discover what serves collective highest good. Practice assuming you have only a part of the full picture, so you remember to seek and value other people's perspectives and intentions. Overcome any prejudice or fear you may have about perspectives different from your own, or that of your gender, your community, your religion, your culture, your political affiliation, or your country.

4. Become good at **Creating "Us"** with others through combining your knowledge and intentions with theirs to co-create solutions that are far better than either of you could have created on your own. Practice finding underlying intentions behind positions so you can synergize solutions honorable both to your own intention and that of the other person, instead of settling for compromises between surface positions. Remember that compromise-based commitments are less likely to be honored than commitments that grow from synergy. Also keep in mind that an equally important part of creating "us" is about connecting beyond words, through having fun and doing things together. Too many relationship experts place too much weight on talking and not enough on connecting. When it comes to creating synergy, talking definitely has its place; however, time spent talking about problems in endless loops would be better spent connecting and playing and having fun together. Get couples counseling or go to couples workshops should you get stuck as a couple, but never make talking more important than connecting through doing. Both are equally important.

5. Become masterful in your ability to use disconnection and conflict to build greater connection so **No Residue** builds up in your relationships. Always remember that differences don't kill relationships, cumulative residue does. Develop your skills at creating commitments you can count on and becoming graceful with holding yourself and others accountable. Upgrade your harvesting skills because they provide the needed foundation for no residue skills development. Then, upgrade your conflict resolution skills if needed.

6. **Relationship Integrity** includes synergy plus being accountable for making good on commitments made. I refer to this as *Commitment Competence*. Acting in integrity with your commitments is as central to relationship integrity as being able to synergize with others to come up with the commitments in the first place. Your relationship integrity can be no better than your personal integrity, and relationship integrity

241

is the prerequisite for leadership integrity. This is why it is impossible to separate personal, relationship and leadership development. The fact that the Seven WisePassions develop all three concurrently and in an integrated way is what makes them so incredibly valuable.

Remember:
Synergize, don't compromise.

CHAPTER 22

WISEPASSION #7:
STEWARDSHIP

*"How can I become really good at discovering and
fully serving the collective highest good?"*

tewardship means serving collective highest good. Stewardship begins
with the passion to make a positive difference in the world. Since
the drive to have impact is one of our three core drives, all of us are
meant to be stewards. Stewardship can be considered the flagship
WisePassion because it is the one the other six WisePassions make
possible. The more you master the art of synergy as described in
the last chapter, the more you can bring this into the realm of stewardship through facilitating synergy in the groups of which you are
a member.

Stewardship means serving through:

❑ Deep teachability and humility.

❑ Clear and healthy boundaries.

❑ A full and loving heart.

❑ Facilitating group synergy.

❑ Inner centeredness that does not depend on the rest of the
world believing what you believe, or changing in the ways
you think change should happen, in order for you to be
okay within yourself (having that need is a form of giving
to get — this motivation contaminates our desire to be of
service).

Serving others or collective highest good out of guilt, or at the
expense of being out of integrity with your relationships or yourself, is not stewardship: it is obsession or addiction. This is a type of

redemption plan that only *looks* like being of service. Serving does not mean thinking you know what's best for others and making them wrong or attacking them if they disagree.

Let me repeat: *Stewardship does* not *mean thinking we know what is best for others or making them wrong or attacking them if they disagree with our perspective.* This isn't stewardship: it is a form of being power-drunk. Stewardship does not mean crusading as though you are God's only savior who knows the real truth and everyone who doesn't think like you is wrong — or even damned for believing. That is fanaticism disorder not stewardship.

The Extreme Do-Gooder

Harold had a deep passion to help make the world a better place. Thinking big, he took a job working for an organization that helps developing countries get a fair shake in the international community. As much as he loved his own country, he was more than willing to move halfway across the world to work for this organization; and, as much as he enjoyed an affluent lifestyle, he contentedly worked for a low wage for the privilege of being able to have impact in the ways that most called to him. After only three months in his new job, Harold's entire world already revolved around the service work about which he felt so passionate. He gave himself a half-day to handle errands on weekends and to relax if there was any time left over; other than that, Harold pretty much worked fifteen hour days, and loved what he was doing.

However his girlfriend of eight years did not. Elena had willingly come with him because she truly supported his desire to make a difference. She managed to find a job that brought in enough extra money so that they could make ends meet. Being a socially gregarious person, she was grateful she made friends quickly and easily. She also understood that she couldn't depend solely on Harold to meet her needs for fun, conversation and nourishment. But, Elena was totally unprepared for how completely Harold disappeared into his work.

Harold had barely enough time left over each day to handle daily life logistics and get some sleep. He was exhausted not only by his work hours but by his frustrations with how dysfunctional he was coming to believe the international community was. Harold's self-care was nowhere near as sufficient for his own good as it needed to be. He began to gain weight, and grew increasingly irritable. Elena not only had barely a few minutes a day with the man she loved, but when they were together he was so depleted and cranky that she could neither feel nor connect with his heart. They now almost never socialized together as a couple. She couldn't remember the last time they went out on a date with one another and their sex life had all but disappeared.

Elena knew Harold loved her, had a good heart and had the greatest of intentions. That knowledge soon became true, but not useful. Eventually, what she knew and loved about Harold's essence paled in comparison to having to live day after day with a self-neglectful relationship abandoner. Not until after Elena had moved out and gone back to their home country to rebuild her life without him did Harold begin to see what he had done. Not long after that he developed diabetes, which the doctor said had been entirely preventable.

Harold the do-gooder paid a huge price for being out of integrity. He didn't realize he had fallen out of integrity because he was an honest, ethical, upstanding, socially concerned man who was genuinely dedicated to making the world a better place. Harold did not understand that 3D Integrity requires making room for each of his three core drives to express themselves. He did not realize that he needed to coordinate among those core drives so that they all supported each other rather than competed against each other. Consequently, his relationship with himself suffered and as a consequence his relationship with the woman he loved ended.

True stewards don't neglect themselves or their loved ones.

It's Not My Problem

Jessica could have been Harold's evil twin sister. Well, forget the evil and twin part; she *was* Harold's sister, and something of a princess at that. She could not imagine how Harold could ever leave the lovely life they had to try to change problems that she thought "little people" like them could never affect. She couldn't believe that Elena actually supported Harold's decision and went with him.

You see, Jessica's world revolved around comfort and fun. She figured that her contribution to the world was to hold down a job, pay her taxes and not land in jail. Beyond that, she was convinced that the world was too broken for anyone, especially someone as "unimportant" as her to make a difference.

In reality, Jessica's attitude was even more self-centered than that. She did not hesitate to go through red lights when she could have stopped before they turned red; and she had no qualms about leaving the remains of her lunch on the park bench where she ate. Jessica went to any lengths to find a way to cut into lines rather than have to wait like everyone else.

Jessica was similar to her brother in that deep down inside she basically had a good heart and good intentions. But, she saw the world as a dog-eat-dog place that left her no choice but to "look after number 1" and leave everyone else to do the same for themselves. Jessica knew nothing about being an everyday steward; she had no idea any such thing existed. (I'll say more about everyday stewardship later in this chapter.)

What Stewardship Is and Isn't

We all are stewards. Some of us get carried away with this role, like Harold, the extreme do-gooder. Others of us deny our stewardship responsibilities, like Jessica, Ms. "It's-Not-My-Problem." Many of us simply don't have enough of a vision of what everyday stewardship is to recognize when they have an opportunity to serve collective highest good.

3D Stewardship is the capacity to synergize with others as your truest self to accurately identify and serve collective highest good. Stewardship includes leading with impeccable integrity in whatever forms and contexts are authentic for you and without doing so at your own expense or the expense of those who are precious to you.

The Key Ingredients of 3D Stewardship

The three key ingredients of 3D Stewardship are: embodying 3D Integrity, facilitating collective highest good, and leading in the ways that are most authentic for you.

Embodying 3D Integrity: First and foremost, stewardship means embodying extraordinary integrity. Integrity requires being profoundly self-responsible, using your personal power fully, compassionately and wisely, and maintaining impeccable alignment between your intentions and actions. 3D Integrity means being in integrity with your own authenticity, in your ways of connecting with others, and in serving collective highest good. Integrity is for all of us and is what makes us all stewards. We are in the midst of the most damaging and dangerous pandemic of lack of integrity that this world has ever seen; it therefore falls squarely on each one of us to first of all embody 3D Integrity ourselves and to then demand it from others, especially our leaders.

Facilitating Collective Highest Good: "Collective highest good" refers to the fact that each of us is deeply interconnected with a larger whole. When we "facilitate" collective highest good, we take our synergy WisePassion one step further. WisePassion #6 focuses on developing your capacity for synergy in order to build happier, stronger, more loving, more productive and more durable personal and work relationships. Stewardship calls upon us to become so good at co-creating synergy that we naturally start demanding it and facilitating it in the groups of which we are a part: our families, our communities, our businesses, and whatever other organizations we are connected with personally, as part of our livelihood or in our service work.

Leading In Ways that Are Most Authentic for You: Who is a leader? Every single one of us. No matter what our age, education or position in life, leadership comes in seven main flavors, some of which you may never before have thought of as leadership. All of us are naturally drawn at least one of them: 1) role-modeling; 2) holding the light; 3) mentoring (teaching/facilitation/eldering); 4) trailblazing (being an innovator); 5) advocating (speaking up on behalf of others, usually those who can't speak up for themselves); 6) underwriting (money/time/activities); and 7) coordinating systems (management, executive and most political roles) on behalf of others. Parenting is a blend of most and sometimes all of these leadership flavors.

WisePassion #7: *Stewardship*

3D Integrity

Being profoundly
self-responsible,
and using your full power
with wisdom and compassion,
in service of aligning and
balancing your authenticity,
your connection with others
and making a positive
difference in the world

**Facilitating
Collective
Highest Good**

Doing all you can
to do what's right,
first on behalf of the
inter-connectedness of
humanity and the planet itself,
and for your own group's
interests within that

**Embracing
Your Leadership**

Leading in ways
that reflect your unique
talents & limitations,
in the contexts that
have the most passion for you,
and in ways that preserve
rather than impair
your 3D Integrity

Your capacity as a steward is directly dependent on how well developed your prior six WisePassions are. That's why stewardship is the capstone of the Seven WisePassions. Far too many leaders have this upside down; they tend to downplay the importance of personal and relationship development as a prerequisite for wise leadership. Most or all of their Seven WisePassions also tend to be insufficiently developed compared to what stewardship-based leadership requires.

More About Embodying 3D Integrity

Remember our three core drives? They are our deep-seated needs to: 1) feel personal well-being and authenticity; 2) enjoy connection with others; and 3) make a positive difference in the world. 3D Integrity means aligning the three core drives so they work with one another rather than compete against each other. 3D Integrity means not sacrificing one for the others but, rather, treating all of them as equally important ingredients in a larger whole. The Seven WisePassions lay the foundation that makes 3D Integrity possible. Embodying 3D Integrity becomes increasingly possible the stronger your stewardship WisePassion becomes. The Integrity Effect is a term for the positive impact you have on the world as a result of embodying 3D Integrity in all your decisions and actions.

More About Collective Highest Good

As I wrote earlier in this chapter, "collective highest good" refers to the fact that each of us is deeply interconnected with a larger whole. The amount of individual freedom we can have over the long run in any society depends upon how well the collective, of which we are a part, functions. When people's individual freedoms are diminished they rebel. When people become self-centered rather than caring for others as well, the collective disintegrates. When people refuse to take self-responsibility and instead expect to be taken care of by others, the collective disintegrates.

Freedom and responsibility are inseparable; freedom alone is narcissism (self-centeredness) and responsibility alone is imprisonment. We are collectively suffering from the effects of too much self-centeredness and too little responsibility. I therefore propose that it may be useful to start using a new word that blends the follow two words: Freedom + Responsibility = Freesponsibility.

The stewardship WisePassion focuses on developing your attentiveness and involvement in contributing to collective highest good because you understand deep down within you that, in the long run, your personal freedom depends on it. Enlightened self-interest requires attention to collective highest good and enlightened self-interest means being "freesponsible."

Remember when I wrote earlier in this book about having been brought to Geneva to train some of the ambassadors to the World Trade Organization (WTO)? I was brought there to train them in intentional effectiveness and synergy so that they could become better at identifying and honoring collective highest good as stewards for both their own country and the larger collective.

Those who brought me there realized that we live in a time when too many people's notions of collective highest good are upside down. They did not want a WTO insider providing this training because they wanted an outside perspective. They wanted me because my perspectives about synergy and collective highest good are definitely those of an outsider.

The word "collective" as I use it in this book refers to the larger wholes of which we are a part. The primary collective, or whole, of which every one of us is a part, is the Earth, including its resources and vulnerabilities. The secondary collective or whole of which we are a part is an inextricably interconnected global economy and politic. The tertiary collectives or wholes of which we are a part, include our own country and culture, and our religious, spiritual or philosophical path. Within that is our business, community, family and support network affiliations. Within that is our primary relationship, if we have one. Within that is our relationship with our inner community of self. This is illustrated in the diagram below.

The Collectives to Which You Belong

We live in a time when too many people's notions of collective highest good are upside down from these primary, secondary and tertiary levels of collective highest good. This is illustrated in the diagram below. As tempting as it may be to view our primary affiliation as being with our tertiary collectives, the urgency of our current global situation calls upon us to make a significant inner shift toward more conscious alignment with our primary and secondary collectives.

The Collectives to Which We Try to Make Others Belong

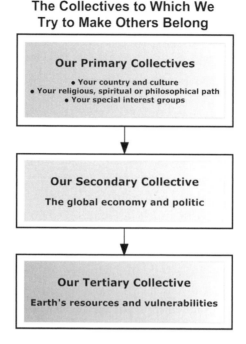

Our Primary Collectives

- Your country and culture
- Your religious, spiritual or philosophical path
- Your special interest groups

Our Secondary Collective

The global economy and politic

Our Tertiary Collective

Earth's resources and vulnerabilities

When special interest groups try to turn their own tertiary collectives into everyone's primary collective, this is group narcissism - otherwise known as fanaticism. This is how fanaticism sabotages true primary and secondary collective highest good from being served. Fanatics want what they want and if what they think they want is not good for "someone else," that is that "someone else's" problem. This is because these twisted versions of special interest groups tend to have no clue about what synergy is or how to create it. Not having mastered the art of synergy, these special interests hope to get their way through coercion, though they will sometimes settle for compromise as a backup plan. (As discussed in the last chapter, coercion and compromise create long-term damage no matter how appealing the short-term gains might be.)

Fanaticism is a manifestation of a group's unwillingness to deal with their own collective Pandora's box. Fanaticism is fed by unwillingness or insufficient skill on the part of those within that group, culture or religion to deal with whatever is causing that fanaticism to become popular. It is also fed by the unwillingness or insufficient skill on the part of other interconnected groups to synergize with the non-fanatics in the culture or religion of which the fanatics are a part.

On September 11, 2001, I was in the New York City area preparing the family home to be sold. My Dad had died years earlier and my elderly Mom had decided she wanted to live in California full time. Having grown up in and around New York City, years earlier I had watched the World Trade Center being built. Now, my original home city had been attacked.

I was profoundly and permanently impacted not as much by the attack (as horrific and unforgettable as that was) as by the initial reaction of most of those in Manhattan closest to Ground Zero. In the week following the attack, an amazing number of impromptu street-side shrines had been created. They were filled with candles, posters looking for lost loved ones who were in or near the World Trade Center at the time of the attack, and deeply moving handwritten notes spilling out their hearts about what had occurred. These notes are what permanently impacted me. I wish I had thought at the time to write all of them down and turn them into a book. Well over 90% of the notes were about love, reconciliation and wanting to understand the problems that could have given rise to this horror, and the role of the United States in those problems; less than 10% of the notes contained angry, vengeful, "nuke the bastards" kinds of messages.

Witnessing this so deeply moved me that I wrote a document called *The Declaration of Global Responsibility*. It proposed a set of principles for dealing with collective highest good regarding terrorism and fanaticism. (A free copy of the document is available through the Freebies section of my website.) That document played a role in my being invited to train the group of World Trade Organization ambasdors I mentioned earlier in the book. Facilitating and teaching my Collective Highest Good Co-Discovery Process is part of my stewardship role in the world.

Facilitating collective highest good requires that the synergy WisePassion be sufficiently developed in all those in leadership positions so they are able to use it to help create synergy in their group, community, business, government or intergovernmental organization. Since the ability to do that rests upon the five WisePassions that precede the synergy WisePassion, it should now be clear that *it is impossible to be a maximally effective leader or a social activist without simultaneously working to attain significant levels of personal and relationship development.*

Imagine what leaders could do in their leadership positions if their stewardship WisePassion (and the other six WisePassions that form its foundation) was highly developed. Can you imagine what changes this would bring about? My impression is that very few leaders, especially at the helm of big business and at the national and international levels in politics, have the Seven WisePassions at their disposal. I am quite convinced that this is why we currently have so many problems as a collective.

You can do something about this as a voter. The more you internalize these Seven WisePassions the more natural it will be for you to intuit which political candidates have developed them the most highly. I personally no longer vote based on party affiliation or candidates' stands on the issues, but rather on the extent to which I sense a candidate's WisePassions are developed. I especially pay attention to the extent to which they seem to embody a blend of healthy power (WisePassion #5), a capacity for synergy (WisePassion #6) and stewardship as I have outlined it here.

Why? If a leader does not have right relationship with her or his personal power, that person is downright dangerous as a leader. If a leader does not know how to synergize, that person will not have the skills necessary to facilitate the co-creation of policies and agreements that combine the wisdom of all who are involved. If a leader does not know how to be a steward, s/he will be susceptible to being co-opted by special interests and thus impaired in his or her ability to serve collective highest good. Such a leader will rule by ideology rather than by the principles of stewardship. The ability to embody healthy power, synergy and stewardship is, to me, the heart of what I call 3D Integrity. It is also the heart of leadership.

(For more about different ways of leading, look for the Service Mission Exercise in the *Workbook*.)

"Don't ask what the world needs. Ask what makes you come alive and go do it. Because what the world needs is people who have come alive." — Howard Thurman

An Example of a True Steward

Ruth is a shining example of the true steward. She is a physician who heads an unusually patient-focused group medical practice. For her, the technical aspects of medicine revolve around and serve her patients' human needs for compassion and understanding. She loves her work, which feels more like a "calling" to her. She is also a philanthropist and has held elected office, among other roles, as part of her dedication to serving collective highest good. Ruth is extremely happy with how she expresses her *impact* core drive.

Ruth is happily married and has two adult children. She and her husband of well over 30 years love and cherish each other. Just as importantly, they continue to enjoy playing together as well as supporting one another's growth. The family loves to spend time together and all are genuinely wonderful supports to each another. Ruth is extremely happy with how her *connection* core drive is fulfilled.

Ruth does an excellent job of honoring all aspects of her self-care. Despite her extremely busy schedule that includes her professional, service and relationship commitments, she always takes time to care for herself in order to keep her energy strong and her enthusiasm replenished. Ruth has also made a priority of pursuing her own interests, including a seemingly unquenchable thirst for travel. She has also worked very hard over many years to overcome the blocks to her being authentic because being everyone else's hero and savior was the cornerstone of her survival and redemption plan. She now experiences herself to be a deeply authentic person who has embraced the high side of her power more than ever.

Ruth is the embodiment of 3D Integrity. Her ethics are impeccable, but ethics are only a part of 3D Integrity. Just as importantly, she has made a priority of honoring and coordinating among all three of her core drives. If you were to ask her to rate how fulfilled she feels in her life these days, she would probably say nine out of ten, simply because she wants to make room for her fulfillment to continue to grow deeper and deeper for the rest of her life.

Ruth would be the first person to say that she was not born this way. She grew up in a challenging family, the repercussions of which have continued with three of her four siblings becoming alcoholics. Her WisePassion development has been hard-fought and hard-won over many years of growth workshops, coaching and psychotherapy. Ruth is a poster child for successful deliberate developers.

How Stewardship is the Embodiment of the Integrity Effect

Leadership Integrity is the third aspect of 3D Integrity. It is the pinnacle of integrity because this aspect of leadership is only possible to the extent that your personal and relationship integrity are developed and aligned with it. Through 3D Integrity alignment, a "Sovereign Servant Leader" leads with impeccable character and superb effectiveness through counterbalancing the following two sets of pulls:

❏ Synergizing his/her own service mission with his/her own wellbeing (self-care) and with the well-being of his/her most precious relationships.

❏ Synergizing the highest good of the collective with the highest good of the larger system of which that collective is a part.

Only to the extent that they create synergy, with these two sets of counterbalancing obligations, can leaders lead in ways that match today's needs. The secret to leadership with integrity is as "simple" as finding your own authentic solution to both of these two counterbalancing obligations. I know no one who has successfully done this without developing all Seven WisePassions, whether intuitively or deliberately.

The essence of the Seven WisePassions:

1. Be eminently **Teachable** because this is where integrity begins.

2. Honor your **Self-Care** needs impeccably.

3. Learning to **Discern** brings you into right relationship with inner and outer input.

4. **Harvest** precious gifts from all your life experiences.

5. Embrace your full **Power** and light with no apologies.

6. **Synergize,** don't compromise.

7. **Steward** collective highest good like it matters, because it does.

The world needs you. Your relationships need you. You need you. This is the recipe for 3D Integrity and 3D Living. It is the recipe for honoring all three of your core drives for personal authenticity, connection with others and making a positive impact in the world.

Three Key Ways Anyone, Including You, Can Be More of an Everyday Steward

Leadership starts with you becoming more of an Everyday Steward. An everyday steward is someone who subtly leads in his or her daily life just as it is right now, today. In other words, you can be an everyday steward without becoming a community activist, running for political office, or becoming the CEO of a company (although all those things are great if they are your service mission's calling). Everyday stewardship simply includes modeling 3D Integrity, serving collective highest good in ways people might not even notice and embodying your Service Mission in all that you do.

1. **Model 3D Integrity at All Times:** The three crucial ingredients to being able to model 3D Integrity are: a) continually upgrade each of your Seven WisePassions and utilize them every day as needed; b) use your harvesting WisePassion to respond to wakeup calls and free yourself from aspects of your survival and redemption plans that will periodically surface; c) be diligent each and every day about attending to, expressing and coordinating all three of your core drives — this is the essence of 3D Integrity. Remember that your authenticity is expressed through WisePassions #1–5, and especially the combination of your self-care and power.

2. **Serve Collective Highest Good in Everyday Ways:** Stewardship is not about being a world leader or even a community leader; it is about having a positive effect on strangers in everyday ways without them even knowing it. Make a list of some of the ways you tend to be oblivious about the potential impact of your actions (or inactions) on others, and of all the little ways you can steward collective highest good. Here are two simple everyday examples having to do with driving: a) Even when you have the right of way, don't drive into an intersection until you can already get all the way through to the other side of it. By doing this, you won't inadvertently block traffic going in the other direction because you are sitting in the middle of the intersection when their light turns green; b) When you park in a lot, park right in the middle of your spot so that those who later pull out or park on either side of you are not inconvenienced. (You will find another example in the Dealing With Internet Alerts part of the Stewardship section of the *Workbook*.)

3. **Discover and Embody Your Service Mission:** The exercise connected with this chapter to clarify the forms and contexts of leadership that fit for you, is an important step in discovering your service mission. Once you are clear about what your service mission is, do whatever you must do in order to be able to accomplish it without neglecting your own wellbeing (including your self-care) or your cherished relationships. (If you would like my complete process for identifying your service mission, see the stewardship WisePassion resources in the Best Resources section on my website.)

(As another act of everyday stewardship, please share your examples of everyday stewardship on my IntegrityWatch Blog, which you can get to through my website. Be sure to post examples of what you do and examples of what you have seen others do. This will help expand everyone else's vision of the forms everyday stewardship can take.)

What happens when you do all three of these things well? 3D Living. The three keys to everyday stewardship described above are your ticket to feeling more fulfilled than ever before. When you live your life as an everyday steward the saying, "What is truly good for you is good for the universe," becomes utterly true. How cool is that?

You can assess the strength of your stewardship WisePassion in the *Workbook*.

Determining Your Current "Priority WisePassion"

I wrote at the beginning of this chapter that stewardship can be considered the flagship WisePassion because it is the one the other six WisePassions make possible. Now is the time to convert that awareness into action.

Look over your self-assessments for each of your other six WisePassions to discover which ones you are weakest in at the present time. The lowest-numbered WisePassion you feel needs the most upgrading is your current *Priority WisePassion*. Focus your attention on that one until your self-assessment results for that WisePassion look strong enough to you for the time being.

Repeat this process with the next lowest numbered WisePassion you feel needs the most upgrading. Continue to strengthen each WisePassion for the rest of your life. Each successive wakeup call you respond to by choosing to surrender into a transformation chapter will give provide you with your best possible opportunities to do that.

This, in a nutshell, is what lifelong integrated adult development is all about. Just remember to enjoy your consolidation periods along the way. And don't forget: life is about living fully. These tools are for helping you do that. *WisePassions are always in fashion.* But, developing your WisePassions is never meant to be a substitute for living. Rather, their purpose is to help you live. I encourage you to treat them accordingly.

Self-Improvers, Connectors and Do-Gooders Revisited

There are **Do-Gooders** in the world who recoil at the idea that personal development and relationship intelligence are prerequisites for wise and effective stewardship. My deep hope, if you have been one of these people, is that by this point in the book you have developed a new or deeper appreciation for why it is an inescapable fact that true leadership is impossible in the absence of sufficient personal development and relationship intelligence. Is it now clear to you that the skill sets (WisePassions) for personal, relationship and leadership development are one and the same?

There are **Self-Improvers** who do not believe in their own power to make a significant positive difference in the world, or who fear that devoting themselves to serving collective highest good will inevitably cause them to have to give up their own personal freedom. My great hope, if you have been one of these people, is that you now recognize at a deeper level than ever before how you cannot be a whole and complete self unless you honor all three of your core drives. Do you now see ways you can become an every-day steward?

There are **Connectors** who fear that committing to making a significant positive difference in the world will result in them neglecting their own most precious relationships. My deep hope, if you have been one of these people, is that you now see that being of service with true integrity requires balance and synergy among your three core drives of authentic self-expression, connection with others and making a positive difference in the world. I hope as well that it is now clear to you just how vitally important the high art of connection is in being able to be of service in making the world a better place. Are you beginning to discover how much richer your connections can become the more you master synergy, and how you can use your gift at connection to facilitate synergy in the groups with which you are already affiliated?

Stewardship WisePassion Summary

1. Your capacity for stewardship can only be as good as your other six WisePassions are strong. It can only be as good as you are free from survival and redemption plan attachment. Your capacity to accurately recognize and effectively serve collective highest good depends on your willingness to continue expanding your 3D Integrity in all the ways described in this book.

2. Don't even try be a steward at the expense of yourself or your most precious relationships; it not only doesn't work, it's also far too costly and it's not stewardship because it's not role modeling 3D Integrity. Neither should you shrink away from being a steward; your drive to have positive impact in the world is one-third of who you are. As stewards we resolve the seeming conflicts among our need for personal well-being and authenticity, for bonding and connection, and for serving the collective by synergizing all three so that they complement rather than compete with each other.

3. Lead in whatever ways you choose. Not out of "shoulds," or because you have certain capabilities, but out of vision, authenticity and passion. Trust that whatever forms your leadership takes make a big difference in the world, that modeling 3D Integrity makes an equally big difference and that serving collective highest good as an everyday steward does as well. Trust that whatever you are not doing as part of your chosen stewardship role is someone else's passion and calling. This is why we need each other. Not one of us is supposed to do it all and every one of us is meant to make a difference in our own unique way without sacrificing our 3D Integrity to do it.

Remember:
Your most important trip is toward stewardship.

SECTION FIVE

THE GRAND UPSHIFT IN HUMANITY AND YOUR ROLE IN HELPING IT EMERGE

CHAPTER 23

IT'S IN EVERY ONE OF US
TO BE WISE

"How can someone in my position make a meaningful difference in helping to create a new era of personal, relationship, collective, and leadership integrity?"

The Top Five Messages This Book Contains

The name of this chapter is the title of a wonderful song written by David Pomeranz. It is also the essence of the wisdom I hope you have taken from this book:

1. **We all have three core drives:** authenticity, connection and impact. Understanding them turns integrity from a vague concept into a practical necessity.

2. **Aligning your three core drives is the essence of integrity.** The secret to true fulfillment is living in integrity with all three of your core drives.

3. **Personal, relationship, leadership and integrity development share the same building blocks**: the Seven WisePassions. Outgrowing your survival and redemption plans, and upgrading your WisePassions, is the key to living in integrity with your three core drives. This outgrowing and upgrading is made possible through cycling through the four LifeZones we naturally move among throughout adulthood.

4. **Humanity must leap forward in integrity if we are to thrive collectively.** They key to this needed upshift in humanity is for each of us to live in increasing integrity with all three of our core drives so we can become equally responsible to ourselves, to all those with whom

we interact, and to collective highest good. The upgrade humanity needs requires as many of us as possible to become the 3D Selves we are designed to be.

5. **Whatever the problem, look to integrity for the remedy.** What is truly good for you is good for the universe...but only when you are a 3D Self.

This final chapter revisits and ties together each of these key messages.

1. We All Have Three Core Drives

You have learned about your three core drives throughout this book. They are your drives for:

1. **Authenticity** — personal wellbeing, self-expression and freedom

2. **Connection** — nourishing and productive co-creation with others

3. **Impact** — making a positive difference in your world

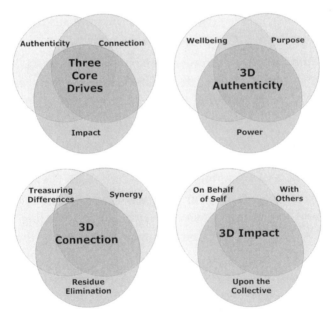

Rather than becoming the 3D Self we are designed to be, most of us define ourselves one-dimensionally.

A one- or two-dimensional sense of self sabotages our quest for inner fulfillment. Imbalance among our three core drives is also what causes so many relationships to be a mess. And it is the hidden key to why the world is facing the most perilous time in the history of humanity.

The way we thrive is through all three core drives.

2. Aligning Your Three Core Drives is the Essence of Integrity

The dictionary definition of integrity includes honesty, wholeness, completeness, unbrokenness and moral soundness. The only antonym to "integrity" that *Roget's Thesaurus* offers is "dishonesty." Lack of integrity takes many more forms than "only" being dishonest. This fact helps explain why so few of us recognize when we are out of integrity.

The most basic form of *honesty* is telling truths and taking actions that are simultaneously good for you, those around you, and the collective. The heart of self-honesty is realizing that you have three core drives and that neglecting any one of them prevents *wholeness* and *completeness*. The key to *unbrokenness* is properly digesting your life experiences through harvesting gifts of great value from them all. A particularly practical way to restore or upgrade your *moral soundness* is to integrate and coordinate among all three of your core drives.

Integrity is thus three-dimensional:

- Being *authentic* is about being in integrity with yourself.
- *Connection* occurs through being in integrity with others.
- *Impact* that is worthwhile comes from being in integrity with collective highest good.

3. Personal, Relationship, Leadership and Integrity Development Share the Same Building Blocks

The split among personal, relationship and leadership development helped create our current age of lack of integrity. This rampant lack of integrity calls upon us to revisit our understanding of how we develop as adults.

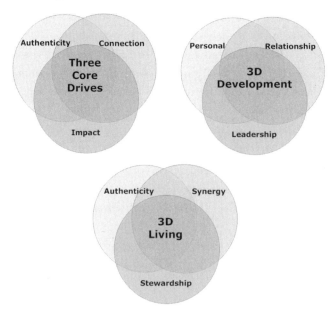

Natural developers have shown us that personal, relationship, leadership and integrity development all require the same sets of skills: the Seven WisePassions of 3D Living. Here is a rhyming summary of each WisePassion:

1. Being **Teachable** makes you reachable.

2. Beware of neglecting your **Self-Care**.

3. The secret to learning is great **Discerning**.

4. To reduce your strife **Harvest** gifts from your life.

5. Embrace your **Power** and your life will flower.

6. **Synergize** don't compromise.

7. Your most important trip is toward **Stewardship**.

Always remember: The Seven WisePassions are always in fashion; they are the backbone of Integrity Intelligence and 3D Living.

4. Humanity Must Leap Forward in Integrity if We Are to Thrive Collectively

Far more of us know that we are in the midst of an era of global lack of integrity than are speaking publicly about it. Four sources have significantly fueled this epidemic:

1. *The self-improvement and self-esteem movements.* These movements have tended to focus in a one-sided way on personal freedom and self-expression. This has unintentionally helped spawn a culture of entitlement and narcissism.

2. *The general attitude among far too many leaders.* Many leaders still resist the idea that there is a crucial connection between lack of personal and relationship development, and leadership incompetence and corruption.

3. *Special interest groups.* Over the past few decades the focus of these groups has shifted from advocating for themselves to imposing their ideologies on others with little regard for the broader collective.

4. *The mass media.* Despite daily reporting of an endless barrage of stories that are actually about lack of integrity, the mass media rarely digs deeply enough into those stories to

expose the lack of integrity that caused them to erupt in the first place.

All of these problems are symptoms of our three core drives competing against, rather than supporting each other. The conflict among our three core drives plays out within individuals, couples, families, groups, communities, businesses, cultures, religions, and humanity as a collective.

Even though lack of integrity is nothing new, what *is* new is our level of interconnectedness and our level of technological development. In the absence of sufficient integrity, interconnectedness and technology have combined to provide individuals and groups with unprecedented power to damage one another and the planet.

Imagine the kind of world that is created when communities, businesses and countries are populated by unfulfilled people who are out of integrity with themselves, their relationships or collective highest good. The picture you will see is the world in which we live today.

The time has come for the next leap forward in humanity's evolution. This will not occur through a new invention or technology. Rather, integrity-focused adult development provides a powerful answer to the call to action Albert Einstein made back in 1946: "The unleashed power of the atom has changed everything save our modes of thinking and we thus drift toward unparalleled catastrophe."

As Einstein understood all too well, the next leap forward in humanity's evolution is in our thinking not our technology. He understood that the more power we have to impact others, the more responsibility we have to upgrade our integrity. Einstein understood that integrity is enlightened self-interest.

Even though personal, relationship, leadership and integrity development all use the same building blocks, these core life skills are not taught in school or in houses of worship. They are not taught in families. They are not taught in business. They are not utilized in government.

Parents need to instill Integrity Intelligence in their children. They need to provide their children with more connection and company-keeping instead of the four forms of disconnection (refer back to Section Two to refresh your memory about these things). Parents need to help their children develop their Seven WisePassions so they don't need to rely too heavily on survival plan skills. Parents themselves need to free themselves from unintentionally inflicting their redemption plans on their children.

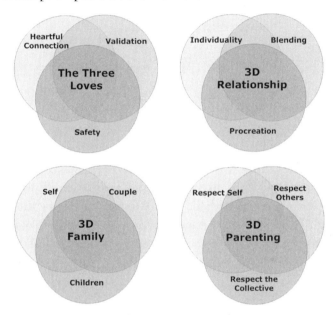

Educators need to infuse training in the Seven WisePassions into school curricula, from elementary school through graduate school. Of all the WisePassions, only one dimension of one WisePassion is actually taught in most schools: the critical thinking dimension of the discernment WisePassion. Educators can use this book as a template for providing what I call an "education in being human we always needed but never got." Think about how much more prepared children will be for their personal, career and service life when they are helped to develop these skills.

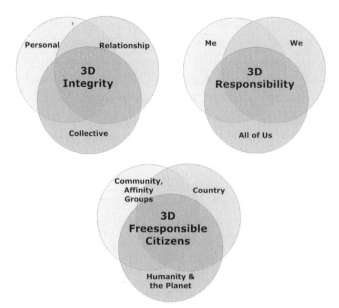

Businesses need to train their executives, managers and staff in the Seven WisePassions. The more literate their employees are in them, the more dependable they will be, the better their work teams will function and the more competently and ethically their executives will lead. Think about all the ways that this will translate into profits.

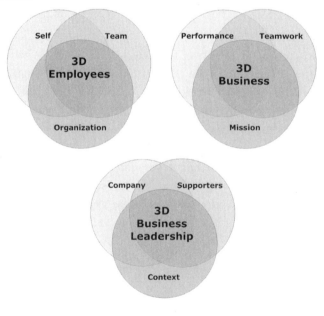

Helping professionals need to make *The New IQ* the cornerstone around which all of the coaching, psychotherapy and treatment they provide revolves. The complete curriculum this book provides opens the door to working with clients in far more powerful and efficient ways. Most helping professionals (social workers excluded) have traditionally avoided using their wisdom to assist with social change. This book has provided a template for integrating social responsibility into your work with clients. Think about how much more helpful and powerful coaching, psychotherapy and treatment can become if you make integrity development the centerpiece of your work with clients.

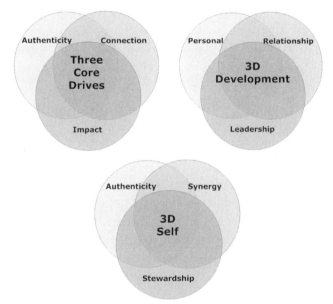

Whatever else we are, all of us are **consumers** of personal, relationship and/or leadership development resources. You have probably noticed that almost every book, method and program claims it is the best thing since sliced bread and that you can't live without it. This book has provided you with an antidote to the resource overwhelm consumers feel every time they look in a bookstore or magazine for a useful development resource. The clearer you are about your predominant LifeZone and your priority WisePassion, the easier it will be to match the resources to your needs. (For more information on how to further reduce resource overwhelm, visit the Success Strategies section of my website.)

Professional athletes, entertainers, public officials and all other social role models need training in how to model integrity rather than entitlement, narcissism and other forms of socially toxic self-centeredness. And not only for the sake of role modeling. When public figures are out of integrity, they hurt their own sports or production team, company, religion or political party. In 2007, Roger Goodell, the commissioner of the United States National Football League (NFL), took a bold new step in professional sports. He started holding players accountable for major misbehavior off the football field. During the 2007 NFL draft, I noticed for the first time that "character" was finally one of the top qualities more football teams than ever were looking for in new players. I am extremely excited about this new insistence on integrity in the world of professional athletics. I hope that all professional athletic organizations follow the example being set by the NFL. I also hope this spreads to all other high profile professions. I'm sure we all can think of at least a couple of celebrities who might benefit from this. As *San Diego Union* columnist Karla Peterson so aptly put it, "So far no celebrity has gone to rehab for being a celebrity…but…perhaps [some] should."

Leaders and opinion-makers of all kinds need to advocate and embody integrity in all that they say and do. It is high time for leaders and opinion-makers to get over the delusion that it's possible to have the impact you most want to have in your heart of hearts without outgrowing your survival and redemption plans, upgrading all Seven WisePassions and living in 3D Integrity. This includes community leaders, clergy, business leaders, politicians at all levels of government, leaders in the international community, and the media.

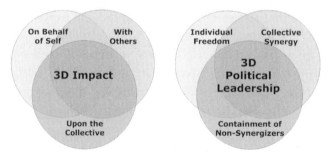

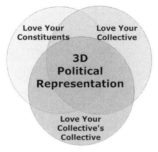

Systems Integrity: Understanding the three core drives is extremely important, not only for individuals but for **systems** such families, communities, businesses, and countries. Take the United States, for instance.

It seems to me that an implicit awareness of our three core drives was built into the profoundly noble and high-minded debates that birthed the United States' Declaration of Independence and the Constitution. In grappling with the tensions between personal liberty and responsibility to the collective, the framers of these documents were dedicated to creating a new form of government. Democracy was built around three fundamental pulls that live at the heart of the human experience: the first was personal liberty; the second was the right to decide how to conduct the private relationships in one's life; and the third was the need to create a collective that was stable, ordered, and attentive to its citizens.

These visionaries had a profound appreciation of the deeply rich and complex interplay between individual freedom and collective good. In the last chapter I referred to this as "freesponsibility." This awareness was perhaps more fully developed than had ever previously occurred when new countries were birthed. Their understanding of the vital importance of accessing collective wisdom that transcends personal egos and ideologies enabled them to co-create a vision that served collective highest good. This, I believe, is a significant part of what makes these documents such remarkable developments in the evolution of humanity.

I believe the United States has unwittingly moved away from the core intentions that birthed these documents. I believe this has unintentionally contributed to the widening split among our three core drives within the United States as well as in how the United

States conducts its foreign policy. It is time for the United States to move back into integrity with the wisdom of its founders about the importance of attending to our three core drives in an equal and coordinated way, not only domestically but with the rest of the world.

If you do not live in the United States, I urge you to look at how your own country deals with these issues. Self-responsibility is a national issue not just a personal one. If you see that your country would benefit from some upgrading in this regard, do your part to help this occur rather than criticizing other countries for falling short in these ways.

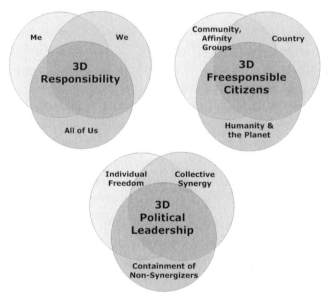

5. Whatever the Problem, Look to Integrity for the Remedy!

Integrity is the key to your own well-being and fulfillment. Integrity makes creating great relationships possible. Integrity makes it possible to truly serve collective highest good. This integration among your three core drives of authenticity, connection and impact is what 3D Integrity and 3D Living are all about.

Integrity — and the lack of it — affects every aspect of life. You have learned in this book what causes a lack of integrity and you have learned specifically and precisely how to upgrade your integrity. Doing this improves every aspect of life. *Upgrading your integrity is your most important contribution to helping the upshift in humanity occur.*

This is why Integrity Intelligence needs to become "The New IQ." This is why personal, relationship and leadership development need to be placed in service of upgrading Integrity Intelligence in all of us. This is how we can individually and collectively contribute to the evolutionary shift humanity so desperately needs at this time.

This book has proposed a new vision of what "having it all" means. It means that your personal freedom and self-expression don't conflict with your need for connection with others. It means that your desire to make a difference in the world doesn't sabotage your self-care or your relationships. This is what 3D Living is all about. It is also what it means to become a 3D Steward.

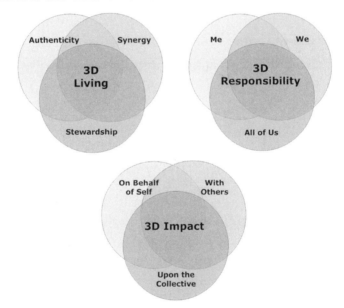

Stewardship, the Seventh WisePassion, includes being as aware of others and the collective as of yourself. This is because integrity means being equally responsible to yourself, to all those with whom you interact, and to collective highest good. "All those with whom you interact" includes anyone you interact with indirectly, such as other drivers, as described in the last chapter. It includes those you know and those you don't know; it includes those you like and those you don't like.

As you learned in the stewardship WisePassion chapter, you are constantly impacting many other people in very significant ways on a daily basis. Far too few of us fully appreciate this. *You do not need to be a world leader to have a huge impact.* Conversely, all those in leadership roles also have a responsibility to be everyday stewards as well.

> *"It is certainly true that*
> *every day we don't strive to live authentically*
> *we do pay a price, with compounded interest...*
> *It is a mistake to accept as our reality, the illusion that*
> *many are called but few are chosen."* — Sara Breathnach

Closing Comments

You now have a complete system for upgrading your 3D Integrity and 3D Living.

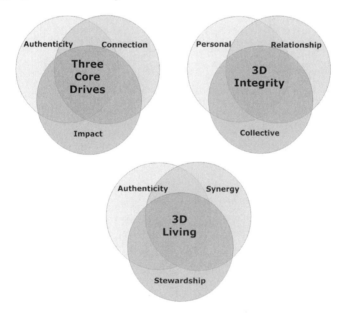

The age of integrity-based integrated adult development is upon us. Outgrowing our survival plan and redemption plan is for all of us. Upgrading our Seven WisePassions is for all of us. Living in 3D Integrity is for all of us. 3D Living is now available to everyone regardless of where you live, the job you hold, or your economic status.

Integrity Intelligence provides the evolutionary leap humanity so desperately seeks: for the sake of ourselves as individuals, for our relationships with others and for humanity as a whole.

As you have probably surmised, this book is not a one-time read. Outgrowing and upgrading is a mission for a lifetime. I encourage you to frequently repeat the exercises in here and in the *Workbook*. I encourage you to revisit my website for my most up-to-date resource recommendations whenever you have a new development focus.

Literally millions of people and perhaps more may well be looking for this kind of book. I therefore hope you will tell all those you know who are searching for this kind of resource about *The New IQ*.

But, whatever you do, don't delay. It is time to stop looking the other way. It is time to stop tolerating lack of integrity in ourselves, in our leaders and in our systems. It is time to set aside our childish beliefs about what the world owes to us. It is time to set aside our equally childish belief that being a true self simply means "looking out for number one."

It is time for the most important revolution of our time — a revolution in how we define "self" and "fulfillment." Embracing a three-dimensional vision of integrity makes this possible. Outgrowing our individual and societal survival and redemption plans, and instead living through our Seven WisePassions, makes this possible. Living a life of 3D Integrity is the best way to experience security in today's world — you won't find it merely through Homeland Security.

Yes, care for yourself. But, truly care for yourself in *all* the ways covered in this book. Embrace in your deepest heart that part of truly caring for *yourself* means caring for those around you and caring for the collectives of which you are a part. As the extraordinary ancient biblical and ethics scholar Hillel said:

"If I am not for myself, who will be?
But if I am for myself only, what am I?
And if not now, when?"

The world needs you. Your relationships need you. You need you. And if not now, when?

APPENDICES

I. GOING FURTHER:
A WEALTH OF RESOURCES

II. GLOSSARY OF TERMS USED
IN THE NEW IQ

III. SELF-ASSESSMENTS
AND EXERCISES

IV. INDEX

GOING FURTHER: A WEALTH OF RESOURCES

The New IQ has provided you with a road map for elevating your integrity and fulfillment. Now it is time to select the resources that can best assist you with whatever portions of this book you have decided are your next step forward. This section is your gateway to those resources.

They include:

- *The New IQ Integrity Makeover Workbook*
- The *Best Resources* Section of *TheNewIQ.com* Website
- The *IntegrityWatch* Blog
- 3D Integrity Support Circles
- Customized Integrity Intelligence Resources

The New IQ Integrity Makeover Workbook

This companion to *The New IQ* is a ten lesson guide to outgrowing your survival and redemption plans and upgrading your WisePassions. It contains a complete set of self-assessments and exercises, a few of which I was able to fit into *The New IQ* and the vast majority of which could not be included due to length limitations.

1. **Integrity Checkup Self-Assessments:** These include your relationship with your three core drives, your survival and redemption plans, your predominant LifeZone and each of your WisePassions. I suggest that you re-take these

assessments every six months, or whenever you are deciding whether to answer a wakeup call, whichever comes
first. This will help you determine which resources are most
likely to help you succeed with your next step.

2. **Integrity Makeover Exercises:** These extensions of the
self-assessments are designed to help you move into integrity with all three of your core drives and upgrade each of
your WisePassions.

3. **Daily Practices:** Included are complete instructions for
using *Ho'oponopono*, Energy Psychology self-help methods
and additional practices that can help you succeed with the
exercises you focus on at any given time.

4. **Success Strategies:** This workbook also includes a special
section on how to select the best resources for you, how to
get the most from your selected resources and how to determine whether it is time to move on to another resource.

5. **Integrity Makeover Bulletin Board Access:** Free access to
reading and posting on a special bulletin board for Integrity
Makeover Workbook users.

To get your copy, go to **www.TheNewIQ.com** and click on
"The New IQ."

The "Best Resources" Section of TheNewIQ.com Website

The "Best Resources" section of my website gives you unprecedented access to discovering the key resources I have culled from
over 35 years of my own personal, relationship and leadership
development, from over 25 years working as a psychotherapist and
coach, and from over 20 years as an expert in self-help methods.

Few of us have the time or expertise to track down the most
useful books, audios, websites and development methods for
outgrowing our survival and redemptions plans, upgrading our
WisePassions and expanding our personal, relationship, collective and leadership integrity. My sincere hope is that the searching I have done over the past few decades, and the failures and
successes I have had with various resources, may be able to save

you time, energy, money and frustration. My dream was to create an extensive resource that could serve as your personal concierge for locating the best resources for your needs at each point along your journey.

Go to **www.TheNewIQ.com** and click on *"Best Resources."*

The IntegrityWatch Blog

As one of your acts of everyday stewardship you explored in the seventh WisePassion chapter (Stewardship), I invite you to make posts on my IntegrityWatch Blog and respond to other people's posts as well as my own. Here are three examples of extremely valuable contributions you can make to this blog:

- ❏ **Examples of Everyday Stewardship:** Share what you do as acts of everyday stewardship and what you have seen others do. The positive impact you will have by doing this will be to expand other people's vision of the many valuable forms everyday stewardship can take.

- ❏ **Examples of the Many Forms Lack of Integrity Takes:** Post examples of lack of integrity that are covered by the media or that you create or witness in your own life. The positive impact you will have by doing this will be to help expand everyone's understanding of the many and varied forms that lack of integrity takes.

- ❏ **Examples of Extraordinary Integrity** (in contrast to everyday stewardship): Post examples of particularly inspiring and impactful acts of integrity that are covered by the media or that you witness in your own life. The positive impact you will have by doing this will be to inspire people by expanding their faith that the Integrity Effect truly does have a larger effect than they might think.

You can access the IntegrityWatch Blog by going to www. TheNewIQ.com and clicking on *"Integrity Blog."*

Start Your Own "3D Integrity Circle"

Virtually all of us need to experience a sense of community. Most people need some amount of support in making changes. *3D Integrity Circles* provide a way for you and those you care about to support one another in recognizing and outgrowing your survival and redemption plans, upgrading your Seven WisePassions and expanding your 3D Integrity and your capacity for 3D Living. 3D Integrity Circles:

❑ Discuss *The New IQ*.

❑ Explore the self-assessments and exercises provided in *The New IQ Integrity Makeover Workbook*.

❑ Utilize the *Best Resources* section of **TheNewIQ.com**.

❑ Help their community become more integrity-conscious.

❑ Communicate with and learn from other 3D Integrity Circles through the *3D Integrity Circles Bulletin Board*.

❑ And much more.

For a free set of guidelines for creating your own *3D Integrity Circle* and to access the *3D Integrity Circles Bulletin Board*, go to **www. TheNewIQ.com** and click on *"Success Strategies."*

Media Integrity Analysis

Invite me to spice up your show or article by putting today's hot-button issues and breaking stories on the couch for an *Integrity Analysis*. Go to **www.TheNewIQ.com** and click on *"Press Kit."*

Speaking, Workshops and Mentoring

I am delighted to provide the following to the extent that my schedule allows:

❑ *Integrity Intelligence Keynotes and Workshops:* My keynotes and skills-building workshops are available for business, politics, religious, education, athletics and mental health audiences as well as the general public. These can introduce attendees to the perspective about integrity proposed in this book or zoom in on any of the specific topics touched upon in this book that are most relevant to your group.

❑ *Integrity Checkups and Makeover Facilitation for Leaders:* Customized mentoring based on *The New IQ Integrity Makeover Workbook* for leaders, executives, entrepreneurs and executive teams.

❑ *Highest Good Co-Discovery Process (HGCP) Facilitation and Training:* This co-creative approach to problem-solving, negotiation and conflict resolution utilizes the perspectives and approaches described in the Synergy and Stewardship WisePassions chapters of this book. Bring me in to facilitate an HGCP for your group or to train people in your organization to be HGCP facilitators.

❑ *Integrity Makeover Facilitator Training for Helping Professionals:* Since I am unavailable to provide Integrity Makeovers to the general public, I am happy to mentor qualified helping professionals in becoming Integrity Makeover Facilitators for individuals and groups.

If you are interested in any of these options, go to **www. TheNewIQ.com** and click on *"Contact."*

GLOSSARY

**(capitalized terms in each definition are also
defined in this glossary)**

3 Core Drives: See Three Core Drives.

3 Loves: See Three Loves.

3D Integrity: Personal, relationship and leadership integrity, in
which our Three Core Drives complement, rather than compete
against, each other; being in integrity with our own authenticity,
in our ways of connecting with others, and in serving Collective
Highest Good.

3D Living: The key to true fulfillment, 3D Living is expressing
our Three Core Drives with integrity in an integrated and coordinated way. 3D Living means living at the intersection of personal
authenticity, synergy with others and stewardship of Collective
Highest Good.

3D Responsibility: Simultaneous and integrated responsibility to
"me," "we" and "us all." We are one-third responsible to and for
ourselves, one-third responsible to those we love and work with
and one-third responsible for serving Collective Highest Good. See
Freesponsibility.

3D Self: Our 3D Self is all of who we are, which is one-third personal authenticity, one-third connection with others and one-third
in service to the greater whole that unites us all. Our 3D Self lives
at the intersection of me, we and us all.

Adult Development LifeZone: See LifeZone.

Adult Development: See Integrated Adult Development.

Adverse Childhood Experience: The term used in Kaiser-Permanente's "ACE" Study, which demonstrated how negative childhood experiences can harm our health as adults unless we resolve them effectively. (See Undigested Life Experiences for more details.)

Anesthesia: Anesthesias used as an element of our Survival Plan are mechanisms for numbing our emotional, spiritual, psychological or physical pain. Survival Plan Anesthesias relieve the pain of having distorted, covered up or abandoned parts of our authentic self, carrying a growing backlog of Undigested Life Experiences and discovering that following our survival plan's rules are not making our Happy Ending Fantasy come true.

Collective Highest Good: Decisions, solutions and actions that best serve the needs of a group. Our primary collective is the earth, including its resources and vulnerabilities. Our secondary collective is our inextricably interconnected global economy and politic. Our tertiary collectives include our own country and culture, and our religious, spiritual or philosophical path. Within that is our business, community, family and support network affiliations. Within that is our primary relationship, if we have one. Within that is our relationship with our inner community of self.

Connection: The experience of being joined with another person, ourselves and our spiritual resources, also known as bonding. Connection is the catalyst necessary for learning how to digest our life experiences and is also the heart of parenting. Connection during difficult life experiences teaches children to be unafraid of life experiences or of their interior reactions to them. This teaches us how to Harvest gifts from our life experiences and encourages us to remain in full embrace of our deepest heart, our true temperament and our personal truths, even during difficult life experiences.

Company-Keeping: See Keeping Company.

Consolidation Period: The LifeZone that follows a Transformation Chapter. Relatively relaxed periods of celebration and joy, heightened well-being and love, particularly high productivity and worldly effectiveness, during which we enjoy the fruits of the labor we performed during our last Transformation Chapter. During Consolidation Periods, we upgrade our integrity and the ways we embody and coordinate our Three Core Drives in a day-to-day way. In time, every Consolidation Period gives way to our next Wakeup Call.

Core Drives: See Three Core Drives.

Deliberate Developer: The majority of us are Deliberate Developers who need to learn the art of Integrated Adult Development, because it is not as intuitively clear to us how to succeed at it as it is for Natural Developers. As we emulate on purpose what Natural Developers seem to do by instinct, we become Successful Deliberate Developers.

Digesting Life Experiences: See Life Experience Digestion and Harvesting.

Discernment (WisePassion #3): Beyond mere listening, discernment is a combination of keen insight and good judgment that gives us right relationship with input. It is the capacity to distinguish between what fits and doesn't fit, to distinguish among truth, partial-truths and lies. It is our ability to recognize and utilize useful input from inner and outer sources that are wiser than the Rules our Inner Critic tries to enforce on behalf of our Survival or Redemption Plan.

Disconnection: An absence of tender-hearted Company-Keeping from another person when we are trying to digest a life experience. Because disconnection is inevitable at times, so are Undigested Life Experiences. The more children experience any of the four forms of disconnection (violation, abandonment, indulgence, and stealing the attention), the more impaired is their ability to digest their life experiences. Frequent disconnection, no matter what the reason for it, prevents children from developing the Seven Wise-Passions they need to develop for adult success and fulfillment. The more disconnection a child experiences, the stronger their Survival Plan becomes.

Energy Psychology: A highly promising new family of methods combining ancient energy techniques with quantum physics and "new biology" principles to rapidly and reliably rebalance emotions and beliefs to remove old blocks, digest life experiences and amplify peak functioning.

Energy System Balancing: Specific Energy Psychology centering and preventive health exercises that appear to help people rapidly regulate their psychophysiology.

Everyday Stewardship: Providing subtle leadership in one's daily life is a centerpiece of WisePassion #7. Everyday stewardship includes modeling 3D Integrity, serving Collective Highest Good in ways people might not even notice and embodying our "service mission" in all that we do. A central aspect of everyday stewardship is practicing Freesponsibility. Leadership begins with becoming more of an everyday steward.

Freesponsibility: Freedom and responsibility are inseparable. Freedom alone is narcissism (self-centeredness). Responsibility alone is imprisonment. Freesponsibility is a word that conveys the inseparability of freedom and responsibility in an attempt to provide an antidote to widespread self-centeredness and lack of responsibility. Freesponsibility is a central aspect of everyday stewardship. Also see 3D Responsibility.

Happy Ending Fantasy (HEF): One of the five elements of our Survival and Redemption Plans, the Happy Ending Fantasy is the most brilliant instinctive childhood empowerment strategy ever created. Our childhood HEF provides the lifesaving hope children need in order to survive. Our HEF says it is possible to get more of the Three Loves (connection, validation, safety) than we are receiving as children. Our HEF says that life will get better if we can only figure out what to do differently in order to get more of the *connection, acceptance and/or safety* we need. One of our most important development challenges as adults is to outgrow our need for an HEF.

Harvesting (WisePassion #4): Harvesting is our capacity to properly digest all of our life experiences in order to restore lost aspects of our authenticity and upgrade our capacity to love, lead and serve collective highest good. Harvesting gathers deep gifts from every life experience no matter how unexpected, unasked-for, unacceptable, traumatic or outside-the-box that experience might be. Successful harvesting is the heart of the human evolution process.

Highest Good: See Collective Highest Good.

Ho'oponopono: A method from the Huna healing traditions of indigenous Hawaiians for restoring spiritual connection and right perception, and accomplishing remarkable healing.

Inner Critic: An internal childhood survival mechanism that remembers and tries to get ourselves and others to obey our Survival Plan and Redemption Plans' rules. Most of us unintentionally bring our Inner Critic with us into our adult life. This wreaks havoc on ourselves and others until we upgrade our discernment WisePassion and replace our Inner Critic with the aspects of our authenticity and integrity we sacrificed as children for the sake of survival.

Integrated Adult Development: Simultaneous personal, relationship and leadership development that focuses on upgrading our Integrity and bringing us into full expression of, and alignment among, our Three Core Drives. Integrated Adult Development entails outgrowing our Survival and Redemption Plans and upgrading our Seven WisePassions. This enables us to live fulfilled lives of personal authenticity and well-being, co-creative synergy with others, and serving the Collective Highest Good of the collectives of which we are a part. Integrated Adult Development occurs through repeated cycles through our four LifeZones.

Integrity: Perhaps the most important form of intelligence needed during this time in history. There are three aspects of integrity: personal, relationship and collective (also see 3D Integrity and Integrity Intelligence). Personal integrity means being true to ourselves. Relationship integrity means connecting and co-creating with others through compassion and respect, and being true to our commitments to them. Collective integrity means doing what serves Collective Highest Good. Leadership integrity is the integration among personal, relationship and collective integrity. Integrity requires being profoundly self-responsible, using our personal power fully, compassionately and wisely, and maintaining impeccable alignment between our intentions and actions. Sacrificing aspects of our integrity begins in childhood for the sake of survival (see also Survival Plan).

Integrity Effect, The: A profound surge in personal, relationship and leadership fulfillment, and in our delight in serving Collective

Highest Good, that occurs when we fully express and align our Three Core Drives.

Integrity Intelligence: The extent to which we align and coordinate our personal authenticity, our ability to co-create mutually satisfying and effective relationships, and our attentiveness to making the world a better place through serving Collective Highest Good. Integrity Intelligence is "The New IQ." The higher our Integrity Intelligence, the stronger the Integrity Effect is in our life.

Integrity Quotient: The amount of Integrity Intelligence we have (see Integrity Intelligence).

Keeping Company: Being a tender-hearted witness who listens attentively and compassionately to someone else's feelings (or your own) without saying how to feel or what to do. Perhaps our most basic connection response, Keeping Company with someone means being fully heart-present to them in ways that encourage them to explore, resolve and learn from their feelings, wants and reactions. The less Company-Keeping we received as children, the more Undigested Life Experiences we accumulated and the stronger our Survival Plan had to grow. (The term "Keeping Company" was first coined by Eugene Gendlin, originator of an extremely important discernment development tool called focusing.)

LifeZones: The four main features of the cycles we repeat as adults in order to grow, expand, transform and evolve — Wakeup Calls, Survival Plan Attachment, Transformation Chapters and Consolidation Periods. The universe offers us Wakeup Calls to try to rouse us from the hypnotic trance created by our Survival and Redemption Plans. We respond to each Wakeup Call either by reinforcing our Survival Plan Attachment or by choosing an Adult Development cycle. If we select Survival Plan Attachment, our life continues on a downward spiral that pushes us further and further out of integrity, and causes our next Wakeup Call to be more intense. If we select Adult Development, we enter a Transformation Chapter which is ideally followed by a Consolidation Period until our next major Wakeup Call occurs. Knowing which LifeZone we are in reveals our most effective course of forward movement, which makes it far easier to select from the vast universe of development resources the best ones for us at any given time. This knowledge helps both consumers and helping professionals reduce Resource Overwhelm.

Life Experience Digestion: Digesting a life experience means harvesting from it hidden gifts that truly make the experience worthwhile, even if the experience was horrible or unacceptable at the time we lived through it. Proper digestion is how we stop being harmed by life experiences. Indigestion is anything short of this. It is never too late to finish digesting a life experience. In fact, the capacity to properly digest life experiences is one of the cornerstones of Integrated Adult Development. (See Harvesting.)

Manifest: Successfully convert intentions into results.

Mask: One of the five elements of our Survival and Redemption Plans, our mask is a partly accurate version of our self that we show to most people, also referred to as our "public self" or "persona." It is a protective mechanism through which we attempt to prevent others from seeing what we have placed in Shadow, in our Pandora's box. Our Mask reflects how we want to be seen. We sometimes develop multiple masks for different situations or people.

Natural Developers: People who succeed at Integrated Adult Development more by intuition than by conscious design. Natural Developers understand that integrity and fulfillment are inseparable. They efficiently integrate their personal, relationship, leadership and integrity development through using the Seven WisePassions in place of the Survival and Redemption Plan skills with which they entered adulthood. The rest of us would be wise to learn how to do on purpose what Natural Developers do intuitively so we, too, can develop as efficiently and successfully as possible.

New IQ: See Integrity Intelligence.

Outside the Box Experience (OBE): See Wakeup Call.

Pandora's Box: One of the five elements of our Survival and Redemption Plans, this metaphorical holding tank from Greco-Roman mythology is our inner treasure chest that holds in safe-keeping whatever we decided we could not show to the world. Our Pandora's box holds the aspects of our authenticity we felt we needed to cover up in order to get more *connection, validation and/or safety.* These aspects include gifts and talents we believe are too much for others to handle and aspects of ourselves that we or others decided were unacceptable to show. It also contains our growing backlog of Undigested Life Experiences waiting to be properly digested. We try to hide the contents of our Pandora's box with our Mask, and we use Anesthesias to try to cope with the pain that comes from keeping the contents of our Pandora's box undealt-with and hidden. (Also see Shadow).

Power (WisePassion #5): Power means being who we truly are when not imprisoned by our Survival or Redemption Plans, or the Undigested Life Experiences that caused them to develop. Power is the core of Personal Integrity. Power is our ability to effectively manifest our intentions through expressing our inner light, strengths, gifts, deepest truths and creativity without holding back, and remaining true to our boundaries. Our capacity for healthy Power builds upon our first four WisePassions (Teachability, Self-care, Discernment and Harvesting).

Redemption Plan: This term does not refer to something religious or spiritual but rather to our ego's idea about how we can prove our worth to ourselves and others as adults. This need to prove ourselves stems from our Survival Plan having failed to get us all the *connection, validation and/or safety* we needed as children. Because we failed to make our Happy Ending Fantasy come true with our childhood caregivers, we have come to believe that we must prove to others and ourselves as adults that we are worthy of experiencing fulfillment and love. In adolescence or early adulthood we transfer our happy ending fantasy from the adult caregivers of our childhood to adult accomplishments, romantic relationships and/or children. We place the other elements of our Survival Plan (our Rules, Pandora's box, Mask, and Anesthesias) in service of making our ego's Redemption Plan come true. Our Redemption Plan cannot succeed at making us feel fulfilled any more than our Survival Plan did, no matter how hard we try. As a result, our Redemption Plan proves to be a bottomless pit. No variety or amount of success can ever fill it. Realizing this marks the beginning of true *adult development.*

Redemption Plan Attachment (RDA): The chronic false hope that succeeding with our next goal, accomplishment or relationship will finally prove that we are not a bad or fundamentally flawed person for having failed to make our Happy Ending Fantasy come true as a child. See Survival Plan Attachment.

Resource Overwhelm: Feeling adrift among the vast sea of the personal, relationship or leadership development resources, unable to determine which to select at this time. Caused by a combination of not knowing: 1) Where you are in your development; 2) The kinds of resources best suited for that location; and 3) How to select from among these your own best choice(s), at least partly because of having difficulty distinguishing between slick marketing and right personal fit.

Rightness: Being closed to evidence that does not support a pre-existing belief. Rightness is a frozen belief that a particular perception or interpretation is the "truth" or "reality" regardless of evidence to the contrary.

Rightness Addiction: An unswerving conviction, sometimes approaching delusional intensity, that one's fundamental beliefs about oneself, others or the world are correct and unchangeable. Rightness Addiction makes being right more important than personal well-being, connection with others or serving Collective Highest Good. It makes us unteachable and blocks us from Harvesting true gifts from our life experiences. Everyday Rightness Addiction takes two forms: blame and shame. Blame means proving how right we are about how wrong someone else is, and that their wrongness is preventing us from having the life experiences we want to have. Shame means proving how wrong (damaged beyond hope) we are because we're not having the life experiences we want. Rightness Addiction, in its extreme, forms the foundation upon which fanaticism is built. Fanaticism is one of the more extreme illnesses that can come from allowing our Undigested Life Experiences to remain undigested.

Rules: One of the five elements of our Survival and Redemption Plans, we search for the Rules we must follow to make our Happy Ending Fantasy come true. These are quite different from Rules that allow systems and societies to function properly. There are two sets of Survival Plan Rules we must discover and obey. The first is Rules about our own authenticity: what we must to cover up, change or overemphasize in ourselves. The second is Rules about how we deal with others: what we must do to help, protect, make things easier for, compensate for, contain or manipulate those around us. These Rules reflect our belief that there are prerequisites to our deserving to be worthy of love, connection, validation and/or being kept safe. Believing in these prerequisites causes us to sacrifice aspects of our authenticity and integrity beginning as children.

Self-Care (WisePassion #2): Daily practices that maintain the abundance of life energy we need for our Three Core Drives (authenticity, connection and service) as well as for completing Transformation Chapters as rapidly and efficiently as possible. Self-care is an important component of personal integrity and is a prerequisite to relationship, leadership and collective integrity. Self-care habits replace our Survival and Redemption Plan strategies of anesthesia, self-neglect and self-indulgence.

Shadow: The term Carl Jung coined for the aspects of ourselves we pretend do not exist but that influence our lives nonetheless. Our Shadow includes the Undigested Life Experiences we try to avoid facing, and our wounds, disowned parts, "faults," basic temperament and undeveloped gifts. Our inner Pandora's box is our shadow's hiding place.

Stewardship (WisePassion #7): One of the Seven WisePassions, Stewardship is our capacity to synergize with others as our truest self to co-discover and serve Collective Highest Good. Stewardship means embodying and leading with 3D Integrity. Stewardship is the flagship WisePassion because it needs the other six WisePassions in order to come into full and healthy expression. Stewardship is not serving out of guilt or at the expense of being out of integrity with our relationships or ourselves. Neither does Stewardship mean thinking we know what is best for others or making them wrong or attacking them if they disagree with our perspective.

Successful Deliberate Developer: Those who are not Natural Developers can learn to do on purpose the same things these intuitively successful developers do by instinct on behalf of their Integrated Adult Development, and with the same extraordinary benefits. Through using these strategies they become Successful Deliberate Developers.

Survival Plan: The brilliant instinctive coping mechanism that develops in children as a result of not receiving enough of the Three Loves, experiencing the four forms of disconnection too often, and accumulating a backlog of Undigested Life Experiences. Our Survival Plan includes five sets of skills: a Happy Ending Fantasy, Rules, a Pandora's box, a Mask and Anesthesias. Our Survival Plan saves our life as children but it cannot get us all of the *connection, validation and/or safety* we need. As we become adolescents and young adults our Survival Plan morphs into a Redemption Plan. Life is designed to help us to outgrow our Survival and Redemption Plans as adults. We do this through upgrading our Seven WisePassions. This transformation from Survival and Redemption Plan Attachment to 3D Integrity and 3D Living is the purpose of Integrated Adult Development. Remaining locked in our Survival and Redemption Plans prevents us from feeling fulfilled.

Survival Plan Anesthesias: See Anesthesia.

Survival Plan Rules: See Rules.

Survival Plan Attachment (SPA): The LifeZone in which we try to cope with a Wakeup Call by further strengthening our pre-existing habits and patterns. SPA focuses on managing or alleviating symptoms rather than on freeing ourselves from the root causes creating those symptoms. It is our best attempt to deal with life when our Seven WisePassions are not sufficiently developed. If we respond to a Wakeup Call through SPA, our life continues on a downward spiral that pushes us further and further out of integrity, and causes our next Wakeup Call to be more intense than our current one. SPA causes a nasty array of symptoms including: 1) bitterness, chronic anger or emotional deadness; 2) frantic escalations in trying to make our Redemption Plan work; and 3) significant increases in Anesthesia usage that create expanding complications in our life. The alternative to SPA is surrendering into a Transformation Chapter. Individuals, couples, families, communities, businesses, religions, educational systems and governments far too frequently function in a state of SPA.

Synergy (WisePassion #6): The art of co-creation. Synergy is combining seemingly separate elements to create new solutions that are even more wonderful than any of these elements by themselves.

Relationship Synergy is co-creating relationships that are collaboration-based, mutually fulfilling, productive and resilient. This is accomplished through synchronizing intentions, boundaries, energy, and Manifestation abilities to create results that are more wonderful than can be created by any one individual or group. Synergy is the core of Relationship Integrity, the heart of healthy, happy, productive and durable relationships, and the key to effective negotiations and conflict resolution. It is the more useful alternative to coercion, capitulation and compromise. How well we can develop our synergy WisePassion depends upon how strong our first five WisePassions are (Teachability, Self-care, Discernment, Harvesting and Power). How developed our capacity for synergy is in turn determines how developed our stewardship WisePassion can become. Synergy is to be used in all of our interactions every day of our life.

Teachability (WisePassion #1): Authentic openness to new ways of understanding and acting that are substantially different from our pre-existing beliefs and habits. Teachability is the opposite of the saying that "insanity is doing the same thing over and over again and expecting different results." Wakeup Calls are the universe's best way of inducing teachability. Teachability is the willingness to discover in unexpected, unasked-for and undesired experiences, pearls of great value about personal authenticity, connection with others and serving highest good. Teachability is thus the doorway into personal, relationship, leadership and integrity development.

The Integrity Effect: See Integrity Effect.

The New IQ: See Integrity Intelligence.

The Three Loves: See Three Loves.

Three Core Drives: The central and deeply interconnected human motivations we must express and coordinate in order to feel fulfilled in life. They are: 1) *Authenticity*, through personal well-being and self-expression; 2) *Connection* with others; and 3) *Impact*, through making a positive difference in the world. Most people are, to varying degrees, out of integrity with their Three Core Drives.

Three Loves: The three experiences that feel like love to children (and adults) — *connection, validation and/or safety.*

Transformation Chapter: The LifeZone in which we respond to a Wakeup Call by entering an intensive inner growth spurt through which we outgrow aspects of our Survival and Redemption Plans and develop or further upgrade our Seven WisePassions. Transformation Chapters significantly expand our capacity for authentic self-expression, synergizing with others, and more fully serving highest good. They are the most efficient ways available for upgrading our relationship with all three of our Core Drives. Transformation Chapters can be as short as a few days for small low-intensity Wakeup Calls. More commonly, they last weeks or months. Occasionally they can last a year or more, depending on how large, complex or life-changing the Wakeup Call is. Completing a Transformation Chapter is ordinarily followed by a Consolidation Period.

Undigested Life Experiences (ULEs): Any life experience we have and from which we do not know how to harvest deep gifts of love for ourselves, for those around us and toward humanity. When a child has a strong negative, positive or confusing reaction to a life experience, and a loving Company-Keeper does not help the child Harvest deep gifts from that experience, that life experience does not get properly digested. The Kaiser study refers to childhood ULEs as "Adverse Childhood Experiences." ULEs disrupt our energy field, our psyche and our body. They disrupt our authenticity and our capacity for connection with others, and they distort the ways we go about trying to be of service in the world. They activate our need to develop a Survival Plan. Learning how to properly digest our prior and current life experiences is a central aspect of Integrated Adult Development. (Also see Disconnection, Connection, Keeping Company, Life Experience Digestion and Harvesting.)

Wakeup Call: The pivotal LifeZone around which the other three LifeZones revolve, a Wakeup Call is any life circumstance that exceeds our current ability to respond to it with centeredness, compassion, integrity, collaboration and life balance. Wakeup Calls are teachability-creation devices. They are life's invitations to us as adults to upgrade our life through outgrowing our Survival and Redemption Plans and further developing our Seven WisePassions.

Ignoring a Wakeup Call means reinforcing our Survival Plan Attachment, which leads to our next Wakeup Call being more intense than the one we choose to ignore.

WisePassion: There seven key life skills that Natural Developers intuitively develop and that Successful Deliberate Developers benefit from developing on purpose. The word "WisePassion" reflects how these skills are the basic ingredients that build wisdom, compassion and passion about life. They are: 1) Teachability; 2) Self-Care; 3) Discernment; 4) Harvesting; 5) Power; 6) Synergy; and 7) Stewardship. These Seven WisePassions make it possible to live a fulfilled, passionate life of personal, relationship and leadership integrity. Pinpointing the WisePassion we would most benefit from developing further, at a given point in time, reveals our most effective course of forward movement. This makes it far easier to select from the vast universe of development resources the best ones for us at any given time. This knowledge helps consumers and helping professionals reduce Resource Overwhelm.

SELF-ASSESSMENTS
AND EXERCISES

Many additional self-assessments and a complete set of exercises are available in *The New IQ Integrity Makeover Workbook*

INDEX